EMPIRE AND LIBERTY

EMPIRE
AND
LIBERTY

AMERICAN RESISTANCE TO BRITISH AUTHORITY
1755 - 1763

Alan Rogers

UNIVERSITY OF CALIFORNIA PRESS

Berkeley • Los Angeles • London

1974

University of California Press
Berkeley and Los Angeles, California

University of California Press, Ltd.
London, England

*For my mother
and for the memory of my father*

CONTENTS

PREFACE

In April 1754 a French expedition from Canada seized a half-constructed log fortress near the forks of the Ohio River in western Pennsylvania. This act of aggression deep in the American wilderness touched off a worldwide conflict between Great Britain and France. Nine years later the British Parliament ratified a peace treaty that ceded all of North America to Great Britain. The birth of the first British Empire was not a completely happy occasion, however. The child, America, was already rebellious and plagued by doubts about the power held by her parent, Great Britain.

In the course of the eighteenth century Americans assimilated a radical political persuasion: a fear of power and a deep concern for liberty were its central tenets. Why did this world view — which played so large a role in the making of the American Revolution — come to be so significant in America? One of the keys to this historical puzzle can be found in the colonists' experience during the Great War for Empire, 1755-1763. While the struggle to drive France from the North American continent was being waged, Americans from every social class experienced firsthand, or had some cause to fear, the use of arbitrary power.

Granted sweeping powers by the Crown, the British generals who commanded in America believed that military necessity was the single most important guide for their actions in the colonies. They imposed embargoes on shipping, ordered press gangs into the streets and countryside to seize men and property, forced citizens to quarter soldiers in their homes, and insisted that the authority of colonial political agencies was subordinate to their own military power.

Individually and through their political representatives Americans contended that their rights as Englishmen could not be disregarded, however grave the crisis. Although the colonists often were able by one means or another to thwart the generals, legally there was no way for Americans to check the power exercised by the British army during the Great War for Empire. In the eyes of many Americans, therefore, the commander in chief appeared to be an arbitrary ruler, a manifestation of what the Crown could do to subvert liberty.

Political problems in America that were left unsolved during the war grew more serious after 1763. Confronted with new economic and political restrictions, American political leaders would complete and formalize the opposition to British imperial power that had been begun during the Great War for Empire.

I have chosen not to write a comprehensive account of what happened in each of the colonies during the Great War for Empire. To have done so would have been unnecessarily repetitious. On the other hand, a purely general description omitting the chief actors and scenes would have robbed the story of its dynamic element. My solution has been to use examples that manifest the impact of the Great War for Empire on the American colonies. Therefore minor variations in the general pattern of opposition to British authority which emerged in the 1750s and 1760s, while of some importance, have not been given detailed study.

I sincerely hope that my friends and colleagues listed below realize that my debt to them is not adequately expressed by the formal phrases of scholarly acknowledgment. Professor Wilbur R. Jacobs first suggested America's response to the Great War for Empire as a fruitful subject for study. His encouragement, counsel, and friendship were a constant incentive to me.

My friend and colleague Karl Hufbauer listened patiently and critically to my ideas and his sharp mind never failed to illuminate troublesome problems.

A University of California Faculty Fellowship in the summer of 1969 helped me gain access to manuscript collections that were indispensable to this study.

I am especially indebted to the excellent staff at the Huntington Library in San Marino for guiding me through their large manuscript collections. My thanks also go to the librarians of the Massachusetts Historical Society, the Massachusetts State Archives, the New York Public Library, the New York Historical Society, the New York City Museum, the Connecticut State Library, the Connecticut Historical Society, the American Philosophical Society, the Historical Society of Pennsylvania, the Library of Congress, and the various campuses of the University of California.

Ms. Cathy Smith is an excellent typist and a friend to whom I am grateful.

A part of Chapter V appeared in the *Western Pennsylvania Historical Magazine* and some of the material in Chapter VII was first presented in *Military Affairs.*

To my wife Anne, who was understanding and encouraging at crucial times and who gave my prose style whatever felicity and clarity it has, I am most deeply and lovingly thankful.

ABBREVIATED TITLES

AB	Abercromby Papers. Henry E. Huntington Library.
Colden Papers	*The Letters and Papers of Cadwallader Colden.* 9 vols. In New York Historical Society, *Collections.* New York, 1928.
Connecticut Colonial Records	Charles J. Hoadly, ed. *The Public Records of the Colony of Connecticut.* 15 vols. Hartford, 1880.
Dinwiddie Correspondence	Louis K. Koontz, ed. *Robert Dinwiddie Correspondence, Illustrative of His Career in American Colonial Government and Westward Expansion.* Berkeley and Los Angeles, 1951.
Dinwiddie Papers	R. A. Brock, ed. *The Official Records of Robert Dinwiddie, Lieutenant Governor of the Colony of Virginia, 1751-1758.* In Virginia Historical Society, *Collections.* Richmond, 1894.
Fitch Papers	*The Fitch Papers: Correspondence and Documents during Thomas Fitch's Governorship at the Colony of Connecticut, 1754-1766.* 2 vols. In Connecticut Historical Society, *Collections.* Hartford, 1918.
Forbes, Writings	James A. Procter, ed. *Writings of General John Forbes, Relating to His Service in North America.* Menasha, Wisc., 1938.
Franklin Papers	Leonard W. Labaree, ed. *The Papers of Benjamin Franklin.* 15 vols. New Haven, 1959——.
HM	Huntington Manuscripts. Henry E. Huntington Library.

Johnson Papers	James Sullivan et al., eds. *The Papers of Sir William Johnson.* 12 vols. Albany, 1921-1964.
Journals, Massachusetts House	*Journals of the Massachusetts House of Representatives, 1715-1761.* 37 vols. Boston, 1919-1966.
LO	Loudoun Papers. Henry E. Huntington Library.
New York Colonial Documents	E.B. O'Callaghan, ed. *Documents Relative to the Colonial History of New York.* 15 vols. Albany, 1856-1907.
Papers of Colonel Bouquet	Sylvester Stevens and Donald Kent, eds. *The Papers of Colonel Henry Bouquet.* Harrisburg, 1941.
Papers of Henry Bouquet	Sylvester K. Stevens and Donald Kent, eds. *The Papers of Henry Bouquet, The Forbes Expedition.* Harrisburg, 1951.
Pennsylvania Archives	Samuel Hazard et al., eds. *Pennsylvania Archives.* 9 ser. 138 vols. Philadelphia and Harrisburg, 1853-1949.
Pennsylvania Colonial Records	*Minutes of the Provincial Council of Pennsylvania from the Organization to the Termination of the Proprietary Government.* 10 vols. Philadelphia, 1851-1853.
Pitt Correspondence	Gertrude Kimball, ed. *The Correspondence of William Pitt.* 2 vols. New York, 1906.
PRO/CO	Public Record Office/Colonial Office
PRO/WO	Public Record Office/War Office.
Rhode Island Colonial Records	J. R. Bartlett, ed. *Records of the Colony of Rhode Island and Providence Plantations in New England.* 10 vols. Providence, 1856-1865.
Shirley Correspondence	Henry Lincoln, ed. *The Correspondence of William Shirley.* 2 vols. New York, 1912.
Votes . . . N.Y., PRO/CO	*Votes and Proceedings of the General Assembly of the Colony of New York.*
Watts Letter Book	*Letter Book of John Watts. In New York Historical Society, Collections.* New York, 1928.

CHAPTER I

ANGLO-AMERICAN POLITICS BEFORE THE GREAT WAR FOR EMPIRE

On the eve of the Great War for Empire colonial politics were Anglo-American, personal, Whiggish, and dynamic. Dominated by ideas and institutions formed in the last quarter of the seventeenth century, the British Empire at midcentury was a patchwork of custom, practice, and tradition loosely stitched together by family connections and patronage. Considered in this light, the politics of Anglo-America were simply English politics writ large. In England a multitude of shifting conflicting factions scrambled continually and singlemindedly for office. The American colonies provided positions for those Englishmen who participated in this race for personal wealth and power.

There was but one basic ideological assumption shared by everyone: the possession of the American colonies helped England accumulate wealth and power. But even this assumption was not consistently pursued. There were few imperial regulations, even fewer men who gave their time and thought to the empire, and practically no enforcement procedures to see to the colonists' acceptance of the fundamental imperial assumptions.

This is not to say that the practices of the empire or Anglo-American politics were static. The British economy was being transformed: large investments in commerce and the accumulation of surplus capital for the development of an industrial technology during the first half of the eighteenth century presaged a new age. The tremendous changes in the economy naturally had important political consequences. Commercial interests sought political power, with a vigor and purpose rarely seen before the opening of the eighteenth century. By the

1740s, Professor Michael Kammen tells us, "various economic and social groups seeking to shape public life and public measures had become larger, louder, stronger, and better organized."[1]

The American colonies, of course, were at once helping to stimulate economic and political change in Britain and being affected by the transformation. In a pamphlet printed in 1754, Benjamin Franklin estimated that America's population would double every twenty-five years, making "a glorious Market wholly in the Power of Britain. . . . Therefore," urged Franklin, "Britain should not too much restrain Manufactures in her Colonies."[2] Franklin perceived both the promise and the threat that were to dominate Anglo-American politics, the economic factors that most politicians barely glimpsed before the Great War for Empire. Patronage and tradition, rather than action based on reality, were still supreme in the early eighteenth century.

Had the Virginian who observed that American governorships were distributed as "the last Rewards for past Services" added "and for family connections," his analysis would have been complete. Professor Stanley Katz points out in his careful study of New York politics that all four of the governors who served prior to the Great War for Empire gained their positions through influential English politicians and relatives. "The road to the governorship," Katz comments, "lay through the favor of the king and his principal officers, and especially by way of connection to Newcastle, for whom personal friendship or political obligation constituted sufficient grounds for preferment."[3] The statement holds true for all of the northern royal colonies. William Shirley's family friendship with Newcastle led first to a lucrative legal practice in Massachusetts, then to his appointment as advocate general of the New England admiralty court; and, finally, after he dispatched his wife to England to prompt Newcastle again, to the governorship of Massachusetts Bay in 1741. Clearly, provincial needs or administrative ability had little, if anything, to do with the selection of a governor.[4]

Once appointed, a governor was even more dependent upon his English connections. He had to retain the favor of his English backers in order to control the distribution of royal patronage in his province. With patronage a governor could build a faction personally loyal to himself. In this way a governor hoped to maintain political stability in his province. Whenever the flow of royal patronage slowed, the governor's opponents were encouraged to seek their own source of favor and, very likely, to increase their opposition to the governor's policies in the assembly.[5] In New York, for example, the faction led by James De Lancey "endeavor'd to persuade the people that the Governors conduct was so blamed that his freinds [*sic*] could not support him and that the Chief Justice [DeLancey] has a better Interest at Court than the Govr . . . which was exceedingly strengthen'd by the Govrs not having been able to procure any thing directly from the ministry in vindication of his conduct."[6] In brief, on one level American politics were, like English politics, simply the maneuvers and joustings of a small elite for power and advantage.

On another level, however, American political life was distinctly different from that of the mother country. To begin with, the circumstances of American politics made it very difficult for even the most adept and favored royal governor to quiet dissent. The electoral system in the northern colonies simply could not be manipulated by royal governors in the manner used by English administrations to insure the election of "friends." The governor did not own any assembly seats; nor were there any rotten boroughs. Moreover, the franchise was relatively widely and equitably distributed. Governor Shirley complained to the Board of Trade in 1743 that the great and rapid increase in membership in the assembly should be stopped. Because each of the 160 towns in Massachusetts had a right to send at least one representative, they had it in their power to dispute "any point with His Majesty's governor which they might suspect their ordinary members would not carry against his influence in the House."[7] Shirley's complaint was well founded. More than 65 percent of the members of the lower house represented small, homogenous farming communities. It is true, of course, as Robert Zemsky points out so clearly in his study of Massachusetts politics before 1754, that representatives from western rural towns rarely rose to positions of leadership. Political leadership in the House was almost exclusively in the hands of men who came from "families of distinction, education and substance."[8] More than 50 percent of the committee assignments in the 1749 assembly, for example, went to twelve wealthy, Harvard-educated, eastern-shore representatives. Yet, Zemsky found, the leader-

ship group was rarely able to persuade the rank and file
members to abandon prior policy commitments. Moreover, both
"backbenchers" and leaders "were uniquely sensitive to
popular opinion within their constituencies."[9] Small homoge-
neous constituencies, yearly elections, and the belief that
politicians had to be watched very carefully lest they succumb
to the temptation to aggrandize political power, produced a
remarkable degree of mutual dependency between the citizen
and the legislator in Massachusetts.

Elsewhere in the northern colonies, where representation was
not quite as responsive or equitably distributed, the assemblies
were nevertheless dynamic, rapidly changing institutions of
government. In Rhode Island the assembly was the focal point
of an economic struggle between Newport and Providence; in
Pennsylvania the Quaker party's contest with the proprietor
and his followers usually kept politics at a fever pitch; and
even in New York, the smallest and most aristocratic of the
northern assemblies, the lower house was the "most rapidly
changing institution in the New York political system. . . ."[10]
Thus in the mid-eighteenth century, the framework and
practice of politics in America were profoundly different from
those of England, where a restricted franchise, placemen, and
patronage determined the tone and the direction of political
life.[11]

There were also important differences in the political
persuasion of American politicians. Those concepts and
principles adhered to by a tiny, insignificant group of
Englishmen who called themselves Real Whigs were central to
a significant number of American politicians. The core of the
Real Whig persuasion, Caroline Robbins has shown, included a
firm belief in the separation of governmental powers, opposition to placemen and personal factions, advocacy of freedom of
thought, an unflagging defense of the constitutional rights of
Englishmen, a distrust of pretentious wealth, and a cluster of
practical political reforms such as the extension of the
franchise, annual parliaments, and compulsory rotation in
office.[12] Of course this political persuasion was not everywhere
uniformly accepted, nor was it always the guide to action, but
the ideas of the Real Whigs still provide the most accurate
conceptual framework for understanding colonial politics
before the Great War for Empire.

Because American colonial politics before 1755 could usually operate smoothly within the loose imperatives of the British Empire, a politician's commitment to the Real Whig persuasion was not frequently tested. But when Americans were led by circumstances to take a political position, they took their stand on Real Whig principles.

In New York, a faction headed by Lewis Morris and his son Lewis, Jr., began publication of a newspaper to articulate the reasons for their political quarrel with Governor William Cosby. In addition to printing essays by the radical libertarians John Trenchard and Thomas Gordon, the *Weekly Journal* printed pseudonymous essays written by members of the Morris faction. The Real Whig persuasion of the latter emerges clearly from these essays.[13]

To begin with, the leaders of this faction printed a solid defense of the need for freedom of the press in a constitutional monarchy. Like Real Whigs in England, the Morris faction feared most the corruption of high government officials. The way to protect liberty and maintain the constitutional balance threatened by political corruption was to expose in the press the misconduct of magistrates who were beyond the reach of normal legal action. By revealing "the glaring truths of his ill administration," and rendering "his actions odious to all honest minds," a free press would be able to curb the appetite of the corrupt, power-hungry politican. Thus, "under a limited monarchy . . . liberty of the press [is] not only consistent with, but a necessary part of, the constitution itself."[14] The assertion that the Morris faction's defense of freedom of the press was simply an opportunistic political maneuver can be maintained only if their Real Whig persuasion is ignored.[15]

Several other of the political imperatives of the Real Whig persuasion appeared in the Morrises' *Weekly Journal* before Governor Cosby ordered its printer John Peter Zenger arrested and charged with printing seditious libels designed to inflame the minds of the people against the government. The *Journal* accused Cosby of subverting the constitutional separation of powers by sitting and voting with the Council. The laws of the province, therefore, were made *"only by one or two branches of the legislature when they ought to be made by three."*[16] Further, Cosby used his power to prorogue the Assembly in an arbitrary manner, raising the fearful possibility that illegal assemblies "will sit and act, and lay burdens upon the subjects. . . ."[17] The fear that arbitrary authority would undermine the

constitutional guarantees that protect a citizen's rights dominated the Real Whig persuasion and, in New York in 1733-1734, it
led the Morris faction to the conclusion that *"as matters now
stand, . . . their* LIBERTIES AND PROPERTIES *are precarious, and that* SLAVERY *is like to be entailed on them and their
posterity, if some past things be not amended."*[18]

To this end, Morris championed a reform program calculated
to preserve the "peoples rights and Liberties" by making
certain that political power would be "Distributed and justly
ballanced and checkt by an independent Council, independent
frequent assembly, independent judges etc." While Morris fell
short of his goal, his vigorous and imaginative opposition to
royal authority did stimulate the development of an anti-
imperialist stance. As Patricia Bonomi puts it in her insightful
survey of New York politics before the Revolution: "now the
words were there, as were the gestures; they had already been
said, and were available to be used again."[19]

By the late 1740s both the Morrises and Cosby were gone
from the New York political scene. Cosby's ultimate successor,
James De Lancey, had carefully paved the way to the
governorship by cultivating relationships with influential
English politicians, including the Archbishop of Canterbury,
the powerful admiral Sir Peter Warren, and the Baker
mercantile syndicate.[20] But because De Lancey and his
followers could not eliminate the Real Whig persuasion from
public consideration, they could not dominate New York
politics. They were challenged in the press, in the Assembly,
and at the polls for more than a decade by the so-called
Presbyterian party, led by William Livingston, John Morin
Scott, and William Smith, Jr. Late in 1752 this trio began
publication of a weekly journal consciously patterned after
Trenchard and Gordon's *Independent Whig.* Dedicated to
"vindicating the *civil and religious* RIGHTS of my Fellow
Creatures: . . . exposing the peculiar Deformity of publick *Vice,*
and *Corruption;* and displaying the amiable Charms of *Liberty,*
with the detestable Nature of *Slavery and Oppression . . . ,"* the
Independent Reflector caused a furor in New York politics.[21]
Whether attacking local political corruption, defending man's
right to religious liberty, hailing the formation of a party
designed to oust corrupt politicians from office, urging
Americans not to be "ambitious by rivalling your Mother
Country" in corrupt election practices, or supporting a
nonsectarian, popularly controlled college, the *Independent*

Reflector was a near-perfect embodiment of the Real Whig persuasion.[22]

While the Livingston faction's record in the Assembly was an imperfect manifestation of their political persuasion, it did support a number of minor reforms that reflected its beliefs. When the De Lanceys challenged the law requiring representatives to the Assembly to be residents of their constituencies, the Livingstons' argument that "a personal residence was a requisite in the elector as communion of interests by a competent freehold" carried the day. The practice of providing only an annual salary grant to administrators — ironically begun by the De Lanceys — was also championed by the Livingstons. The Livingstons also called for publicly supported grammar schools, another position embraced by the Real Whigs.[23]

Opposition factions, such as those led by Morris and Livingston, were not the sole advocates of the Real Whig persuasion. Even imperial officials, like the De Lanceys, occasionally voiced such ideas. But the fact is that as a chief justice and governor with influential English allies, James De Lancey was an enormously powerful political figure. He was the consummate Anglo-American politician. Imperial concerns were at least as important to him as provincial matters. It is hardly surprising, therefore, that for New York provincial politicians — anxious about the dangers of autocratic government — opposition to established authority and the Real Whig persuasion became nearly synonymous before the Great War for Empire.

Politics in other northern colonies — heatedly contested and Whig oriented — were very much like those of New York. In Pennsylvania the conflict between governors determined to uphold executive authority and local politicians eager to defend and extend the "liberties and privileges" of the people was nearly as old as the colony itself.[24] For the first third of the eighteenth century the struggle for liberty was led by David Lloyd, a fiery Welshman who held public office for forty-two years, serving many times as speaker of the Pennsylvania Assembly. Lloyd attacked the proprietary prerogative at every opportunity. In 1704 he and five other assemblymen dashed off a sharply worded "Remonstrance" against the Penns which Lloyd's most recent biographer terms "the boldest attack ever made on the Proprietor in the history of the province."[25] When Governor Charles Gookin's anxious inquiries to the Assembly

suggested he would accept any legislation if his salary were
forthcoming, Lloyd seized the opportunity to gain control of
the purse strings and the right to regulate the province's
judiciary. Both, of course, had been powers wielded by the
executive.[26] Near the end of his long career, Lloyd entered into
a pamphlet war with James Logan, proprietary agent, about the
proper structure of government. Lloyd's position, spelled out in
two lengthy pamphlets issued in 1724 and 1725, was
unequivocal. The legislative authority exercised for the freemen
of Pennsylvania by their elected representatives in the
Assembly was not a proprietary grant, but flowed from the
colony's royal charter. Neither the Penns nor their deputy nor
the council could legally intervene in the legislative process.
Therefore, proprietary attempts to expand executive power
beyond the limits set by the constitution would change
Pennsylvania politics "from a State of Freedom . . . into an
Arbitrary Government, subjected to the Power of one Person.
. . ."[27]

In the decades following Lloyd's defense of the "liberties
and privileges" of Pennsylvanians, the Quaker party continued
the assault on proprietary prerogatives. "Whiggish almost to a
man," the Quakers and Benjamin Franklin, party leader in the
1750s, largely determined their political behavior according to
the Real Whig persuasion.[28] To be sure, Franklin and the
Quaker party were not democrats; they believed, along with the
most advanced liberal thinkers of their time, in an elitist social
structure. But, in true Whig fashion, they championed the
rights of Englishmen guaranteed by the constitution, espoused
freedom of thought, shunned undue luxury, fought for an
environment that would encourage public virtue, and opposed
the proprietary prerogative as arbitrary.

Franklin had embraced this persuasion before he was elected
to the Assembly in 1751. When Franklin took his seat in the
lower house, Professor Ralph Ketcham contends, he "knew
perfectly well *what* he wanted and *how* he would seek his
ends."[29] He wanted above all to preserve the liberty and
happiness of the people of Pennsylvania. To do this, Franklin
committed himself to strengthening those personal and social
values that, in his opinion, held a free society together. The
"junto" he organized among his fellow tradesmen, his efforts to
establish an academy and a hospital in Philadelphia, and the
voluntary militia scheme were all designed to improve the

community in which he lived, to help people to lead virtuous lives. If this could not be accomplished by individual citizens, Franklin was willing to act in concert with others of like mind, as he did increasingly after his election to the Assembly in 1751.[30]

From the moment he took his seat in the Assembly, Franklin stoutly defended the right of the elected representatives of the people to govern Pennsylvania. In the winter of 1754-55 he attacked the Penns' practice of giving their colonial deputy secret instructions. He found the instructions objectionable because they aimed at "extending the Prerogative beyond its due Bounds" and "abridging the just Liberties of the People. . . ."[31] Governor Robert Hunter Morris was correct, it seems, when early in 1755 he concluded that Franklin had "very out of the way notions of the power of the People and is as much a favourer of the unreasonable claims of American Assemblies as any man whatever."[32]

In many ways, of course, Franklin was the perfect example of the Real Whig persuasion, but he was certainly not unique. William Livingston's thoughts and activities in New York closely paralleled Franklin's in Pennsylvania. Both men founded clubs for personal and civic improvement; both published essays designed to instruct their fellow citizens, to help them make rational political decisions. Livingston and Franklin defended man's right to freedom of thought. Each firmly believed — and in this Livingston and Franklin were joined by lesser-known leaders in other northern colonies — that the liberties of the people had to be defended continuously "against the attacks of lawless and arbitrary Sway."[33]

The Whiggish nature of American politics was more fully developed during the Great War for Empire. Viewing events from the perspective of the Real Whig persuasion, Americans on all social levels saw what they regarded as arbitrary violations of their rights and took steps to defend those rights. This movement toward ideological conflict within the British Empire was accelerated by the changes in imperial politics introduced during the war. The conduct of a war on such a grand scale required careful planning and tight administration. In 1754 it was thought that American liberty could be maintained while imperial authority was increased. By the war's end that belief had been seriously questioned.

CHAPTER II

AMERICANS AND COLONIAL UNION, 1754-1755

By 1754 it was clear to a great many Englishmen on both sides of the Atlantic that the long-standing quarrel between France and Britain was about to erupt into warfare once again. For this reason, the Crown directed the governor of New York to invite representatives from the governments of Virginia, Maryland, Pennsylvania, New Jersey, New Hampshire, and Massachusetts to a conference with the Six Nations Indians, whose friendship was considered indispensable in the event of a war.[1] All but Virginia and New Jersey agreed to meet in Albany, New York, on June 15 in order to carry out the Crown's instructions. At the same time, on their own volition, some colonial politicians decided to place the matter of building an intercolonial union on the Albany agenda. Indeed, this latter aspect quickly became more important than the proposed Indian treaty.[2]

Faced with a new French threat, many Anglo-American leaders responded with alacrity to the opportunity to work out a plan of union, a political system that would make it possible for the combined strength of all the American colonies to be brought against the French in North America. Unless the colonies united, Governor William Shirley warned the Massachusetts General Court, the French — who were both united and belligerent — would seize the rich Ohio Valley. Such a move would not only hem in the English colonies, but it would also deprive them of the profits arising from the fur trade with the western Indians. Moreover, by occupying the Ohio Valley, the French would gain an important military advantage, for they would then be able to instigate Indian attacks on vulnerable frontier settlements. "What fatal Consequences such an Army of Warriours (a few of which have been found sufficient to keep a large Frontier in continual Alarm) would have...," Shirley concluded darkly, "it is easy to conceive...."[3] The only way to stave off this disaster, in Shirley's opinion, was for the colonies to unite.

In Pennsylvania, Benjamin Franklin dramatically demonstrated his general agreement with the Massachusetts governor. Beneath a woodcut depicting a snake cut into thirteen parts with the motto "Join or Die," Franklin wrote:

> The confidence in the French in this undertaking [the occupation of the Ohio Valley] seems well grounded on the present disunited state of the British colonies, and the extreme difficulty of bringing so many different governments and assemblies to agree in any speedy and effectual measures for our common defense and security, while our enemies have the very great advantage of being under one direction, with one council and one purse.[4]

Franklin had believed in the need for some sort of colonial confederation since at least 1751. In that year he had written a letter describing a plan of union he thought would be effective.[5] The increasing danger of French encroachments strengthened his conviction that the colonies had to unite.

Despite his considerable powers of persuasion, Franklin was unable to convince the Pennsylvania Assembly that there was a need for new intercolonial political machinery. Thus, on April 12, 1754, the Assembly pointedly omitted any mention of colonial union, although it approved Governor James Hamilton's choice of commissioners to represent the colony at Albany and appropriated £500 to buy presents for the Indians who were to be in attendance.[6] About a month later, responding to several speeches by the governor, who was an avid proponent of colonial unity, the Assembly made its opposition to intercolonial union unmistakably clear. Pennsylvania's commissioners to the Albany conference should only "answer the Ends proposed in the Letter from the Lords of Trade...." Thus, the commission issued to Franklin and the other delegates made no reference whatsoever to political union. They were instructed simply to enter into a treaty of friendship with the Iroquois and to give them the presents provided by the Assembly.[7]

With the exception of Massachusetts, all of the other colonies sending representatives to Albany generally followed the restrictive formula adopted by Pennsylvania.[8] Representatives

from Connecticut and New Hampshire were instructed by their
assemblies to talk only about Indian affairs. Those from
Maryland and Rhode Island had authority to discuss colonial
union, but they could not commit their colonies to a particular
plan. Governor James De Lancey could speak for his colony,
but because he did not invite any members of the lower house
to participate in the deliberations, it was obvious to the other
delegates that New York could not be relied upon to approve
whatever plan of union finally emerged from the conference.[9]
In short, as the conference opened, the outlook for union was
clouded with uncertainty.

But just four days after the conference began the delegates
brushed aside their restrictive instructions and resolved
unanimously to consider the question of intercolonial union. A
committee consisting of one member from each delegation was
directed to "prepare and receive Plans or Schemes" for union
and to "digest them into one general plan for the inspection of
this Board."[10]

At the first meeting of the committee, Franklin submitted a
copy of his plan, "Short Hints towards a Scheme for a General
Union of the British Colonies on the Continent." He had
drafted the plan in New York while on his way to Albany and
had shown it to James Alexander and Archibald Kennedy,
members of the New York Council who had long been
interested in intercolonial cooperation.[11]

Franklin's proposal called for the selection by the King of a
Governor General, a "Military man," paid by the Crown and
empowered to veto all of the acts of the Grand Council. The
representatives to the latter were to be chosen by the
assemblies of the various colonies. Each colony was to have at
least one representative and the larger colonies two or more "in
proportion to the Sums they pay Yearly into the General
Treasurey." The Governor General and the Grand Council
were authorized to negotiate Indian treaties and land purchases, to initiate and maintain new settlements, raise soldiers,
build forts, outfit warships and "every thing that shall be
found necessary for the defence and support of the Colonies in
General, and encreasing and extending their settlements, etc."[12]

The chief difference between the plan Franklin had drawn
up in 1751 and the one he submitted to the Albany
conference's committee on union was that in the earlier plan
the colonies' entrance into a union was to be voluntary. By

1754, however, he had come to believe an act of Parliament
was necessary to bring about colonial unity. He later explained
the reasons for this change:

> When it was considered that the colonies were seldom all
> in equal danger at the same time, or equally near the
> danger, or equally sensible of it; that some of them had
> particular interests to manage, with which a union might
> interfere; and that they were extremely jealous of each
> other; it was thought impracticable to obtain a joint
> agreement of all the colonies to a union, in which the
> expence and burthen of defending any of them should be
> divided among them all; and if ever acts of assembly in
> all the colonies should be obtained for that purpose, yet as
> any colony, on the least dissatisfaction, might repeal its
> own act and thereby withdraw itself from the union, it
> would not be a stable one, or such as could be depended
> on. . . . Therefore, the commissioners came to another
> previous resolution, viz. *that it was necessary the union
> should be established by act of parliament.*[13]

Although it was not the only one discussed by the committee,
Franklin's plan was recommended to the conference as the
basis for the proposed union. Copies of it were distributed to
the delegates for study and were "debated" or "considered" on
eight occasions after June 28.[14] On July 10, the plan was read
and debated paragraph by paragraph. Finally, late in the
afternoon, the Albany Plan of Union was officially approved,
though the Connecticut delegation and several unofficial
representatives from New York opposed the plan.

As adopted by the Congress at Albany, the Plan of Union
was more detailed than Franklin's "Short Hints," though the
two documents were very similar in many respects. Franklin's
"Short Hints" had called for a union of the northern colonies
only; but the Plan of Union specifically named all of the
continental colonies from New Hampshire to South Carolina,
deliberately omitting Nova Scotia and Georgia. While Franklin's proposal did not mention a speaker for the General
Council, the Albany Plan provided for the election of a speaker
who, upon the death of the President General, succeeded
temporarily to that office.[15] The Albany Plan was also more
specific in the matter of representation to be allowed each
colony in the Grand Council. Representatives to the proposed
intercolonial legislature were to be chosen by the lower houses

of assembly. The larger colonies were to have seven representatives, and the smaller at least two. The proportion of representatives assigned to each colony was to be altered from time to time in order to correspond with changes in their relative contributions to the general treasury.

In regard to military matters, the Plan of Union was at once more specific and more cautious than Franklin's "Short Hints" had been. First, the Albany Plan simply eliminated Franklin's notion that the President General must be a military man. Second, the Plan of Union stipulated that officers for the proposed intercolonial army had to be approved by the Grand Council. In this way the people, represented by the legislature, had an effective voice in the composition and thus in the character of the officer corps that would be created in a time of crisis. Third, the Grand Council was specifically prohibited from impressing soldiers in a colony without the consent of that colony's lower house of assembly.[16]

In this — the guarded relationship between civilian authority and the military — as well as in numerous other respects, the Albany Plan was a good reflection of the broad outlines of American political thought at midcentury. As we have seen, the political persuasion of colonial America was largely determined by Whig ideas and beliefs. But while America's politics were similar to England's in many ways, significant differences were developing.

Like their contemporaries in England, the colonists accepted the antinomy of power and liberty as the central fact of politics. To the colonists, power meant the rule of some men over others. The essential characteristic of power was its aggressiveness, its unrelenting attack upon liberty. As seen by the Albany commissioners, for example, the political world was divided into two antagonistic spheres: the sphere of power and the sphere of liberty. The former had to be resisted; the latter defended.[17]

The chief aim of government was to harness these contending forces for the mutual benefit of all. The British constitution accomplished this extraordinarily difficult task by balancing and checking the basic forces within society. It was common knowledge that British society consisted of three social orders, of which each would be best served by a different form of government: royalty, whose natural form of government was monarchy; the nobility, whose natural form was aristocracy; the commons, or people, whose form was democracy. The functions of government were carefully distributed among these three socioconstitutional orders so that no one order dominated the others. This "mixed constitution" created a framework that insured stability and the preservation of the rights of all men.

The difficult task confronting the delegates at Albany in 1754 was to incorporate the central ideas of English constitutional theory into the realities of American politics. The delegates assumed that power and liberty were contending forces: "The Just Prerogative of the Crown must be preserved . . . [and] the Just Liberties of the People must be Secured . . . ," declared the opening statement of the drafting committee's report to the conference.[18] The delegates also assumed there were socioconstitutional elements that had to be checked and balanced in order to bring about stability and preserve liberty.

At this point, the commissioners to the Albany conference encountered a complicated constitutional problem. The English constitutional miracle was achieved by mixing three orders — king, nobles, and commons. In America, however, there were only two socioconstitutional elements — the Crown and the people. Therefore, the Plan of Union divided political power into two parts. Franklin explained the division as follows: "The choice of members for the grand council is placed in the house of representatives of each government, in order to give the people a share in this new general government, as the crown has its share by the appointment of the President General."[19]

New York's representatives objected to this division of power because they claimed it excluded the governors and councilors from the government. But Franklin argued convincingly that the governors and councilors were not a distinct socioconstitutional element, but part of the Crown's sphere of influence because the majority of them were appointed by the King. If the governors and councilors were given a special role in the new constitution, the Crown would control two-thirds of the governmental power. Therefore, the majority of the Albany delegates settled on the bipartite arrangement as the most equitable and realistic formula for the new constitution.[20]

While the proportions of the constitutional mixture created at Albany were somewhat novel, the approach was very traditional. But a new and distinctly American idea did emerge from the Albany conference. It was that the new constitution had to be ratified by the people. The idea was not fully articulated, but it was implicit in all the discussions of the ratification procedure. To be sure, the delegates voted that an act of Parliament should be obtained to put the projected Plan of Union into effect. But to interpret this bit of practical politics either as evidence that most Americans believed that "Parliament possessed the authority to alter the basic constitutional arrangements within the Empire . . . " or that a union simply could be imposed on the colonies misreads both the fundamental constitutional beliefs of most Americans and the ratification procedure set in motion by the Albany commissioners.[21] To begin with, the Plan of Union was supposed to be submitted to Parliament only after it had been altered and approved by the colonists.[22] Secondly, none of the delegates who are recorded as having participated in the debate on the question of parliamentary enactment thought the Plan of Union would be significantly altered by Parliament after it received American approval.[23] Finally, the very fact that the delegates decided to send the new constitution to the lower houses of assembly implies they believed the people had the right to construct a government. The people — the "democratic part" of the socioconstitutional orders — apparently were seen, in R. R. Palmer's phrase, "as a constituent power."[24]

The first colony to consider the Plan of Union was Pennsylvania. Less than a month after the Albany conference had concluded its work, Governor James Hamilton laid the Plan before his assembly, urging its adoption. But the Assembly unceremoniously refused to cooperate with the governor. On August 17, 1754, the lower house voted not to refer the Albany constitution to the next session of the Assembly for consideration. Franklin later recalled that the "House . . . by the management of a certain number, took it [the Plan of Union] up when I happened to be absent, which I thought not very fair, and reprobated it without paying any attention to it at all, to my no small mortification."[25]

The Plan of Union received much more attention in Connecticut than it had in Pennsylvania. As soon as the Assembly reconvened in October 1754 a committee was appointed to study the proposed constitution. The committee's report was unfavorable. It objected to the union for several reasons.

First, it maintained that an intercolonial union would be too large to be governed effectively. In this opinion, the Connecticut assemblymen were probably reflecting their own political experience. As a small corporate colony they enjoyed a very large measure of self-government. The lesson they seemed to have drawn from this experience was that an extensive government, distant from the people, would tend to become tyrannical. Following this line of reasoning, the Assembly suggested that "the government should be lessened, and divided into two districts."[26]

Second, the committee report attacked the President General's authority as being too broad and too loosely defined.[27] The executive's power to nominate and commission all military officers caused the committee dark and anxious thoughts. It plainly feared that the President General would bring in non-American officers who would "press" men into service, a "hard and grievous" action. Moreover, the committee did not think the executive of the proposed union should have the power to veto acts of legislation. The executive might not act in the people's best interests and this would discourage immigration, since the promise of liberty brought many settlers to the colonies.

Further, the Assembly committee saw the proposal allowing the President General and the Grand Council to levy taxes, "throughout this extensive government," as contrary to the rights of Englishmen and a violation of Connecticut's charter privileges. A practical objection to additional taxation was also raised by the committee. The shortage of money among the inhabitants of the northern colonies, coupled with new heavy taxes, "must occasion grievous complaints."[28]

Finally, the committee held up the specter of independence. A growing population, "brought into one point, all to move under the direction of such President General and Council, might in time be of dangerous consequences to his Majesty's interest. . . ."[29] Indeed, the Connecticut legislature was so anxious to protect the Crown's interests that it instructed the colony's agent in England to use every means available to defeat the Plan when it came before Parliament.[30]

Both the lower and upper house quickly accepted the committee's adverse report. They agreed that the Plan of Union represented a clear threat to liberty as liberty was defined and manifested in Connecticut. Therefore, as viewed by Connecticut legislators, the proposed government was fraught with danger, not promise.

Critics of the Albany Plan of Union in Rhode Island came to the same pessimistic conclusion. "Philolethes," the author of a pamphlet sharply attacking the Albany Plan, asserted that "the instant it was established . . . [it would] revoke all his Majesty's Governors Commissions in North America, and destroy every Charter by erecting a Power above Law, over the several Legislatures." Moreover, "Philolethes" tried to stir up intercolonial jealousy by charging that western landowners would make substantial profits when the proposed union purchased sites for frontier forts.[31]

Although opposition to the Albany Plan was intense in Rhode Island, the union did have some influential supporters, including Stephen Hopkins, a powerful member of the lower house of assembly. Early in 1755 he published *A True Representation of the Plan Formed at Albany*, a somewhat uncertain defense of the conduct of the commissioners. Hopkins's effort apparently was responsible for postponing a vote in the lower house, thus staving off outright rejection of the Plan of Union.[32]

In March 1755, however, Governor William Greene, describing the Albany Plan as a scheme designed to deprive Rhode Island of its charter rights, demanded that the upper house vote against it. A few days later both houses approved a letter to the colony's London agent, urging him to "be upon his Watch and if any Thing should be moved in parliament respecting the Plan for an Union of the Colonies formed at Albany which may have a Tendency to infringe on our Privileges that he use his best Endeavours to get the same put off till we are furnished with a Copy thereof and have Time to answer the same."[33] In this way Rhode Island achieved two ends: although it did not openly reject the proposed union, it did ward off a supposed threat to its liberty.

In Massachusetts, the Plan of Union had the enthusiastic support of Governor William Shirley. On October 18, 1754, he laid the Albany Plan before the legislature with his earnest recommendation that the proposal be given "the Speediest Dispatch, to ripen it for the Consideration of the British Parliament. . . . "[34] Four days later the legislature appointed a joint committee to study the Plan.[35] Nearly two months of hearings were held by the committee before it reported back to the General Court.

Although the committee's report tended to be favorable to the idea of union, a majority in the House became critical soon after debate began. The legislators' antagonism was initiated by a letter from the colony's agent in London, William Bollan. He warned the legislature that under guise of a plan for "raising, collecting and uniting the Forces of all the Colonies" members of Parliament actually contemplated "a Design of gaining power over the Colonies."[36]

Despite Bollan's ominous message, there was still enough sentiment in favor of intercolonial cooperation to push through a resolution authorizing additional consideration by the joint committee of "such Plan of an Union as to them appears to be most salutary." In a short time, the committee advanced an alternative to the Albany Plan. It suggested a temporary union of New York and New England for the purpose of coordinating military and Indian affairs.[37]

On December 12, the House began debate on the committee's plan for a partial union, the Albany Plan, and the idea of a general union. The Albany Plan was rejected without the necessity of a roll-call vote. But by a close vote of forty-one to thirty-seven, the legislators showed their enthusiasm for an intercolonial union and repudiated the alternative plan for a partial union. A new committee was appointed, new recommendations made, and another debate held in the House on December 26. This time a vote of forty-eight to thirty-one postponed indefinitely any further consideration of the question of a general union.[38] Four days later the House directed Bollan to oppose any plan of union on the grounds that it would be

> subversive of the most valuable rights and Liberties of the several Colonies included in it. As a new Civil Government is hereby proposed to be established over them with great and extraordinary power to be exercis'd in time of Peace, as well as War; ... These powers are in the judgment of the two Houses inconsistent with the fundamental rights of these Colonies, and would be destructive of our happy Constitution.[39]

As if to strengthen the legislators' resolve, the Boston town meeting voted on January 17, 1755, that colonial union — in whatever form — endangered the liberties of the people and should therefore be opposed.[40]

Those who hoped for an American confederation were sorely disappointed when the Albany Plan of Union was rejected by all of the colonies. Governor Shirley concluded glumly that their "different constitutions, situations, circumstances, and tempers, will ever be found an invincible obstacle to their agreement upon any one plan. . . . " He was now convinced that Parliament had to impose union on the colonies, "without further consulting them upon any points whatsoever."[41] Furthermore, he maintained that the parliamentary union must be less "Republican" and more imperialistic than the Albany Plan had been. While adhering to the Albany proposal for a President General appointed by the Crown, Shirley now advocated the Crown's appointment of the Grand Council as well. And he insisted that parliamentary taxation of the colonies was necessary in order to guarantee the existence of a common defense fund.[42] He submitted these ideas to Franklin, who was in Boston in December 1754.

Franklin strongly objected to Shirley's proposals. To have the Grand Council appointed by the Crown and taxes imposed by Parliament would deprive Americans of the "undoubted Right of Englishmen not to be taxed but by their own Consent given thro' their representatives."[43] Indeed, according to Franklin's assessment, there were a great many loyal Americans who considered an imperial tax to raise money for defense completely unnecessary. The Crown had no reason to think that the colonies would not provide for their own defense. Therefore, local autonomy in military matters should continue. Franklin contended:

. . . the People in the Colonies, who are to feel the immediate Mischiefs of Invasion and Conquest by an Enemy, in the Loss of their Estates, Lives and Liberties, are likely to be better Judges of the Quantity of Forces necessary to be rais'd and maintain'd, Forts to be built and supported, and of their own Abilities to bear the Expense, than the Parliament of England at so great a Distance.[44]

It would be undercutting the liberties of the people to permit someone other than the people affected to make these and other vital military and political decisions.[45]

This was not to say, however, that Americans should bear the cost of defense alone. "The Frontiers of an Empire," Franklin asserted, "are properly defended at the Joint Expence of the Body of the People in Such Empire." And Americans contributed to the defense of the empire not only directly in the form of taxes but indirectly as well, because of the trade laws. Specifically, the difference between what Americans obtained for their goods in England and what they might get in some other market was, in effect, a tax. Therefore, Franklin argued, all discriminatory trade regulations were arbitrary and should be repealed even if the colonies were given representation in Parliament.[46]

Franklin concluded his remarks on Shirley's proposal with a plea for the Albany Plan. Acceptance of the Albany Plan would eliminate potentially explosive sources of friction between England and the colonies by making clearer the relationship between them and by providing a process for resolving differences. In looking back nearly forty years after its rejection, Franklin opined that if it "or something like it, had been adopted and carried into Execution, the subsequent Separation of the Colonies from the Mother Country might not so soon have happened . . . [but] the Crown disapprov'd it, as having plac'd too much Weight in the democratic Part of the Constitution; and every Assembly as having allow'd too much to Prerogative."[47]

Together with the discussions focusing on the Albany Plan, Franklin's comments on Shirley's plan form a good picture of American political thought on the eve of the Great War for Empire. One central theme emerges clearly. Although Americans feared the danger of a French attack, their apprehension could not overcome their parallel dread of losing their liberty.

This was ignored when the Crown created a commander in chief with extraordinarily broad powers to conduct the war in America. It could be expected, therefore, that the colonists would react with hostility toward the imposition of military power in spheres they only recently had claimed as belonging to the people.

CHAPTER III

INDIAN AFFAIRS

When the Great War for Empire began in 1755, British efforts to win over the Indian tribes occupying the frontier between New France and the American colonies were intensified. British officials immediately took steps to centralize authority over Indian affairs, placing them under the jurisdiction of the Commander in Chief of the British forces in North America and appointing two Indian superintendents to implement Crown policy decisions.[1] While these steps had some beneficial results, they also stirred up bitter controversies between Anglo-American leaders and also between colonial legislatures and British imperial authorities.

The war with France convinced the British Crown of the need for a unified power structure to deal with Indian affairs; some Anglo-Americans had long advocated such a move. The French government, it was pointed out, owed its successes in Indian affairs to the development of a highly structured Indian trading system.[2] The governor-general of New France headed a network of government representatives whose function was the distribution of presents — the single most important part of wilderness politics, as Professor Wilbur Jacobs has ably demonstrated.[3] French missionaries, soldiers, fur traders, and French Canadians who lived among the Indian tribes all had a hand in maintaining good relations with the natives. This grass-roots organization enabled the governor-general to recruit warriors easily in the first years of the Great War for Empire.[4]

While centralization characterized the French administration of Indian affairs, the Anglo-American system was highly decentralized until 1755. Traders, agents of the Crown, Quakers, army officers, provincial assemblies, and governors all haphazardly distributed presents to the Indians, hoping to win favor for their special interest. At times, of course, the aims of these groups conflicted, though this was not a serious problem during peace time. But when it became evident there was going to be another war between France and Britain, fought in North America with Indians playing a crucial part, many Anglo-Americans realized that imperial authority had to assume a larger role in Indian affairs. "However insignificant the Remains of the Indian Natives might appear to shallow Politicians in Times of Peace and Security," the Boston *Evening Post* noted shortly after the war with France began, "every Man must now be convinced that they are the most important Allies and the most formidable Enemies; and consequently no Pains or Expence should be spared to regain or secure their Friendship or at least their Neutrality."[5]

A few astute observers of the Anglo-American scene saw the truth of this position even before the war began. In 1751 Archibald Kennedy, a member of the New York Council, advocated a new approach to Indian problems. In a widely circulated pamphlet, Kennedy proposed that a superintendent of Indian affairs be appointed who would report to the New York legislature and the Board of Trade. The superintendent would establish a public trading system that would set fair standards for private Indian traders to follow. The money to administer this system would come from duties levied in England on goods sent to America for Indian trade and on furs imported from America.[6]

Kennedy sent a copy of his pamphlet to Cadwallader Colden, another New York politician who had shown an interest in Indians.[7] Inspired by Kennedy's proposals, Colden prepared a comprehensive report on Indian affairs and sent it to the Board of Trade in October 1751. Colden took a broader view of the problem; that is, he suggested the superintendent should be responsible to all the colonial governors, not simply New York's. Furthermore, he recommended that the superintendent be appointed by the Crown and supported by a special duty on wines and spirits imported into the colonies so that he would not be dependent upon the colonial assemblies for support.[8]

Yet another Anglo-American placeman, Edmond Atkin, attempted to persuade the Crown to centralize the administration of Indian affairs.[9] Atkin's exhaustive account to the Board of Trade in 1755 argued that it was in the Crown's interest to assume control of all negotiations with the Indians. Permitting each colonial assembly to deal with the Indians on its borders had produced for the Crown a long list of negative results, including missed commercial opportunities, an inadequate defense system, and the loss of invaluable Indian allies in the struggle with France. (The Indians, observed Atkin, are "the Cheapest and strongest Barrier for the Protection of our Settlements."[10]) To remedy this situation, Atkin called for the establishment of two Indian superintendents, appointed and supported by the Crown, with exclusive responsibility for negotiating with all North American Indian nations. Only such a centralized system, Atkin wrote, would reverse the current unfortunate practice of placing Indian affairs "almost entirely in the hands of the People."[11]

None of the proposals for strengthening the Crown's control over Indian affairs received much attention in England. Still, as Britain and France edged closer to war, it became apparent to politicians on both sides of the Atlantic that something had to be done to unify the administration of Indian affairs. American political leaders — "the People" in Atkin's analysis — met in Albany in June 1754 to discuss and act on proposals for improving relations with the tribes of the Six Nations. The Albany Congress heard from Thomas Pownall, a minor English bureaucrat with influential friends in England; William Johnson, a highly successful Indian trader who had served New York as commissioner to the Six Nations from 1746 to 1751; and from some of the Six Nations Indians themselves.[12]

Both Pownall and the representatives from the Six Nations argued that one person should be put in charge of Indian affairs, and they had William Johnson in mind.[13] In many ways, of course, Johnson was the most suitable person for the job. He was both experienced and well liked by the Six Nations Indians. Furthermore, Johnson was especially anxious to have a royal office; his own speech to the Congress clearly implied that he was the only man who might be able to succeed in winning the powerful Six Nations to the Anglo-American side. Several Six Nations spokesmen echoed Johnson's self-evaluation and pleaded that he be made superintendent. One of the Indians told the delegates dramatically: "If he [Johnson] fails us, we die."[14]

Despite these recommendations on Johnson's behalf, the delegates to the Albany Congress did not make him Indian superintendent. Indeed, they rejected the concept of a single man being in charge of Indian affairs, and also the idea of his being responsible only to the Crown. Instead they decided to have a president chosen by the Crown and a Grand Council elected by the colonial legislatures.[15] In this way, the delegates apparently hoped to achieve a united Anglo-American Indian policy without surrendering all of the power held by their local assemblies.

But this attempt at compromise was not even considered, for about six weeks before the reports from Albany reached England, the Duke of Newcastle, head of the Cabinet, had decided against any kind of colonial union. If legislation calling for union were introduced in Parliament, Newcastle told his cabinet, it would arouse latent fears about America's drift toward independence and thus stir up a hornet's nest which might prove fatal to the ministry's weak coalition.[16] Lord Halifax, a member of the Board of Trade and an influential adviser to Sir Thomas Robinson, Newcastle's secretary of state for the southern department, then suggested simply that two commissary-generals be appointed to manage both treaty and trade relations with the North American Indians.[17] Shortly after the Board met to consider Halifax's proposal, the journals and minutes from the Albany Congress arrived in England. According to Newcastle's instructions, the Board put aside the Plan of Union adopted at Albany and read with approval only the testimony by Thomas Pownall, Johnson, and the Six Nations Indians, which supported Halifax's scheme. Therefore, it was hardly surprising that when Major General Edward Braddock left for America early in 1755 to take charge of the war effort there, he carried with him a commission naming William Johnson superintendent of northern Indian affairs.[18]

Meanwhile, every one of the American legislatures turned down the Albany Plan of Union. While the reasons for doing so varied widely, it seems clear that the colonists' fear that the British government might use the confederation as a weapon to curb political autonomy underlay most of the votes against the proposed union. The Pennsylvania Assembly, for example, declared flatly that "no Propositions for an Union of the Colonies, in Indian Affairs, can effectually answer the good Purposes, or be binding, farther than are confirmed by Laws, enacted under the several Governments, comprized in that Union."[19]

Johnson's appointment did little to assuage colonial anxiety on that score. Indeed, the creation of a powerful imperial office

outside of colonial political control ran directly counter to
nearly a century of American political development. By 1755
most colonial lower houses of assembly had won the right to
determine policy in areas such as Indian affairs which vitally
affected their interests.[20] Thus, several northern assemblies
·moved immediately to create a lever which they might use to
control Johnson's Indian policy decisions. Specifically, Massachusetts, New Hampshire, and New York sought to check
Johnson's activities by making him dependent upon them for
the money he needed to manage his office.[21]

Governor William Shirley of Massachusetts, whom Braddock
had made second in command with some general responsibility
for military operations in New York, including supervisory
authority over Johnson's management of Indian affairs, adhered
to the assemblies' point of view.[22] That is, he believed that
Johnson was subject to the customary colonial political
processes; therefore, according to Shirley, the Indian superintendent had to wait for interested provincial assemblies to
appropriate money for gifts before Johnson could act. Johnson
was adamantly opposed to this mode of operation. He insisted
throughout his controversy with Shirley that he alone could
determine how and when to wield the power that had been
granted him over Indian affairs.[23] This profound disagreement
over the distribution and manipulation of colonial political
power lay at the bottom of the bitter quarrel between Johnson
and Shirley.[24]

Johnson interpreted his commission from Braddock to mean
that he was independent from both military and civilian
control. Shirley, on the other hand, believed that Johnson was
subordinate to both. In part, of course, this confusion was
attributable to Braddock's vagueness. The general had issued
two conflicting commissions during the conference at Alexandria in April 1755. Johnson's commission empowering him to
act as Indian superintendent gave him "the Sole Management
and direction of the Affairs of the Six Nations and their Allies
. . . ." At the same time, however, Braddock named the
governor of Massachusetts his second in command with
authority over northern military operations.[25] Assuming that his
new military position elevated him above the Indian superintendent, Shirley sent Johnson a set of general instructions.
"You are," he told Johnson just two days after the Alexandria
conference ended, "to give me a regular and constant Account

of what you do in discharge of the Trust reposed in you."[26] In the same letter, Shirley asked Johnson to recruit some Indians for the former's Oswego campaign.

Nearly two months passed before Johnson responded to Shirley's request. The delay was deliberate. A coterie of New York politicians easily persuaded the ambitious Johnson that he had to undercut Shirley's political support at home in order to build a power base for himself.[27] What better way to achieve this goal than by holding back the Indian warriors Shirley needed?

The superintendent's letter to Shirley was, therefore, purposefully vague and unpromising: "If the Indians can be brought to act with us against the French," he wrote, "I will endeavour to prevail on a sufft. Number to attend your Excellency." Three days earlier Johnson had manifested no such doubts. He boasted to his new political ally Oliver De Lancey: "If the Forces were ready now to March I could get as many Warriours to go with me as I pleased."[28]

Johnson's New York clique was especially anxious to win over General Braddock. Reports from Johnson to the commander in chief were filled with complaints about Shirley and the threat of colonial political control that he symbolized to the New Yorkers. Johnson viewed the colonial effort to work out an equitable division of the money needed for Indian gifts as a threat to his hoped-for independence. In his letters to Braddock he condemned this halting step toward greater colonial unity as evidence of "an ill judged parsimonious and partial Spirit" and insisted that "the administration at home . . . support me hereafter in my Management of Indian affairs."[29] A guaranteed annual income from the Crown was, of course, one of the indispensable steps toward political autonomy.

But the very first step toward that goal was the elimination of Governor Shirley from the Anglo-American political scene. To this end, Johnson and his New York friends set off a devastating propaganda barrage aimed at destroying Shirley's political support. Johnson fired the opening salvo. He told Braddock that Shirley's clumsy attempt to recruit Indians for his Oswego campaign was not only an unwarranted infringement on the officially defined duties of the Indian superintendent, but also might well cause the powerful Six Nations to go over to the French.[30]

As proof of this dangerous possibility, Johnson maintained

that his conference with the Six Nations in June and July 1755 was nearly destroyed by the presence of one of Shirley's men. During those proceedings, one of the Indians had pointed to Shirley's agent, Colonel John Lydius, and declared, "that man sitting there is a Devil and has stole our Lands." The following day Johnson replied to the accusation against Lydius; he agreed fully with the Indians' characterization![31] Lydius was thereupon barred from the conference. According to notes made by Johnson's personal secretary, Peter Wraxall, the Six Nations were so pleased by this and other displays of empathy that they subsequently agreed to remain neutral during the war. Johnson immediately hailed the decision as a momentous diplomatic victory.[32]

Other members of the New York clique were equally prompt to label Johnson's conference a triumph. Thomas Pownall, a Johnson partisan who also hoped to launch his own career in the colonial service, saw to it that his friends on the Board of Trade knew about Shirley's "Abuse and Mismanagement of Indian Affairs . . . ." Lieutenant Governor James De Lancey also was active in Johnson's behalf. He assiduously cultivated the political support of New York's new governor, Sir Charles Hardy. De Lancey was able to assure Johnson that Hardy "is sensible of your merit and influence with the Indians and will do you justice at home on this article."[33]

All of Johnson's friends hammered at a single point: Indian management had to be centralized and Johnson was the only suitable administrator. "To be subjected to the caprice or political views of governours," Johnson wrote to the Board of Trade in September 1755, "I cannot think will ever harmonize with that uniform direction of Indian Affairs which . . . is the only judicious plan which can be pursued."[34] The Board of Trade, of course, had long been anxious to centralize at least the crucial administrative aspects of the empire. Plans designed to accomplish this were under serious consideration just prior to the outbreak of the war with France. For this reason, the recommendation made by Johnson's friends was very favorably received by the Board. In February 1756 Johnson received a royal commission giving him exclusive control of northern Indian affairs, including a separate income.[35]

The Board's action pleased Johnson and his clique enormously, but some political leaders reacted adversely to the

enlargement of the Crown's involvement in colonial government. When British military force — or the threat of it — was
used to back up Johnson's claims to absolute power in an area
long considered democratized by the colonies, the stage was set
for conflict, the kind of conflict which, as Bernard Bailyn has
posited, "raised in minds steeped in the political culture of
eighteenth-century Britain the specter of catastrophe."[36]

In New York, Governor Hardy, who had originally supported
Johnson's attack upon Shirley, now had second thoughts. He
suddenly found himself excluded from an extremely important
area of his colony's political and economic life. His switch
apparently began with doubts about Johnson's military compet-
ence. Specifically, Hardy was irritated by Johnson's refusal to
follow up his victory at Lake George with an attack upon
Crown Point. Hardy impatiently told Johnson's emissary that
he should either attack or "prove plainly" that his council of
war was responsible for the halt.[37] While Johnson stalled, New
York's so-called Presbyterian party countered the De Lancey
faction's advocacy of Johnson by circulating the story that he
"only went into the Army to Retrieve a broken Fortune. That
he owes about £5000 to Sir Peter Warren's Estate and that
Oliver De Lancey is Security for payment of that debt."[38]
Whether it was this propaganda, or Johnson's continued refusal
to move his army toward Crown Point, or the governor's
realization that he had been led astray by the De Lanceys that
changed Hardy's mind, the fact is by January 1756 he was no
longer a staunch supporter of Johnson. Reversing his earlier
position, Hardy wrote the Board of Trade suggesting that
Indian affairs in New York be put directly under the governor's
control.[39] Only Hardy's political naivete kept him from realizing
that the opportunity for change had passed. Johnson's new
position placed him largely outside Anglo-American political
manipulation.

A decline in political influence at home was not the only
setback Hardy suffered in 1755-1756. The race for power in
New York between the De Lancey faction and the so-called
Presbyterian party also had the effect of undermining the
governor's authority. In the process the Assembly developed
both articulate leaders and political maturity and greatly
increased its control over local affairs.[40] Thus, an anomalous
situation existed; New York's political system was self-
contradictory in its structure. On the one hand, the Assembly

had achieved political dominance by triumphing over a succession of royal governors; on the other hand, the Assembly had been rendered powerless in an important area by the new imperial agency of control Johnson headed.[41]

The pattern of politics in the proprietary colony of Pennsylvania was also significantly influenced by Indian problems. Pennsylvania's politics were different in form but not in substance from those which emerged in New York during the Great War for Empire. In Pennsylvania there was the same conflict between an ambitious assembly, a weak executive, and an assertive imperialism exercised by both proprietary and English officials. The Assembly—or to be precise, the dominant Quaker party—sometimes sided with the Crown against the proprietors, sometimes with the proprietors against the Crown; but in either case the goal of the lower house was the same: a bigger voice in Pennsylvania politics.

When hostile Indians launched a series of brutal attacks against the Pennsylvania frontier early in the spring of 1756, the colony's political leaders separately—if temporarily—agreed on what should be done to protect the frontiersmen. Governor Robert Morris issued a declaration of war against the Delaware and other Indians allied with them who were responsible for the attacks.[42] The powerful Assembly committee controlling defense expenditures immediately supported the governor's decision by establishing bounties for the scalps of those Indians named in the declaration.[43] In brief, both proprietary and Assembly interests assumed that Pennsylvania's government could determine its own best course of action.

Within a very short time, however, Crown officials intervened, denying Pennsylvania its act of governmental autonomy. Johnson contended that Pennsylvania's war was undermining his official policy of maintaining friendship with the Delaware through their obedience to the Six Nations. General Shirley, now commander in chief of the British forces in North America, also pressured Governor Morris to rescind his proclamation.[44] In the face of such pressure, Pennsylvania ended its war against the Delaware, thus reluctantly acknowledging Johnson's right to determine the colony's Indian policy in the future.[45]

Early in July 1756, Johnson boasted that his policy had succeeded where Pennsylvania's had failed. He had persuaded the Six Nations to absolve the Delaware of their subservient status, thus making separate peace treaties possible. At the conclusion of the Onondaga conference, therefore, both the Six Nations and the Delaware agreed to cease their attacks on the Pennsylvania frontier.[46]

Still, several Pennsylvania politicians had doubts about the efficacy of imperial intervention. Benjamin Franklin, for example, believed that Johnson put too much trust in the Six Nations. "The Six Nations," Franklin charged, "have privily encourag'd these Indians [Delaware] to fall upon us; they have taken no Step to defend us . . . nor to prevent the Mischief done us." For this reason, the Quaker party leader told Thomas Pownall, agreeing to Johnson's policy was "the most unfortunate Step we ever took. . . . For we tied up the Hands of our People till we heard the Result of that Application."[47] On the opposite end of the political spectrum, Richard Peters, titular head of the proprietary party, also complained loudly about Johnson's intervention in Pennsylvania affairs.[48]

In October the question of Pennsylvania's right to negotiate with the Indians became a matter of public debate. At that time Lord Loudoun, Shirley's replacement as commander in chief, told Governor William Denny that Pennsylvania was not to confer with the Six Nations or their allies "in any shape, on any account whatsoever."[49] The Council, consisting chiefly of men committed to the proprietary faction, objected strenuously. Loudoun's blunt order was discussed heatedly "and many observations made upon the Style as well as the matter of the said Letter." The Councilors took the position that a stipulation in the colony's royal charter guaranteeing the Penns "full right, power and authority of Treating with the Indians and declaring War against them if necessary . . ." was inviolable, and could not be altered by either the commander in chief or the Indian superintendent. For this reason, the Council refused to recognize the validity of Loudoun's order and it advised Governor Denny to bring the matter before the lower house.[50]

Denny's request for advice forced Assembly leaders to walk a political tightwire. On the one hand, the Quaker party was extremely reluctant to side with the proprietary faction on any issue; but, on the other, it was opposed to the Crown's arbitrary usurpation of an important part of the colony's political power. Appointed chairman of a committee to draft a reply to the governor, Franklin formulated a brilliant solution which the House quickly accepted. The Assembly first stated that it

supported the idea of multicolony treaties. But then the
Assembly argued that because former Governor Morris had
committed Pennsylvania to meet with the Delaware "before Sir
William Johnson's Powers were made known," Governor
Denny should follow through "lest the Indians be disgusted,
and the Opportunity of bringing them to a general Peace with
all the British Colonies be lost." Whatever agreements were
reached at the proposed conference should then be submitted
to Johnson for ratification.[51]

This scheme deftly avoided full support for proprietary
claims to the exclusive right to negotiate with the Indians by
vaguely encouraging imperial plans for "a more general
Direction" for Indian affairs. At the same time, the proposal
skirted Loudoun's order banning colonial participation in
Indian politics by allowing Johnson to make the final —
though essentially meaningless — decision about accepting or
rejecting a treaty that had already been concluded. In short,
Franklin's plan was designed to prevent either the proprietors
or the Crown from taking power away from the Assembly.

Denny immediately accepted Franklin's proposal, thus
opening the way for the Pennsylvania government to continue
its negotiations free from imperial intervention. Johnson
complained that his authority had been usurped by this
procedure, but neither Lord Loudoun nor his immediate
successor as commander in chief was able to prevent the
conferences from being held.[52] The negotiations came to a
successful conclusion in the summer of 1758. In return for the
Indians' solemn pledge not to attack frontier settlements, the
proprietors released all claims to land west of the Alleghenies,
thus removing the single most important source of Indian
discontent.[53] The Assembly boasted that the Easton treaty
represented the fulfillment of its general Indian policy, as well
as specifically accounting for the abandonment of Fort
Duquesne by the French, who were now without Indian
support.[54]

But both the Assembly's political independence and its
diplomatic success were relatively short-lived. When General
Jeffery Amherst assumed the office of commander in chief late
in 1758, he soon made it clear that his convictions on the
Indian question were directly contrary to those of the
Pennsylvania government and that unlike his predecessors, he
intended to put his ideas into practice.

To begin with, Amherst, like most British military men, had a very low opinion of American political processes. He found totally unacceptable the idea that local assemblies could, or should, determine what direction Indian affairs would take. "I have no Sort of Dependence whatever on them," he wrote of colonial political agencies on the eve of Pontiac's uprising.[55]

Secondly, Amherst firmly believed that most colonials had been far too willing to buy the Indians' friendship, rather than demanding it as recognition of England's superior power. Economic assistance should be given only for services performed. If the Indians failed to follow imperial directives, all aid should be ended immediately. "I am well convinced a due observance of this alone," he wrote arrogantly, "will soon produce more than can ever be Expected from Bribing them." In keeping with this hard line, Johnson's budget was pared down; local assemblies were prohibited from giving gifts; and only carefully licensed traders were permitted to transact business with the Indians.[56]

For those in authority, however, centralized control had its rewards. Amherst callously disregarded the Indians' bitter and repeated opposition to any further aggrandizement of their lands. In April 1761 he issued permits to a number of his fellow officers who were anxious to settle near Niagara Falls — the very region where colonial governors had been ordered to deny grants. Later, when the Privy Council insisted that Amherst break up the settlement, the general claimed he had not known of the Crown's prohibition against land grants.[57]

Finally, Amherst allowed his personal hatred for Indians to blind him to their past record of military effectiveness and to the difficulties of combating such an elusive enemy. Americans, of course, had long acknowledged that hit-and-run raids by Indian warriors were nearly impossible to defend against. Indeed, recognition of this fact provided the rationale for Pennsylvania's practice of befriending those Indians on its borders.[58] Amherst pointedly rejected such a peaceful approach to Indian-white relations, choosing instead to make the Indians subservient by denying them the goods they needed to be autonomous. If the Indians sought to get what they needed by force, they would be crushed — which, according to Amherst, would be an easy task. "Upon the first Hostilities they [the western Indians] May be Guilty of," the general vainly told Johnson, "they Must not only Expect the Severest Retaliation,

but an Entire Destruction of all their Nations, for I am firmly
Resolved, Whenever they give me an Occasion to Extirpate
them Root and branch. . . ."⁵⁹

In May 1763, the Indians launched a series of attacks against
the British forts guarding the frontier. By the end of June, the
garrisons at Sandusky (Ohio), St. Joseph (Niles, Michigan),
Miami (Fort Wayne, Indiana), Le Boeuf, Venango, and Presque
Isle (western Pennsylvania) had been wiped out.⁶⁰ Despite
Amherst's earlier boast, it took the British army nearly two
years to restore peace to western America.

Pontiac's uprising caused considerable comment on both
sides of the Atlantic; in England most of it centered on
Amherst's part in bringing on the war. "Gineral Amhirsts
Conduct is Condemned by Everybody and has been pelted
away in the papers," Johnson's semiliterate assistant George
Croghan reported from London early in 1764. "The Army
Curse him in publick as well as the merchants . . . in Short he
is No body heer nor has he been askt aqustion with Respect to
the affairs of amerrica Sence he Came over which a gentelman
might nott ask his footman."⁶¹ Captain Robert Stewart, a friend
of George Washington, wrote that "the Conduct of the Late
Commander in Chief in that Country . . . his Errors, contempt
of Indians, ill tim'd parsimony . . . is expos'd to the publick by
some very keene and able Pens. . . ."⁶² At least one high-ranking
British government official reflected this popular excitement.
The cabinet officer chiefly responsible for colonial affairs
commented candidly, though discreetly, to Amherst's replacement General Thomas Gage, that many officials "are of [the]
Opinion that the Indians have of late years been too much
neglected, and that the Commencement, and Continuation, of
Their present Hostilities, have been in a great Measure owing
to an apparent Contempt of their Consequence, either as
Friends, or Foes."⁶³

Understandably, Americans heatedly condemned Amherst's
failure to protect their frontiers. William Livingston, leader of
New York's Presbyterian party, attributed Pontiac's uprising to
Amherst's "blundering and disdainful Conduct towards the
distant Tribes." In Pennsylvania, wealthy Samuel Morris
blamed the corrupt land schemes of Amherst and "some other
stupid officers" for stirring up the Indians. Similarly, letters
and articles appearing in the colonial press named Amherst as

"the sole cause of the cruel war which inflicts horror and desolation on our suffering colonies."[64]

Amherst's failure to deal effectively with the Indians also provided Americans with an opportunity to express their deep resentment toward the British army.[65] Shortly after Amherst's recall, the Massachusetts House of Representatives instructed its agent, Jasper Mauduit, to protest the Grenville ministry's plan to maintain an army in the colonies. "What merit can there be in a Submission to such an unconstitutional Measure?" the House asked. "These Colonies," Mauduit was reminded, "Subsisted for more than a Century and defended themselves against the French and Indians with very little assistance from England."[66] Cortland Skinner, a high-ranking New Jersey official, echoed the sentiments of the Massachusetts legislature. "What occasion is there for garrisons and forts hundreds of miles in the Indian country? These are so far from protecting that they are the very cause of our Indian wars. . . ." Remove the British army, Skinner told Governor Thomas Boone of Georgia, and "we shall live in all the security we have hitherto enjoyed, when a few independent companies were sufficient for the continent."[67] The conclusion seems unmistakable: according to the view of many Americans, the danger to liberty posed by a standing army far outweighed the doubtful value of maintaining the British army as a barrier against Indian attack.

When the Great War for Empire began, British officials took important and far-reaching steps to centralize the management of Indian affairs. The Board of Trade maintained that however well intentioned or well designed, provincial legislation was simply an unsatisfactory solution to the related problems of American security and Indian affairs. "We are of opinion," the Board asserted in 1757, "that the only effectual method of conducting Indian affairs will be to establish one general system under the sole direction of the crown and its officers. . . ."[68]

The Crown's drive to create a more rational administrative organization did not eliminate intercolonial rivalry. When the Indian trade was reopened following the capture of Fort Duquesne in 1758, merchants from Pennsylvania and Virginia still behaved more like competitors than compatriots; and within these two provinces in particular rival trading interests continued to stimulate political factionalism until Pontiac's uprising forced all the traders out of the Ohio Valley.[69] But provincial rivalry is by no means the complete story. The effort to rationalize Indian affairs was regarded by some Americans as a potentially dangerous challenge to their political autonomy. Lord Loudoun was correct: Americans contended for the right to control Indian affairs "from a Jealousy of the Power being taken out of their hands. . . ."[70]

CHAPTER IV
IMPRESSMENT AND RECRUITMENT
IN THE TOWNS

Nearly five thousand Americans enlisted in the British army during the first two years of the Great War for Empire. After 1756, however, British recruiting parties had very little success, despite a lowering of the physical requirements and extravagant inducements for enlistment.[1] There are several reasons for this sharp drop in the number of Americans who chose to serve with the British army. First, colonial crowds exerted direct and powerful pressure on recruiting parties, significantly reducing their effectiveness. Second, colonial political agencies developed arguments against impressment and the recruitment of servants which tended to cast the whole matter of military service in an unfavorable political light. Third, Braddock's ignoble defeat and Dunbar's humiliating retreat severely undermined the status of the British army in colonial eyes.

The largest number of incidents of crowd activity before the Stamp Act demonstrations occurred just prior to and during the Great War for Empire. Repeatedly, crowds surged into the streets to protest the methods used by the royal navy and army to fill their ranks. Was this simply a spontaneous, mindless outburst of a "lawless rabble"? Were they a reflection of the selfish attitude of the majority of colonials who "expected the mother country to bear the chief burden of protecting them and their interests, while leaving them undisturbed in their pursuits"?[2] Or should these crowds be regarded as "the first outward and visible signs of the profound revolt of the Western World against aristocratic rule. . . ."?[3] The numerous outbursts which rocked colonial America during the war years were neither as petty nor as grandiose as these views imply. In order to determine the historical significance of these outbursts against the British military, the beliefs, motives, composition, and achievements of the crowds must be carefully analyzed, along with the general ideological context.

George Rudé's provocative study, *The Crowd in History: A Study of Popular Disturbances in France and England, 1730-1848*, offers a model that can be utilized fruitfully by the historian of colonial America.[4] Rudé claims that the eighteenth-century crowd was unusually rational with a "remarkable single-mindedness and discriminating purposefulness." "In fact," he writes, "the study of the preindustrial crowd suggests that it rioted for precise objects and rarely engaged in indiscriminate attacks on either properties or persons." Furthermore, those who assume that crowds had "no worthwhile aspirations of their own and, being naturally venal, can be prodded into activity only by the promise of a reward by outside agents or 'conspirators' " are very wide of the mark. According to Rudé, crowds in France and England were not composed solely of riffraff, but included a representative cross section of the working class and occasionally men of the "better sort."[5] Crowds of this type were not bloodthirsty. There was often widespread destruction of property, but very few deaths except when authorities sought to disperse the crowd by force.[6]

Of course, the historical and social background of the particular causes of popular tumult in America were very different from those in Europe. There were no bread riots, no uprisings of the poor, in the colonies. Yet, Rudé's implied thesis that preindustrial outbursts were a form of political protest inevitable in an increasingly democratic society that lacked the political institutions to successfully express or repress that protest seems especially applicable to America in the mid-eighteenth century. The crowds that attacked British recruiting officers and impressment gangs were protesting what they considered violations of their rights as Englishmen. They were militantly expressing a position long advocated by various colonial political agencies, but unfortunately ignored by British authorities.[7]

Before the Great War for Empire even began, a crowd in at least one major colonial city had rushed into the streets to protest the practice of impressing civilians into the royal navy. On the night of November 16, 1747, Commodore Charles Knowles sent a press gang into Boston to round up replacements for his squadrons. The gang moved along the waterfront area collaring a number of apprentices, craftsmen, and laborers as well as seamen. By ten o'clock the following morning a crowd of several hundred people had gathered, determined to take some direct action. The crowd surged through the city looking for British naval officers and British property upon which it could vent its anger and frustration. Several naval officers were taken as hostages by the crowd as it moved toward Province House. Once there, the crowd, now numbering several thousand, hurled bricks through the windows and pounded on the doors. Governor William Shirley spoke to the throng, demanding that it disperse. One of the men in the crowd shouted back that because he had issued a press warrant the governor was responsible for creating the disturbance. Shirley insisted that his order was meant to apply only to "outsiders and not New Englanders," but his words were not audible over the derisive shouts. Although it was hostile, the crowd was not bloodthirsty, as evidenced by the fact that Shirley himself was allowed to collect the four naval officers and escort them into Province House.

On November 18 the governor ordered out the militia to suppress the crowd. Only the officers responded to Shirley's call. He then went to the legislature, asking it to investigate the causes of the rioting, to condemn the militiamen for not obeying orders, and to issue a proclamation calling for the apprehension of the ringleaders of the crowd. At this point the crowd appeared outside the Court House. Two of the councilors attempted to appease them without success. Shirley again spoke to the people and apparently convinced them that the legislators could do nothing about the matter of impressment. Frustrated in its attempt to find an institutional channel for its protest, the crowd turned to the dockyards "to burn a twenty gun ship now building there for His Majesty."

While the crowd burned British property, Shirley and a group of legislators returned to Province House. They had armed themselves and were prepared to make a stand inside the governor's mansion. Within a short time the mob appeared and prepared to rush the house, but when it became evident that the lawmakers were determined to use their muskets, the crowd retreated into the night.

The governor nevertheless fled to the safety of Castle William, from which he announced that he expected the town to apologize "for insults to His Majesty George II." The following Sunday, Shirley accepted the Boston Town Meeting's carefully worded apology, issued a proclamation ordering the rioters to surrender themselves to the King's mercy, and then wisely considered the matter closed.[8]

At its peak, the crowd protesting the use of impressment gangs numbered several thousand. Governor Shirley first claimed that it was composed chiefly of sailors, Negroes, laborers, and other "lewd and Profligate Persons." Later, after some reflection, the governor's analysis of the November 17th uprising strongly implied that he knew the crowd was not made up only of the riffraff of Boston but included a representative cross section of the citizenry. "The principal cause of the Mobbish turn in this Town is it's [sic] Constitution," Shirley told the Lords of Trade, adding significantly that "the Management of it is devolv'd upon the populace assembled in their Town Meetings; where . . . the meanest inhabitants who by their Constant attendance there are generally in the Majority and outvote the Gentlemen, Merchants, Substantial Traders and all the better part of the inhabitants to whom it is irksome to attend."[9] In short, it seems very likely, judging from Shirley's own testimony, that numerous freemen who normally participated in community politics were in the crowd which had protested against impressment. The militia's refusal to respond to Shirley's order to disperse the crowd reinforces this contention. Likewise, a writer to the *Independent Advertiser* argued that the crowd's behavior did not reflect unfavorably on the character of the people. The citizens of Boston, he remarked, are not usually "disposed to Riots" but they had been "subjected to peculiar Temptations."[10]

The belief that impressment was illegal, so violently expressed by the Boston crowd, was widely shared in the colonies. When, at the beginning of the Great War for Empire, the Massachusetts House of Representatives was asked to permit an impress, it replied by branding the practice "a Thing abhorrent to the English Constitution and particularly odious in this Country. . . ."[11] Late in 1756, Thomas Hutchinson, then a member of the Council, made his position clear. He sided with the people. In a letter to the colony's agent to Parliament, Hutchinson labeled it "absurd" that a naval commander had the right to take a man out of the colony. He called for the immediate cessation of the practice of impressment.[12]

Political leaders in other colonies with major seaports were not as outspoken, but in no case did a colonial legislature favor a request for permission to impress.[13] In fact, colonial hostility against the practice ran so deep that Lord Loudoun informed one naval commander that "without a Land Force to support you . . . there is nothing to be done ashore."[14]

In the spring of 1757 Loudoun's soldiers came to the aid of frustrated navy press gangs in New York City. Loudoun first threw an embargo on all shipping, cinched the net with three battalions of redcoats, and then, beginning at 2:00 A.M. on the morning of May 20, conducted a house-to-house search for "deserters." By 6:00 A.M. somewhere between 800 and 1,100 men had been pulled in. Professor Jesse Lemisch estimates that this figure represented more than one-quarter of New York's adult male population.[15]

Given this kind of brutal, arbitrary use of royal authority, it is hardly surprising that American politicians and newspapers denounced impressment as a violation of the rights of Englishmen. The New York *Gazette,* for example, branded impressment illegal under British law and inconsistent with "the Natural Rights of Mankind." It is even less surprising that American seamen militantly resisted press gangs; pitched battles between Americans and British sailors and soldiers were fought in the streets of every major port in America during the Great War for Empire. Men on both sides were killed. On a single spring day in 1758, two men—one British, one American—lost their lives as a result of gun battles between soldiers and civilians in New York City.[16]

Victory over France in 1763 brought no decline in the number of confrontations between militant American crowds and British press gangs. Wherever and whenever the British navy tried to "procure" men, Americans resisted. In Newport and New York during the summer of 1764, in the same ports the following year, in Norfolk in 1767, and in Boston in 1768, crowds militantly opposed impressment with the weapon their wartime experience led them to believe was most effective— riot. American civil authorities looked on passively, if not approvingly.[17]

Unlike impressment, army recruitment in the colonies was

legal, but it also aroused a good deal of resentment which often culminated in direct popular action in defense of what Americans believed to be their traditional rights. The first such incidents occurred when British recruiters enlisted "servants," men legally bound to an employer for a period of time. "Violences have been committed" over the enlistment of indentured servants in Maryland, Governor Horatio Sharpe reported early in 1756. He warned General Shirley: "unless their Cause of Complaint be remov'd an Insurrection of the People is likely to ensue."[18] In Philadelphia a mob seized an army recruiting party, beating one sergeant to death and putting the rest in the city jail. All the men who had been enlisted were then released.[19]

Within a short time the Pennsylvania Assembly legitimized the mob's hostility. In an angry letter to Governor Robert Morris the legislators condemned the enlistment of apprentices and other servants as "an unconstitutional and arbitrary Invasion of our Rights and Properties. . . ."[20] Morris admitted that enlisting indentured servants involved some complex legal questions, but he insisted that only the King could provide the answers. Therefore he told the Assembly that its proclamation ordering magistrates to help employers keep their indentured servants out of the army was presumptive and illegal.[21] General Shirley supported Morris in a letter intended for the Assembly. "When a Country is in Danger of being lost to the Enemy it is not a time for the Government of it to enter into critical dissertations [about] the enlisting of indented Servants. . . ." It is the Assembly's obligation to provide some financial relief for those people who have lost their workers, or to petition the King to change the recruiting laws. These constitutional channels, Shirley told the lawmakers, would be "a more Eligible method of proceeding than to incite the populace to pursue violent measures. . . ."[22]

Despite Shirley's warning, the populace continued to use violence as a countermeasure against the recruiting of apprentices and domestic workers in Philadelphia. Several times during the months of March and April 1756 hostile crowds forced British recruiting officers to surrender the men they had enlisted. Moreover, city officials followed the Assemblymen's suggestion and cooperated with the people by arresting and jailing recruiters.[23]

The British government moved to end these conflicts

between soldiers and civilians over the enlisting of indentured servants. In March 1756 Secretary of State Henry Fox proposed that each colony create a fund to pay employers whose contracted workers enlisted in the regular army. Colonial politicians handled Fox's plan roughly. Maryland and Massachusetts flatly refused to establish such a fund; the New York Assembly tacitly approved the procedure, but failed to appropriate any money; Colonel George Washington told the governor of Virginia that he had no intention of enlisting indentured servants until the House of Burgesses actually provided the money to pay their owners; and, finally, the New Jersey legislature passed a law prohibiting the enlistment of indentured servants under any circumstances.[24] Only Pennsylvania seemed to be willing to cooperate with the ministry's proposal. The Assembly advertised for owners to bring in their accounts, apparently intending to pay them out of province funds. The catch was that the Assembly included its appropriation for the fund to reimburse employers as a rider on the total budget, which the governor refused to approve because it initiated a tax on proprietary estates.[25] As matters stood in mid-1756, not one colony had established a fund to pay masters of indentured servants who enlisted in the British army. Indeed, a sizable number of colonial politicans had either encouraged crowds who assaulted recruiting parties or had translated those violent protests into political opposition.

When Lord Loudoun arrived in America in July 1756, he brought with him an act of Parliament specifically designed to end the bitterness between the colonists and the King's officers over the enlistment of apprentices. The new law required a recruiting officer to pay the remaining portion of the master's original investment according to the number of years left to be served in the indenture.[26] But the dissatisfaction of the masters was by no means completely assuaged. As Benjamin Franklin pointed out, the last two or three years of an apprentice's indenture were worth far more than the early years, for only after a young man had become somewhat skilled in his trade did a master begin to get a good return on his investment. Moreover, Franklin continued, there was a shortage of labor in the colonies and therefore it was very difficult to replace a man who went into the army. In complex businesses the loss of one man could mean a complete breakdown. "For instance," he wrote, "Taking the Spinners from a Ropewalk, the other

Servants who know not how to spin, tho' they do not inlist, cannot go on with the Business, and must stand idle."[27] If an indentured servant were returned because a recruiter decided the price he was required by law to pay was too high, the chances were good that the master had to pay back the enlistment money, for "the Servant very probably has spent it in Drink with the Sergeant and his Fellow Recruits. . . ." This whole clumsy, irritating process, Franklin concluded, would lead to an increase in the number of slaves brought into the colonies.[28]

At the very least, recruiting continued to arouse a good deal of animosity. A Maryland planter, disclaiming any political motives, complained bitterly to Governor Sharpe of the "illegal, nay felonious" acts of a British recruiter who "made our Servants Drunk, forced them to enlist and carried them off. . . ."[29] Complaints of this nature were so numerous that Franklin suggested that Loudoun appoint someone to investigate them. Such a move, noted the politically wise Franklin, would "quiet the Minds of the Sufferers, as well as show your Lordships Regard for Justice."[30] But Loudoun was absolutely convinced that his position was the only right one and for that reason he characteristically refused to make any concessions.

Besides, the general was nearly as unhappy with the existing law as the colonists were. It had not brought about good relations between recruiters and civilians as the ministry had hoped, nor had it facilitated recruitment. According to Loudoun, "The general resistance of the People continued, and the Justices insisted they were the Judges of the Sum, the Man is worth to his Master, without calculating the Original Price and ordering in proportion to the Years remaining to Serve." Frustrated at every turn, Loudoun issued an order prohibiting the enlistment of any man to whose master a justice awarded more than £3.[31] Despite an act of Parliament and the power of the British army, American crowds and political agencies had successfully obstructed army recruiters from tapping the best source of military manpower in the colonies.

Furthermore, the arguments and actions directed against the enlistment of indentured servants soon affected all recruiting. The Mutiny Act provided numerous legal safeguards for the recruit and American politicians often used these safeguards as a means to obstruct recruiting.[32] Of course, the British army was not altogether blameless. The methods used by recruiting parties were often either illegal or so distasteful that they actually prevented the ministry from getting what it wanted — enough American recruits to fill the ranks of the regular British regiments.

New Englanders were usually considered by British officers to make the best soldiers. But in 1755 British recruiters in Nova Scotia behaved so badly toward some New England troops then stationed there that they alienated most New Englanders for the remainder of the war. When the one-year terms of the provincial soldiers were nearly completed, British recruiters used every conceivable means of inducement to get these New Englanders to enlist in the regular army.[33] Colonel John Winslow, commander of the New England troops, complained to both the British regular officers and to Charles Lawrence, governor of Nova Scotia. "It is an Impolitical Step," Winslow warned, "as these Men are Sons of some of the best Yeomen in New England . . . and if Disappointed and their Children kept, there will be an End Put to any future Assistance. . . ."[34] After a long and unnecessary delay, Lawrence finally replied to Winslow's request that British recruiters be kept away from his New England troops. Lawrence claimed that he could do nothing to prevent men from enlisting.[35] Winslow then brought the matter to the attention of the Massachusetts legislature, which promptly objected to Governor Shirley. The House noted angrily that it had received reports of invidious distinctions being made between the regulars and the New England troops. This, together with the "unwarrantable" efforts made to draw men into the regular army, led the House to demand that the troops be brought home immediately. The issue soon "inflam'd the whole Province," forcing Shirley to bow to public opinion. Early in February 1756 the governor ordered home all the New England troops in Nova Scotia, including those who had enlisted in the British army but now wanted to be released from their commitment.[36]

Shirley's appeasement policy temporarily satisfied the legislators, but recruiting was still "an unfavoured Cause" in Massachusetts. Jeremiah Gridley claimed that he nearly lost his seat on the Council because he had defended two British soldiers charged with recruiting irregularities. Moreover, most of the civil magistrates eagerly reflected the people's opposition to the regular army. Among other things, the magistrates allowed civil suits to be lodged against recruiting officers, when they knew very well, according to Gridley, that this was simply a means of obstructing the British army.[37] Gridley was also kept busy freeing recruiting officers who were jailed for various offenses. When Captain Harry Charteris of the Royal Americans, for example, tried to capture a deserter whom he believed was being hidden by a Cambridge magistrate, he and several of his men were arrested for trespassing by order of a Boston justice of the peace. Gridley eventually freed the redcoats, but meanwhile, of course, the deserter had fled.[38]

Although there was some truth to Gridley's charge that the magistrates were deliberately harassing the recruiting officers, it was also true that the British were often guilty of flagrant violations of the detailed provisions which guarded a prospective soldier's rights. "To see a Drunken man lugged through the streets on a souldiers [sic] back guarded by others . . . ," Governor Thomas Pownall once remarked, "must certainly give a strange impression of the method of enlisting."[39]

In Connecticut, Governor Thomas Fitch discovered that a recruiting party was "Guilty of very unjustifiable Conduct in the Manner in which they Attempted to inlist a Man into the King's Service, and were Guilty of Using Violence against his Person, contrary to the known Laws of the Land. . . ."[40] For this reason, the governor refused to interfere when a justice of the peace in New London ordered the sheriff to take a group of citizens and "rescue" a recruit from the soldiers. To see that his order was carried out, the justice of the peace accompanied the sheriff and his party and, according to a British officer, struck one of the redcoats and refused to examine the enlistment contract. When he heard of this, Lord Loudoun demanded that Fitch remove the justice from office. The governor politely but firmly informed Loudoun that only the Connecticut Assembly could remove an official from his post.

An investigation of the incident revealed that the New London magistrate had acted justly, if precipitously. Witnesses testified that Woodward, the recruit in question, had sold a turkey to the owner of a house where some soldiers were resting. The owner told Woodward he did not have exact change and one of the soldiers offered to pay. When Woodward accepted the money, however, the soldier insisted that he was now "a King's soldier, for he had got the King's money," and he was forcibly carried off.[41]

New Yorkers also complained to Loudoun about the illegal

methods used by recruiting parties. One, they said, had "listed by force first the son and then the father and let them both off for money." Another group of soldiers "got a man to . . . buy some papper [sic] and then insisted he was enlisted by the money they gave him to pay for it and took a pistole from him to lett him off."[42]

These methods had two immediate results: fewer colonials volunteered for the British army, and angry crowds attacked recruiters with increasing frequency as the war continued. Loudoun told Secretary of State Henry Fox late in 1756 that he had had three recruiting parties in New England for over two months and they were unable to enlist a single man! "The Whole Country are Against the Regulars," lamented Lieutenant George Cottnam.[43] In fact, only 1,200 colonials — less than half the number that had been recruited in previous years — volunteered to serve with the British army during 1757. And in 1762 only 670 colonials became redcoats.[44]

Furthermore, in order to get these relatively few men, recruiters had to face hostile crowds in nearly every colony. On three occasions in 1757 soldiers and civilians fought in the streets of New York City.[45] Captain Samuel Mackay reported that he encountered similar hostility in Portsmouth, Maine. "I have had my party out in the Country," he wrote in December 1757, "but they generally get Mob'd; and one of them was beat in the Streets the other evening. . . ." Another time, a throng of about 300 people, most of whom were respectable townsmen "drest [sic] like Sailors drag'd the [H.M.S. Mermaid's] long boat about two Mile in the Country and there left her; the people who were in her," Mackay added, "are not yet heard of." In Brintwood, New Hampshire, an army recruiting party had to slip out of town before dawn after a crowd "Beset the House where They had fled for Shelter" earlier in the previous day.[46]

Pitt's policy of relying upon regulars sent from Great Britain, rather than trying to recruit large numbers of colonials, greatly reduced the number of clashes between British soldiers and American civilians during the latter part of the war. It did not eliminate the basic problem: the intense feelings of distrust and hostility some Americans had for British redcoats. The "imperious Insolence" that seemed to some Americans to characterize British officers and soldiers still stimulated militant and occasionally violent demonstrations against the

British army. Crowds attacked redcoats in Massachusetts, Connecticut, and western Pennsylvania in 1758 and 1760. Late in the war one of General Jeffery Amherst's staff officers wanted permission to use soldiers to put down what he termed "anti-military riots" in Philadelphia. And in January 1764 a crowd of New Yorkers engaged in a shooting battle with a group of British soldiers.[47]

The crowds who assaulted British redcoats seemed to have been composed of a representative sampling of colonial society. In New Hampshire, members of the crowd were identified as respectable townsmen; in Massachusetts, as voters and jurors. Connecticut citizens who joined crowds attacking recruiters were men whose opinions the governor of that colony respected, and in Pennsylvania both craftsmen and employers participated in violent acts against the British army.[48] To be sure, sailors, young apprentices, and idle ruffians were also in the crowds. But there is no evidence to suggest that this element predominated. Certainly, colonial political agencies would not have sided with the crowds so readily if the politicans had not been convinced of the crowds' respectability and in agreement with their aims.

From the outset colonial politicians refused to condone the military's illegal or distasteful methods of recruiting. Judges and jurors, sheriffs and justices of the peace, assemblymen, councilors and even a governor or two made it perfectly clear to the British soldiers in the colonies that they intended to protect the rights of Englishmen as they were interpreted in America. Recruiting methods infringing upon "Old Charter Privileges" or the "Laws of the Land" or the rights of "a freeborn British subject" were repeatedly denounced. Moreover, while colonial assemblies could not stop recruiting, they could, and did obstruct the process. Colonial legislatures bickered well into the recruiting season about how many men they would raise; they offered higher bounties and easier terms of service to men who enlisted in the provincial armies, while encouraging vagrants and criminals to enlist in the British army.

While unsavory and unconstitutional methods provided an immediate rationalization for attacking recruiters, the British army's humiliating loss in July 1755 was also an important factor in accounting for the sharp drop in colonial enlistments and in emboldening hostile crowds. Braddock's defeat at once undermined the status of the British regulars and reinforced the colonists' biased regard for their own military prowess.

Scores of American sermons and articles written in the months immediately after the battle seriously questioned the British regulars' fighting fitness and bravery, while praising the American soldiers' ability and willingness to fight in the wilderness.[49] Archibald Kennedy, a member of the New York Council, suggested that if Americans were allowed to fight in their own way the French could be quickly defeated. British officers simply did not understand how to wage war in America. Their techniques were suited for the drill field or the plains of Europe, but not the American forest. Nor were British soldiers equipped to fight in this kind of terrain. "I compute," wrote Kennedy in a pamphlet printed late in 1755, "An *English* soldier stands encumbered with a Weight of about Forty or Fifty Pounds, while that of a *Frenchman* or *Indian* is not above twelve or Fifteen. What Service can be expected from Men thus encumbered . . . ?" Kennedy concluded by urging the colonies to unite. Disunity was the only thing that prevented Americans "from being Masters of this Continent. . . ."[50]

According to Charles Chauncey, a Boston clergyman writing at the same time as Kennedy, Braddock's defeat had made it clear that the British could not succeed in the war against France without American assistance. "The plain truth is," declared Chauncey, "*Regular* Troops in this Wilderness country, are just the same as *irregulars* would be in *Flanders*."[51] William Vinal told his Newport congregation that Braddock's defeat was due to the sinfulness of Americans, especially the sin of pride. Indeed, the "sin" was so widespread that Vinal himself succumbed to its temptations. He gave as the second reason for the disastrous loss the fact that the British army was not trained in the superior "American Way of Fighting."[52]

In addition to special pamphlets devoted to the subject, there were numerous articles in colonial newspapers commenting unfavorably on the quality of the British army in North America. It was commonly believed that Braddock had not used sound military judgment during his fateful march along the banks of the Monongahela River. The Boston *Evening Post* sarcastically pointed out that the general had ignored basic tactical procedure by not having flankers out to protect his army from ambush. In December 1755, the *Evening Post* suggested that Braddock's expedition was undertaken merely to line the pockets "of a friend to the ministry. . . ."[53] While the New York *Mercury* and the *Pennsylvania Gazette* did not raise the issue of corruption, they strongly implied that British soldiers were cowardly. It was not simply the ability to fight in the wilderness that redcoats lacked; their main failing was one of personal courage. Moreover, the *Mercury* thought it knew why Americans were braver under fire than Englishmen. Americans fought for freedom, not simply for money as did the regulars.[54]

Legislative bodies, especially those in colonies with unprotected frontiers, were also publicly critical of the actions of the British army. The people of Virginia were shocked when Colonel Thomas Dunbar ordered his troops into winter quarters early, leaving the frontier completely unprotected. Dunbar's retreat, the House of Burgesses maintained, would "leave the Frontiers expos'd to the incroachments, nay Murders and Robberies of an Inhuman Enemy."[55]

The Pennsylvania Assembly was a bit more tactful than the Burgesses, but still very critical of Dunbar's retreat from the frontier. His flight left the people "under great Apprehensions of Danger, and ready to abandon their Settlements." If the army could not fight, it should be stationed "in such Places, as may be most suitable for the Protection of the Frontier Inhabitants of this and the neighbouring Colonies . . . ." Certainly this would be preferable to having the soldiers "Lying idle in this City, where such of them as do not desert will be continually drunk."[56] It seems clear that after Braddock's defeat, colonials were convinced that the British soldier was an unsavory character, ill-suited in every way for fighting in the American wilderness. Without question these opinions made the recruiters' job much more difficult and, therefore, help explain' why fewer Americans enlisted in the British army after 1756.

When the Great War for Empire began, the ministry had planned to recruit enough soldiers in the colonies to fill both the depleted ranks of the British regiments sent to America and two regular American regiments. By 1757 that plan had to be scrapped. Working together, American crowds, politicians, and writers obstructed recruiting to the point that the ministry was forced to abandon its original policy. The effectiveness of community action was a lesson that Americans who came to political consciousness in the 1750s and 1760s would not soon forget.

CHAPTER V

IMPRESSMENT IN THE COUNTRYSIDE

On the eve of the American Revolution, General Thomas Gage, commander in chief of the British army in North America, was asked what he considered to be the single most important reason for General Edward Braddock's defeat at the hands of the French in 1755. Unhesitatingly, Gage answered, "the cause of General Braddock's disaster is to be attributed first, to [Pennsylvania's] disappointing him in the carriages and provisions, they engaged to furnish by a stated time, by which he was detained several weeks, when otherwise ready to proceed. . . ."[1] Gage went on to defend Braddock's successors who, when faced with similar problems, seized whatever their armies needed from American civilians. About the same time Gage was being interviewed, Thomas Pownall, one of a very few Englishmen who qualified as a knowledgeable observer of American politics, declared that British military power had to be subordinated to civil authority in America. The onetime governor of Massachusetts believed, for example, that the seizure of a citizen's property by the army was a "terrible infringement . . . on the Liberty of the Subject. . . ."[2]

This mixture of politics and military logistics has not claimed the attention of contemporary historians of the Great War for Empire. To historians sympathetic with the problems faced by British generals in the conduct of the war, the Americans who either refused or were reluctant to provide the army with the supplies and transport it needed were obstructionists whose selfish interests threatened to betray British military leaders. A less harsh critique finds the Americans merely acquisitive. If the farmers who had wagons had been paid more by the army's contractors, there would have been no problem.[3]

There is truth in both these interpretations. But it is not

enough to say there was difficulty between Americans and Englishmen over the matter of impressment of supplies. It is necessary to know how this problem in civil-military relations was postponed, compromised, or decided; what the colonists thought was at stake; and how the incidents that arose in connection with the impressment of transport were interpreted by British officials and by American farmers and politicians.

Late in 1754 the Crown decided that in certain cases civil authority would be subordinate to military power in America during the war with France. The governors, for example, were instructed to obey whatever orders the commander .in chief issued for "impressing carriages and providing all necessaries . . ." for the British army. In short, the Crown brushed aside the customary legal safeguards that in England protected a citizen from the arbitrary impressment of his property.[4] The use of such arbitrary power on a people as devoted to liberty as were eighteenth-century Americans elevated the resultant disputes from prosaic incidents to matters of political importance.

Armed with the Crown's sweeping directive, General Braddock arrived in America early in 1755 to drive the French from the Ohio Valley. The governors of Virginia and Maryland had assured him that wagons, horses, and forage would be assembled at Fort Cumberland upon his arrival, but they were not. Instead of 200 wagons, there were but 20; instead of 2,500 horses, there were only 200.[5] Braddock's quartermaster general, Colonel John St. Clair, was outraged. He told a group of Pennsylvania politicians that

> instead of marching to the Ohio he would in nine days march his army into Cumberland County to cut the Roads, press Horses, Wagons, etc.; that he would not suffer a Soldier to handle an Axe, but by Fire and Sword oblige the Inhabitants to do it, and take away every Man that refused to the Ohio as he had yesterday some of the Virginians; that he would kill all kind of Cattle and carry the Horses, burn the Houses, etc., and that if the French defeated them by the Delays . . . he would with his Sword drawn pass thro' the Province and treat the Inhabitants as a Parcel of Traitors to his Master.[6]

Although he was not as imperious as St. Clair, Braddock did threaten to use his discretionary power to impress horses and wagons from local farmers.

At this point, Benjamin Franklin arrived on the scene, ostensibly on post office business; in truth he had been sent by the Pennsylvania Assembly to explain proprietary politics to the general.[7] Learning of Braddock's plight, Franklin offered to assume responsibility for obtaining transport. He composed an advertisement promising fifteen shillings per day for a team of four horses, a wagon, and a driver; seven days' pay in advance, and the reassurance that the drivers would not be "called upon to do the duty of soldiers. . . ." In addition, he addressed an open letter to the residents of Pennsylvania's western counties, outlining the problem and the need for a prompt response. "If you do not do this Service to your King and Country voluntarily, when such good Pay and reasonable Terms are offered you," Franklin warned, "your Loyalty will be strongly suspected; . . . violent Measures will probably be used . . . [and] Sir John St. Clair the Hussar, with a Body of Soldiers will immediately enter the Province for the Purpose aforesaid. . . ."[8] This skillful mixture of promise and threat turned the trick. Within two weeks Franklin had 150 wagons and 259 horses, with more coming in daily. Braddock warmly praised Franklin in his report to the secretary of state. When the governors of Maryland and Virginia failed to provide wagons, Franklin took on the job, "which he . . . executed with great punctuality and integrity, and is almost the only Instance of Ability and Honesty I have known in these Provinces."[9]

Franklin's success was only temporary, however. He had done nothing to bridge permanently the gap separating the army and the farmers of western Pennsylvania. Suspicion and hostility still characterized the relationship between soldiers and civilians. Only a short time after Franklin's initial success, for example, Governor Robert Morris experienced considerable difficulty obtaining additional wagons for Braddock. He had to resort to the issuance of threatening warrants to the magistrates of four counties and pay from £5 to £15 over the usual rate of 15 shillings a day merely to get forty-one additional wagons.[10]

Undoubtedly, the people's reluctance to rent their wagons to the army stemmed in part from the fact that payment due them was exasperatingly slow in coming. Six months after the army had used the wagons Franklin had contracted for, the process of payment had only begun. It was not completed until April 1756, nearly a year after the transactions had been initiated. Even then, however, many debts were not satisfied. For in order to collect what was due him, a farmer had to go to Philadelphia, an expensive and time-consuming trip many chose not to make.[11]

There is some evidence to indicate that the people's dissatisfaction with the army's impressment system was politicized. In the fall elections of 1755, half of the sheriffs who had been instrumental in acquiring wagons for the army in the western counties were not returned to office.[12]

In New York the conflicts that arose over transport problems were even more deep-seated. There was a continuing dispute between those who exercised public power—the army and certain government officials—and those who sought to maintain private rights—individual citizens and some politicians. Early in 1756 Governor Charles Hardy asked the Assembly to establish a ceiling on the rates that could be charged for wagons and horses and wages. If they failed to act, Hardy told the legislators, the army would be forced to pay whatever the people demanded. The Assembly took no action.[13]

Having failed to win legislative support, Hardy utilized his executive powers. He issued impress warrants which allowed army officers to seize transport and to prevent workers from leaving their jobs when their demands for higher wages were not met. But some of the county sheriffs with whom the army ultimately had to deal refused to carry out Hardy's orders. The commanding general of the British army in America, Lord Loudoun, complained to Hardy about this insubordination. The governor increased the fine for disobeying orders and announced that the colony's attorney general, not local juries, would try men who would not comply with the impress laws.[14]

Still Loudoun complained. "We can come to no Resolution on this Point," he wrote, "for the evil lies in the Disposition of the People, who will have no Consideration for the Necessity of the times."[15] Finally, with Hardy's approbation, the British army resorted to force to get what it needed. Squads of redcoats swept through the Albany countryside, seizing supplies and transport and jailing everyone who refused to cooperate.[16]

The application of force had the effect of raising the level of the conflict between the army and the people of New York. The farmers affected turned to the courts, to the legislature, and to acts of civil disobedience in order to protect their private rights. Local officials helped the farmers resist by jailing army

officers for past due debts. "Civil officers . . . in general,"
wrote a captain vainly trying to obtain horses and wagons in
Albany county, "are either a Bar themselves to publick
Business or under the Direction of those who are."[17] While
farmers and local politicans did not see their grievances in an
overall political context, their actions make it quite clear that
they looked upon the army's discretionary powers with
concern.

Everywhere the British army operated one finds a record of
conflict generated by the use of arbitrary military power. The
Pennsylvania frontier in 1758 was no exception. There General
John Forbes, painfully ill and often irascible, and Colonel
Henry Bouquet, a highly competent soldier of fortune who
assumed the role of military manager during the campaign,
were determined not to allow "the horrible roguery and
Rascality in the Country people" to keep the British army from
taking Fort Duquesne.[18] Only if military success is taken as
sufficient justification for the methods they employed can their
record be praised. Judged by any other standard, their rough
treatment of Pennsylvania's farmers must be seen as one of the
factors contributing to the growth of an anti-British sentiment.

Bouquet and Forbes seem to have regarded the colonists as
childlike: the frontiersmen could be easily manipulated with a
little flattery and a little scolding. Like children, however, the
Americans were untrustworthy. The fact is, Bouquet wrote
Forbes, "no one in this country can be relied on." This was
true, according to Bouquet, in large part because those in
authority did not instill the people with the virtues of
obedience. Forbes did not intend to make the same mistake. He
told the Pennsylvania Assembly in September 1758 that unless
he got enough wagons, he would "call in the whole troops
from their Eastern frontier and sweep the whole Country
indiscriminately of every Waggon, Cart, or Horse, that he could
find."[19] The Forbes-Bouquet method enabled the army to
overcome the difficult logistical problem of transporting
supplies from Philadelphia to the frontier outposts, but it
aroused considerable resentment among the people directly
affected as well as in their elected representatives.

The farmers' anger was manifested in several ways. First,
they harassed the army impressment officers who were sent
into the western counties by bringing lawsuits against them

and by having them jailed for unpaid debts. Second, they
apparently threatened officers and magistrates with violence.
One of the army's agents confessed he was "affraid some
obstinate Wretches will be too many for the Constable" to
handle. Third, the issue of impressment became an important
one in the elections of 1758. In the opinion of some observers,
these elections showed the people were angry about "the
Conduct of some of the Military Gentl. towards such as have
supplied Our Western Army with carriages. . . ."[20]

Given this manifestation of discontent at the polls, it is not
surprising that the Pennsylvania Assembly adopted a firmer
line toward the British military in the spring of 1759. The
lower house noted that a considerable number of the wagons
and horses impressed into service during Forbes's successful
drive against Fort Duquesne had been destroyed, abandoned,
or returned to their owners in very poor condition. Moreover,
the farmers had not yet been paid. Warming to its subject, the
Assembly charged that "both Officers and Soldiers have paid
so little regard [to the provincial law] in the manner of
procuring them, that some have terrified, abused, and insulted
the Inhabitants. . . ."[21]

The commander in chief of the British army, General Jeffery
Amherst, took strong exception to the Assembly's assertions.
Amherst gave the Assembly a quick lesson in the use of
military power. The Assemblymen "have . . . mistaken the
Extent of the Laws," for if transport could not be hired then it
was the army's "Duty and incumbent on them, for the Good of
the Service, to impress them." In short, the general told the
Assemblymen that military necessity superseded civil law.[22] As
if to underscore that statement, Amherst added that he was
coming to Philadelphia to see what could be done "at this
present important Crisis."

In an unprecedented and bold move, Amherst instructed his
area commander, General John Stanwix, to write a transport
bill that would best serve the interests of the army. Amherst
then encouraged one of the Pennsylvania legislators to
introduce the bill in the Assembly. When the Assembly referred
the general's bill to a study committee, the army began to apply
pressure on influential Pennsylvanians to get the bill passed.
Colonel Bouquet, for example, commented ominously that if
the Assembly did not approve the general's bill, "we should
fall upon proper Methods to compel the unwilling to do their

Duty, beginning with those who are most inclined to obstruct the Service."[23]

The Assembly fought back. If General Forbes had fulfilled the contracts he made last year, there would be no problem now, the House told Governor William Denny. Therefore, before any new law was passed, General Amherst must "order immediate Payment on the Old Contracts." Furthermore, no new law would be passed until the army provided some assurance that it would obey the law.[24]

The Assembly's defiant attitude apparently encouraged county magistrates and the farmers themselves to resist the army's efforts to impress transport. An angry Colonel Bouquet reported to Governor Denny that the impress warrant sent to local magistrates over a month ago had been "secreted" and that "the rest of the Justices do not seem dispos'd to forward the Service." Indeed, the sheriffs refused to levy the fine prescribed by the existing law on those who attempted to avoid impressment.[25] Finally, influential political leaders, such as John Hughes, an Assemblyman from Philadelphia County and Franklin's lieutenant in the Quaker party, actively began to support the westerners in their struggle against army impressment procedures. Hughes accused Bouquet of deliberately misleading the people, of doing "a dishonest thing." "If Gentlemen the Complaints of the Country People are of Little Significance with You . . . it is not my case by any Means . . . ," declared Hughes.[26]

Hughes's statement and the action taken by local politicians in Pennsylvania and New York should be seen as a manifestation of the emergence of a new politics in America. While there was no movement toward "democracy," the Great War for Empire did stimulate a profound change in the colonies' political life. Stated simply, it was that the popular will could not be disregarded. Politicians anxious to ensure wider popular support for their views soon realized they could not be insensitive to the grievances of the people. Thus, the assemblies and other local political agencies often refused to support unpopular measures such as the army's impressment of property. In this way a link was forged between the people and the colonial legislators which shocked army officers and other imperial officials accustomed to the exercise of governmental power in England.

One way or another, the British army got the transport it

needed to carry on the war in America, but it ultimately paid a
high political price for its brashness.[27] For those farmers who
had property seized by British soldiers, future warnings from
colonial politicians about the dangers of arbitrary power
needed no explanation.

CHAPTER VI

REGULARS AND PROVINCIALS
The Two Armies Look At Each Other

The French were driven from North America by the combined strengths of the British and American armies. But, ironically, the relationship between Americans and Englishmen deteriorated during the Great War for Empire. At the same time, the war stimulated the growth of an American self-awareness, a sense of pride in being different from the British soldiers who came to fight the French. For these reasons, the victory over France did not mean the same thing to all members of the British Empire.

Until late 1756 colonial troops enjoyed a considerable degree of autonomy. In other words, there was not one British army led by a supreme commander, but two separate armies.[1] The first three British commanders accepted this separate but equal arrangement of the military forces in America. Most American politicians preferred this command structure and, until Lord Loudoun assumed command in July 1756, no British general had either the power or the incentive to alter it. Loudoun was the first British general who tried to unify all of the troops under his command, a move that was passionately resisted by American military men and civilians. To colonial army officers, integration with regular troops meant loss of their rank; to soldiers in the ranks it meant subjection to a harsh code of military conduct, with swift, brutal punishment for infractions. Finally, many civilians regarded the policy that brought British regulars and colonial volunteers together in a single unit as a grave threat to the virtue of American soldiers. Therefore, when it came, or was threatened, integration brought about open conflict between British and American soldiers and stirred up resentment among the colonial populace at large.

Loudoun attempted to override colonial antagonism arising from this issue, while General Jeffery Amherst thought to reduce hostility by assigning colonial soldiers a subordinate role in the conduct of the war. Neither method successfully bridged the gulf separating Americans from Englishmen during the Great War for Empire.

To begin with, American soldiers and officers were vastly different from the Britons who were sent to fight in North America. There were important sociological differences separating the men who composed the two armies. The kind and degree of military skill possessed by American and British soldiers varied markedly. When these real differences were combined with other imagined and exaggerated differences, the result was that Englishmen and Americans came to have a poor opinion of one another.

All British officers who served in America during the Great War for Empire were not aristocrats, but the image of the officer corps was definitely aristocratic. Most officers had paid dearly for their commissions and even when they could not afford it, British officers were expected to live in a style commensurate with their rank.[2] They were, above all, anxious to maintain the notion that a British officer was, *ipso facto,* a gentleman. The officers who served in America were more heterogeneous than the British officer corps as a whole, but the general picture that emerges still fits the aristocratic stereotype.

John Campbell, the fourth Earl of Loudoun and commander in chief of the British armies from mid-1756 to the end of 1757, was one of the few genuine aristocrats who served in America before 1763, but a number of other British officers were closely connected to the aristocracy. Jeffery Amherst's career was aided by the Duke of Cumberland and Sir John Ligonier.[3] Sir Peter Halkett, a colonel in the 44th Regiment, was a member of Parliament who also had influential friends. Many more officers, such as James Wolfe and Edward Braddock, were sons of army officers who, though not socially prominent, enjoyed the prestige of an army career. Even the foreign officers — the Swiss and Germans who commanded the newly created Royal Americans — were praised as gentlemen.[4]

Two additional points need to be made about the British officers who fought in the Great War for Empire. First, and almost without exception, British officers had been in the army for a long time. Better than 90 per cent of all the colonels of regiments during the period 1714-1763 had more than fifteen years of military service. Men who had reached the rank of general had served an average of twenty-five years in the army. As might be expected, most officers were not young men. Generals were about fifty-five years old in 1755, while the average age of a colonel was about fifty.[5] In brief, British officers tended to be middle-aged gentlemen with decades of military experience.

American officers, on the other hand, tended to be young, middle-class men with very little, if any, military experience. To be sure, colonials believed just as the English did that the prerequisite for command was the status of a gentleman. "To be an Officer," the Boston *Evening Post* commented, "there is no Necessity of being inspired with supernatural Talents. *Common Sense* and the *Deportment of a Gentleman are sufficient.*"[6] But the men whom colonials described as gentlemen were not regarded as social equals by British officers. For while most of the New England officers had had some education, nearly all of the high-ranking officers were also small businessmen or farmers or "pettifoggers" — certainly not gentlemen's callings by English standards. General John Forbes characterized the American officers he encountered as "an extreme bad collection of broken innkeepers, horse jockeys and Indian traders."[7]

American officers were not only less genteel than the British, but they were younger as well. The average age for a general in the provincial army was forty-three, and Americans with the rank of colonel were on the average almost twenty-three years younger than British colonels. Finally, although these youngsters had virtually no military experience, they fully expected to be treated as equals by the older professionals who commanded the British army.[8]

The differences between enlisted men were nearly as striking as those between officers. Colonial soldiers were much better off economically and far more pious than British redcoats. Although both armies had a relatively high proportion of lower-class men in their ranks, there were more skilled craftsmen and farmers in the provincial armies, young men who probably could make good use of the bounty money and wages offered to them for enlistment.[9] It was probably these men who set the pious tone that characterized the provincial armies. There were strict regulations against profanity and cardplaying, and usually two religious services were held in camp each Sunday.[10]

Thousands of colonial volunteers came face to face with redcoats for the first time during the Great War for Empire and by and large Americans came away from their encounter thinking the British were immoral. In a stroll around an encampment near Ticonderoga, for example, Private Joseph Nichols "observ'd but little profanity among our Provantials: But among the Regulars much profaneness." Unlike the pious Americans, British soldiers regarded the Lord's day as any other day. They sang bawdy songs and carried on business as usual.[11] Ezra Stiles, Congregational minister and future president of Yale, was worried that continued contact with British soldiers would undermine American morality. "I imagine the American morals and religion were never in so much danger as from our commerce with the Europeans in the present war," he wrote the Reverend Jared Eliot in 1759. "The religion of the army is infidelity and gratification of the appetites . . . I look upon it that our officers are in danger of being corrupted with vicious principles. . . ."[12] Colonial newspapers frequently printed stories about British regulars which supported the opinions of American soldiers in the field. Incidents of drunkenness, thievery, and murder involving redcoats were dutifully reported. When a New Haven man killed a British soldier who was drunkenly assaulting another citizen, the *Pennsylvania Gazette* commented: "The conduct of Seeley [the soldier's assailant] seems to meet with general Approbation, except in his surrendering at last into the hands of such ————— ————."[13]

Moreover, because most Americans assumed that morality and victory were closely linked, the string of British losses which extended through 1758 seemed to confirm their judgment of the regulars' character.[14] At the same time, the conquest of Fort Frontenac by Colonel John Bradstreet's provincial army stimulated the growth of American pride. "Saying that provincials are worthless troops, wont go down now," Edward Shippen, a Pennsylvania merchant and politician, wrote his son in the wake of Bradstreet's victory. "Provincials," he rejoiced, "marched into the very heart of the enemy's country and took a fortress which is the very key to all the French settlements on the Lakes."[15]

British officers firmly believed that American soldiers had nothing to be proud of. This belief was based in part on professional military judgment, but the wedge that was driven between Americans and British soldiers was composed chiefly of unsubstantiated opinions and prejudices. British professionals arrived in America with a jaundiced view of colonial soldiers which, despite a great deal of evidence to the contrary, they rarely changed.[16] "The Americans are in general the dirtiest, the most contemptible, cowardly dogs that you can conceive," wrote Colonel James Wolfe from Louisbourg in 1758. "There is no depending upon them in action. They fall down dead in their own dirt and desert by battalions, officers and all."[17] Many of Wolfe's brother officers shared his low opinion of American soldiers. General Braddock had hardly begun his ill-fated assault on Fort Duquesne when he concluded that American soldiers' "Slothfull and Languid Disposition renders them very unfit for Military Service."[18] Lord Loudoun's estimation of the character of Americans was no better. Even the New Englanders who had gained a reputation as being America's best soldiers as a result of their capture of Louisbourg in 1745 were "frighten'd out of their senses at the Name of a Frenchman ...," according to Loudoun.[19] Not surprisingly, this line of thought often led British officers to conclude that Americans were largely responsible for whatever defeats the French were able to inflict upon the British forces. General James Abercromby's bloody defeat at Ticonderoga in July 1758 was excused by many British observers simply because about 10,000 of his army of 16,000 men were provincials.[20]

Moreover, to the dismay of British military leaders, the defects they saw in the American character were reflected and magnified by the peculiar political thought and practices of the colonists. British army officers assumed that unquestioned obedience and the subordination of personal freedom to military necessity were prerequisites to victory. To colonials long accustomed to a large measure of political freedom, such restrictions were unacceptable. They were willing to serve in an army, but they were unwilling to surrender all of their personal freedom as the British generals seemed to demand. In short, military service was defined differently by colonial volunteers than it was by British professionals.

Governor Robert Dinwiddie was one of the few imperial

officers to recognize the dilemma inherent in the role of citizen-soldier. He warned the Board of Trade not to expect many Virginians to be willing to serve in the armed forces. Most of the people, he pointed out early in the war, were freeholders whose elected representatives "strenuously insist on their Privileges."[21] Among other things, this meant the House of Burgesses refused to put Virginia troops completely under the control of the military. The governor had to approve all court martials, and the defendant had the right to appeal to the House of Burgesses. This arrangement exasperated Colonel George Washington. Civilian interference in military affairs, the young officer complained to Loudoun, is designed to make "Command Intricate and precarious; and to render it difficult to support Authority and not offend the Civil Powers, who tenacious of Liberty and prone to Censure, condemn all Proceedings that are not exactly Lawful, never considering what Cases may arise to make it necessary and excusable."[22] Harassed by what he considered a lack of cooperation, Loudoun joined with Washington in condemning civilian interference in military matters. In fact, after only six weeks in America, Loudoun was convinced that colonial governments were more a hindrance than a help. "Till we have every thing necessary, for carrying on the War here, within ourselves, independent of Aid from this Country," he wrote the Duke of Cumberland, "we shall go on very slowly."[23]

Above all, of course, Loudoun wanted to be free from any dependence upon colonial troops. According to professional military standards, American volunteers simply were not trained soldiers. By a trained soldier, British officers meant a highly disciplined career man; one who was able to execute the 184 movements in the manual of arms, while under fire if necessary; a man who would stand and face an enemy across an open field; a man who fought because he was ordered to.[24]

American volunteers did not measure up to these professional standards. Indeed, it seems unlikely that many colonials would evaluate their military service by the yardstick of British standards. The standard for military behavior used by Americans was their experience with local militia units, and militiamen were required to make only a slight adjustment in their usual patterns of behavior. There was some drilling and some-shooting at the periodic training sessions for militiamen, but the habits of command and obedience, which were prerequisites for a well-trained army, were not inculcated. Because militia officers were either elected by the men or selected by the legislature, their position of authority was ultimately subject to popular control, hardly an ideal military situation.[25] In short, the colonial militia was an almost perfect reflection of American society.

This was not nearly so true of the provincial army units. While they did not compare favorably with the British army, they were a long way from casual militia units. Discipline was stricter, duty harder and longer, and the rewards were unlikely to be compensatory with the risks. Therefore, the New England colonies who supplied most of the provincial troops had to devise a variety of inducements and penalties in order to fill their quotas. To begin with, they offered high wages and a bounty upon enlistment. A Connecticut volunteer, for example, earned about 10d. sterling per day. (A British regular, by comparison, was paid less than half that amount.) There were other incentives designed to promote enlistments in the provincial forces: volunteers were often exempted from taxation; soldiers were allowed to keep their equipment after serving for one campaign; and they were paid subsistence money while they were en route to and from the battle area.[26]

Still there were not enough volunteers to fill the quotas. Therefore, from time to time draft laws were reluctantly enacted by the New York, Massachusetts, and Connecticut legislatures. Generally, the laws required all able-bodied men between the ages of sixteen and fifty to report to their local militia unit. There, a predetermined number of men were impressed for service in the provincial army.[27]

This was not a popular procedure with either the lawmakers, who much preferred to entice volunteers into the army, or with the citizens, who were loath to leave their families to fight on some distant battlefield. Not surprisingly, therefore, some Americans decided not to obey the draft laws. "A Considerable Number of persons belonging to the 7th Regiment who have been detached for his Majesty's Service . . . have Neglected and Refused to go into the Service . . . ," Samuel Willard told the Connecticut Assembly late in 1757. Likewise, Governor De Lancey was astonished to discover that New Yorkers were fleeing their military obligations. Despite military pressure, however, both Connecticut and New York made only half-hearted attempts to enforce their impressment procedures.[28]

For those men who enlisted or were unlucky enough to be drafted, life in a provincial regiment was often a grim experience. Death lurked everywhere—on the battlefield, along a wilderness trail, and especially in camps. Because they were not adequately equipped and trained to survive long encampments, colonial soldiers were disastrously vulnerable to disease. "Our Provantial Forces Dye More or Less almost every day . . . ," noted Private Joseph Nichols sadly in August 1758. By September, when cold rains began to fall, the number of healthy, effective men in a provincial regiment was generally very low.[29]

The number of American soldiers available for duty was further reduced by a high desertion rate. When conditions became intolerable, or when a battle was won or lost, or simply when the men "got home in their heads," they left the army in droves. According to the Mutiny Act, which after 1756 applied to all British soldiers, desertion was punishable by death. But with this, as with other matters of military discipline, officers in the colonial armies only rarely allowed the maximum penalty to be carried out. If they were caught, deserters were tried, convicted, and sentenced; but then a provincial officer almost always stepped in and spared the man's life. If he got beyond the confines of the camp, the deserter had clear sailing, for the laws against harboring such men were universally ignored. Therefore the customary method used in America to round up deserters was for the governor to issue a proclamation pardoning all men who voluntarily returned to the army.[30]

This typically American remedy appalled British officers. It seemed to support their biased opinions about the character of Americans and it led them to the conclusion that provincials were too undependable to be used as fighting men. For this reason colonial troops were either assigned to unimportant posts or used as common laborers. Provincial soldiers "may be usefully employed with an Army," Loudoun told William Pitt, "in the deserted back parts of the Country . . . [thus] preventing the wearing out of the [regular] Troops before they come to Action." Or colonials could be strategically sacrificed. Americans were stationed at Fort William Henry in 1756 and Fort Cumberland in 1758 because British professionals believed these were not defensible positions. As the war progressed, American volunteers were employed increasingly in noncombat roles, or as James Otis later put it, as the "hewers of wood and drawers of water." "The Provincials," wrote Colonel James Robertson with disarming candor, are "sufficient to work out Boats, drive our Waggons, and fell our Trees, and do the Works that in inhabited Countrys are performed by Peasants."[31]

Some American volunteers refused to play such a menial role; many others did so only after a good bit of grumbling.[32] One Massachusetts officer confided to his cousin that he agreed with the opinion being expressed by his soldiers. Americans, they were saying, would be better off without "a Loudoun or a Webb or both." Should colonial officers always follow orders from British commanders, he wondered?[33] Although other colonial officers and soldiers may have had similar thoughts, nearly all of them did whatever they were ordered to do.

The mere fact that most Americans dutifully obeyed British orders and thus in some minor way participated in driving France from North America is certainly not in itself evidence of Anglo-American solidarity.[34] Indeed, the discriminatory military structure that grew up during the war, based as it was on "national" differences, contributed to the widening chasm between Great Britain and the colonies. For, paradoxically, while Americans were cast in a subordinate role, they thought of themselves as superior to the British. The seeds of this belief were sown in the early years of the war and although its nourishment was sometimes reduced to a trickle, an American self-confidence flowered nevertheless.

The development of this American self-awareness may be measured both quantitatively and qualitatively by using techniques pioneered by Richard Merritt and Ithiel de Sola Pool.[35] By counting the number of American, British, and other (European, South American, African) symbols used in the news columns of four randomly selected issues per year of newspapers published in Boston, New York, Charleston, Philadelphia, and Williamsburg, Professor Merritt was able to determine statistically the steady growth of an American self-awareness. His work indicates that the percentage of American place-name symbols in the colonial press reached a new high in 1755, the year of Braddock's defeat. The papers were filled with articles boasting about the American soldier's fighting prowess. As British regulars assumed the dominant role in the war's prosecution, the number of British symbols used in the colonial press declined sharply. Thus for the first time,

American symbols appeared more often in colonial newspaper columns than did British symbols.[36]

Furthermore, American symbols were used increasingly in favorable contexts, while British symbols were used unfavorably in the decade after 1755. This was especially true for symbols used in descriptions of military affairs. Immediately following Braddock's defeat, for example, there was much public comment, most of which decried the shortcomings of British regulars and extolled the virtues of American volunteers. The quality of the symbols used in these writings may be computed by applying a formula worked out by Ithiel de Sola Pool. In 1755 twenty pamphlets that dealt with Braddock's loss were published by Americans. American soldiers received four times as much favorable as unfavorable mention. Conversely, British regulars were written about unfavorably twice as often as they were favorably in these tracts.[37] Later in the war the virtues of the American volunteer were talked about less frequently, but this drop was not accompanied by an increase in British popularity.[38] In short, Americans did not come to regard redcoats more favorably because they were winning battles. There were only three victory sermons printed in America when the war ended in 1763 and they praised God, not the British army. Clearly, Americans were not as emotionally involved with the war in 1763 as they had been in 1755 when colonial soldiers seemed to offer the only hope for victory.

Of course, not all Americans thought highly of colonial soldiers. Although his provincial troops defeated a French army at Lake George, William Johnson believed that Americans were not "fitt for the various Duties and Services of a Campaign of any continuance. . . . "[39] Another American general, Phineas Lyman of Connecticut, agreed that colonials did not make outstanding soldiers and he thought he knew why. They were free men and "the proper habits of mind which Constitute ye soldier can not be raised in such a way, humain [sic] Nature does not Admit of it. . . . "[40]

The real and imagined differences between American and British soldiers created a situation that put these two protagonists on a collision course. Especially during the early years of the war — before American troops had been relegated to second-class status — there were a number of serious clashes between British and American officers. The root of the problem, which first came to the surface in the summer of 1756, was that by royal order American officers of whatever rank were to be regarded as captains with the least seniority whenever the provincial troops they commanded were joined with regular troops.[41] The order made it clear that the British government had no confidence in American officers, no understanding of the way in which a volunteer army was recruited in the colonies, and no concern for colonial legislative authority.

Until 1756 regulars and provincials were carefully kept apart, but when General James Abercromby was appointed commander in chief, the status of colonials became a hotly debated question. Early in that year, General John Winslow of Massachusetts was commissioned commander in chief of the troops raised by the New England colonies for an expedition against Crown Point. In May, a meeting attended by civilian representatives from each of the colonies participating in the assault was held in Albany. The independent mood of the conference was soon apparent. Governor Charles Hardy, a naval officer who had recently been appointed royal governor of New York, was shocked when his suggestion for a mixed force of regulars and provincials was overwhelmingly defeated. All but Hardy agreed with the representatives from Massachusetts, who stated that "they hoped never to see the day that their Troops should be under the Command of the King's Officer."[42] The conference decided, therefore, that the provincial troops would attack Crown Point alone, while the regular troops garrisoned the forts along the route.

General Winslow and his staff were highly pleased with this plan, for it specifically prevented "a Mixture of our Troops with the Regulars . . . which is a thing our people are strongly disaffected too. . . . "[43] Thus, on July 15, 1756, Winslow began to move his provincial soldiers toward Crown Point. But he had gone only a short distance when he was ordered to return to Albany by General James Abercromby, the newly appointed commander in chief of the British forces. The British general asked Winslow what would happen if his provincial soldiers were joined with the regular troops and their officers. Winslow answered bluntly: "It would occasion almost an universal desertion among the Provincials, because they were raised to serve solely under the command of their own Officers. . . . " In light of this strong testimony, the council of war summoned by

General Abercromby concluded that it would be "extremely unadvisable" to join regulars and provincials. Indeed, to do so "might be of fatal consequence to the public Service."[44]

After five days of debate, the provincial officers at Fort Edward came to the same conclusion. Unless the provincial officers were treated as equals, merging the troops would cause a "Dissolution of the greater part of the Army and have a direct tendency to prevent the raising of any Provincial Troops for his Majesty's Service for the future."[45] Winslow reported this resolution to General Abercromby, adding weakly that he still had some hope that some "means might be found that a Union might be made to destroy the common Enemy . . . and altho' we do not mix our persons, yet that our minds are bent the same way. . . ."[46]

Thinking the matter was settled, Winslow again began to move his army toward Crown Point. Once again, however, he and his staff were asked to return to Albany to confer with the new commander in chief, Lord Loudoun. When Loudoun discovered the bargain that had been struck between the regulars and provincials, he was enraged. He viewed the arrangement in an entirely different light than his predecessors. To Loudoun the plan represented an attempt by a clique of Massachusetts officers, secretly led by former Governor William Shirley, to subvert the authority vested by the Crown in the commander in chief.[47] Indeed, Loudoun interpreted the provincial officers' recommendation against a merger as a positive manifestation that Americans would not obey "his Majesty's Commands." In short, he refused to accept the separate but equal arrangement which Generals Braddock, Shirley, and Abercromby had tacitly approved in past years.

Winslow was bewildered. He wrote Shirley, reminding him of his earlier commitment to the New England governors which permitted the provincial troops to move against Crown Point unaided by regulars. It was on the basis of that agreement that men were recruited. In other words, according to Winslow's interpretation, the provincial officers had entered into a contractual arrangement with the soldiers who had enlisted. The officers were, therefore,

> Executors in Trust which was not in their power to resign, and, even should they do it, it would end in a DISSOLUTION OF THE ARMY as the Privates Universally hold it as one part of the Terms on which they

Enlisted that they were to be Commanded by their own Officers and this is a Principle so strongly Imbib'd that it is not in the Power of Man to remove it.[48]

Shirley countered by arguing that the people of New England did not support the independent stance assumed by Winslow and his staff. The officers were commissioned and the men recruited to drive the French from North America. This goal only could be achieved if the provincials cooperated with the commander in chief. Governor Thomas Fitch supported Shirley. We "must not goe Counter to the plans Laid . . . ," the Connecticut governor told Winslow, and "run the Risque of those Dreadful Consequences which may follow a Refusal."[49]

Loudoun's response to Winslow's argument was equally uncompromising: he ordered Winslow to come to Albany immediately. When the provincial general arrived, Loudoun demanded to know whether the American troops would "Act in Conjunction with His Majesty's Troops, and under the Command of His Commander in Chief. . . . " Furthermore, Loudoun insisted upon an "immediate answer . . . in writing." On August 10, Winslow formally capitulated; he declared that he would always carry out the instructions of the King's general, though he asked as a favor that Loudoun permit the American troops to act separately insofar as that was possible.[50]

Winslow now thought he had Loudoun's consent to move ahead, for on August 19 he issued orders to move supplies from Lake George to an advanced post, five miles south of Crown Point. The following day, however, Winslow's plans were checked once more, for Loudoun had received news of the loss of Oswego, which he believed changed the whole military picture. Should the provincial troops "meet with any Misfortune" the enemy would be able to drive deep into their territory. Therefore, Loudoun ordered Winslow simply to establish a strong defensive position near Fort Edward rather than launching the long-planned offensive against Crown Point. Through the winter months of 1756, American soldiers waited for the expected attack by the French. It never came. On November 11, when their enlistments expired, the first contingent of provincials marched from Lake George to Albany, where they were discharged from the service.[51]

The deep resentment felt by colonial officers who lost their rank when British officers assumed command of an operation manifested itself repeatedly during the Great War for Empire.

William Williams, a young Massachusetts officer, complained bitterly that British officers treated the Americans like "Orderly Serjeants." "We must do what we are biden and if not, Threatened with this and the Other Thing," he wrote his cousin, Israel Williams. "If things are not put upon some other Footing," he concluded, "I am of the Mind tis not worth while to proceed."[52] Thomas Hutchinson heard similar hostile opinions expressed by other Americans. "There are a thousand stories all over the Country" having to do with how shabbily provincials were treated by British officers, "which it's impossible to satisfy people about."[53]

The low opinions that Americans and Englishmen formed about one another during the Great War for Empire were not quickly forgotten. In the sharp verbal exchanges prior to the American Revolution, these opinions became important factors in the decisions made on both sides of the Atlantic to wage war in 1776. British officers who had served in America prior to 1763 spoke contemptuously in the House of Commons about the military qualities of the colonists. The First Lord of the Admiralty asserted that the Americans were "raw, undisciplined, cowardly men. I wish instead of 40 to 50,000 of these brave fellows, they would produce in the field [against us] at least 200,000, the more the better . . . if they didn't run away, they would starve themselves into compliance. . . ."[54] General James Grant, who had served with little distinction in Forbes's assault on Fort Duquesne in 1758, also publicly condemned American soldiers. According to Grant, Americans were neither as brave nor as devoted to the protection of women as were the British. And he boasted that during the Great War for Empire British officers such as himself had taken the measure of provincial soldiers and decided they should be treated simply as beasts of burden.[55]

While he was in England, Benjamin Franklin assumed the task of replying to these slurs on American valor. In an anonymous letter to the *Public Advertiser* in February 1775, he pointed to instances of American bravery, including the battles at Louisbourg and Lake George, and praised colonial troops for "having covered the Retreat of the British Regulars and saved them from utter Destruction in the Expedition under Braddock." Turning to British failures in America, Franklin listed General Grant's rout by Indians in 1758, as well as several other "Campaigns of shameful Defeats or as shameful Inactivity."[56]

Despite the efforts of Franklin and a few others, including General Thomas Gage, the British ministry remained absolutely confident that their professional army could crush America's amateur troops. In the spring of 1775, shortly before he left England, Franklin heard a British army officer who had once served in America boast that "with a thousand British grenadiers he would undertake to go from one end of America to the other, and geld all the males, partly by force and partly by a little coaxing."[57]

In the colonies, the Reverend Myles Cooper, president of King's College and an active Tory writer, made the same argument: Americans simply were no match for British professionals. Cooper's *Friendly Address to All Reasonable Americans* maintained that resistance to British regulars was useless. It was absurd, Cooper contended, for undisciplined and unorganized Americans to think of opposing British veterans, especially in light of the fact that the British had done the major part of the fighting during the Great War for Empire.[58]

Cooper's disquieting pamphlet was answered by Charles Lee, a lieutenant colonel in the British army who nevertheless supported the American cause in 1775. Lee effectively demolished Cooper's contentions. He ridiculed the achievements of the British regulars in the Great War for Empire, pointing out that it had taken them several years to learn to cope with American conditions. The parade maneuvers in which the redcoats were so thoroughly trained were of no military value, Lee argued. Finally, he observed that the British army was not as well commanded in 1775 as it had been during the campaign against the French in America.[59] According to the editor of the Salem *Essex Gazette,* Lee's pamphlet definitely reduced the awe some people had for British soldiers.[60]

Large numbers of Americans and Englishmen came together for the first time during the Great War for Empire. They emerged from this experience thinking less of one another than they had before the war. To be sure, the images Americans had of themselves and of the Englishmen they encountered were not wholly accurate.[61] On the one hand, when Americans thought of British soldiers they thought of Braddock's defeat, of Loudoun's ineptness, and, in general, of the redcoats' inability to fight in the American environment. On the other hand, as a result of their wartime experiences, Americans thought of themselves as men of the highest character, motivated to fight by the highest ideals, and especially able to fight in the wilderness. Although these myths did not determine the events that led to the breakup of the British Empire, they did make Americans less fearful of British threats after 1763.

CHAPTER VII

CONTROVERSY OVER THE QUARTERING OF SOLDIERS

Nearly a century and a half of resistance to arbitrary military power, with which the colonists were as familiar as any Englishman, was ignored when the Crown left the quartering of troops in America to the British army during the Great War for Empire. Americans vigorously opposed the forced quartering of troops as a violation of the constitutional guarantee that the army must be subordinate to civil authority. Moreover, the colonists went beyond legalistic objections to the actions of the British army to a defense of the underlying principle articulated by that provision of the constitution. Specifically, they feared that if British military power were allowed to reign unchecked — as the Crown's new policy seemed to threaten — liberty itself would be destroyed.

Students of colonial history have not defined the issues as clearly as the colonists did. Historians of the Great War for Empire who are interested in the problems faced by British leaders in its prosecution usually picture the colonists who spoke out against forced quartering as shortsighted obstructionists whose petty arguments undermined the war for empire. Those historians intent on tracing the development of political ideology have described the controversy over quartering simply as one more milestone on the colonists' march to democracy. Other historians have viewed the whole business as a power struggle masquerading as a constitutional debate. For instance, it is maintained that the Pennsylvania Assembly used the quartering issue to make gains in its contest with the governor for political supremacy. And finally, one student finds that the " 'ideological' differences were overshadowed by the sure consequences of appearing laggard in the King's service."[1]

While this interpretation explains generally why the struggle over quartering was not more bitter than it was, it does not provide much insight into the precise nature and the long-range effect of the issue.

Since the revolutionary settlement of 1689, Parliament had enacted an annual Mutiny Act which expressly prohibited quartering on private citizens against their will. Whenever the army marched out of its barracks, local governmental officials were to make arrangements with innkeepers to provide for the troops. Proprietors of inns and public houses were allowed to choose between supplying officers and men quarters with food and drink at an established rate or providing quarters with free incidentals, such as candles, vinegar, salt, a maximum of five pints of beer or cider daily, utensils, and firewood. When the army moved on, the quartermaster paid the innkeeper the legal charges for quartering; any expenses were considered a tax on the proprietor, which was sometimes paid by Parliament.[2] In 1723, 1754, and 1756 certain provisions of the Mutiny Act were specifically stated by Parliament to be applicable in the colonies, but the sections on quartering were not extended to America until the war there had ended.

During the war Americans were told only that they must follow the orders issued by the commanders in chief for quartering soldiers.[3] This use of arbitrary power raised in American minds the "specter of catastrophe," the fear that civil government would be overwhelmed by military power.[4] For this reason, General Edward Braddock and the Earl of Loudoun became the targets for colonial opposition to an assertive British imperialism.

Early in 1755 General Braddock acridly told the Pennsylvania Assembly that, as the assigning of quarters for the army was his province, he would "take due care to burthen those colonies the most, that show the least loyalty to his Majesty." Edward Shippen, a wealthy Lancaster merchant, wrote his son that the Assembly "know not how to stomach this military address, but tis thought it will frighten them into some reasonable measures as it must be a vain thing to contend with a General at the head of an army, though he should act an arbitrary part; especially in all probability he will be supported in everything at home."[5]

The general did not live to carry out his threat. He and nearly half his men were killed in an ambush near the banks of the Monongahela River in July 1755. Upon Braddock's death,

Colonel Thomas Dunbar assumed command and immediately ordered that once vain army to Philadelphia. Both Governor Robert Morris and the Pennsylvania Assembly reacted incredulously. It was only the middle of July, but Dunbar was pulling the army off the frontier and marching it into "winter" quarters. Even while the Assembly met in special session to consider steps "to retrieve the glory of His Majesty's Arms," Dunbar's beaten army moved closer to Philadelphia. His assurances that he would not require Pennsylvania to provide his men with free quarters, as "General Braddock threatened," were received coolly.[6]

On August 1, Morris reluctantly asked the mayor and corporation of Philadelphia to arrange quarters for 100 officers and 1,200 soldiers. When the city officials replied that they "have it not in our powers to Obey your Order," the governor asked the Assembly to draft a law that would enable the magistrates to quarter Dunbar's troops.[7] The Assembly responded immediately; a committee was appointed and a bill drafted and passed by the House within a day after Morris's request had been made. The legislators used the Mutiny Act as their model, and therefore they included in their bill the hallowed rights of Englishmen as embodied in the Petition of Rights and the Bill of Rights.[8] Since Dunbar's troops were not quartered in Philadelphia as expected, the new law was not actually tested. But the constitutional issue that lay at the heart of subsequent controversies over quartering had been raised, and it would not fade away as easily as had Dunbar's defeated troops.

Indeed, the issue was rudely thrust into the political arena in July 1756 when the Privy Council decided that Pennsylvania's quartering act should be disallowed. Attorney General William Murray told the Council that the law would "Cramp the Public Service and obstruct the defense of the Province. That it assumes propositions true in the Mother Country, rightly asserted in the Reigns of Charles the First and Charles the Second in time of Peace, when Soldiers were kept up without Consent of Parliament." Murray added, however, "the application of such propositions to a Colony in time of War, in the Case of Troops raised for their Protection by the Authority of the Parliament of *Great Britain* made the first time by an Assembly, many of whom plead what they call Conscience, for not making or assisting Military operations to resist the Enemy, should not be allowed to stand as Law."[9] Obviously, the

attorney general's decision was motivated at least as much by
his disdain for Quaker pacifism and by the immediate needs of
the army as by the technical question of legal privilege. In
other words, Pennsylvania's claims to the historic rights of
Englishmen to refuse to quarter soldiers was measured against
military necessity and found wanting. The stage was thus set
for another confrontation between the army and the legislature.

Lord Loudoun, who arrived in July 1756 to resume the
military campaign in America, was well aware that the legal
basis of his demands for quarters was ill-defined. But he was
determined to get what he needed, by force if necessary. "As to
quarters at Philadelphia and every other place," he instructed
one of his senior officers in September 1756, "where I find it
Necessary to have Troops [quartered], I have a Right to them,
and must have them; I would have you go gently with the
People at First, but [you] must not give up. . . ."[10]

In October, Loudoun wrote Governor William Denny of
Pennsylvania informing him that one battalion of royal troops
was to be quartered in Philadelphia. Loudoun disingenuously
added that he thought it unnecessary to spell out the army's
needs because as a former army officer, Denny was "so
thoroughly acquainted with the Quartering in England in Time
of Peace, and what Things are furnished in Quarters, for the
Officers and Soldiers, and how much further Quartering
extends in Time of War, and even must do so from the Nature
of Things."[11] In fact, neither Denny nor anyone else, including
Loudoun, knew what effect war had on the provisions of the
Mutiny Act because there had been no clear precedents for
quartering in Great Britain in wartime since 1689.

Once again, therefore, the Assembly turned to the Mutiny Act
as the only possible source of guidance available to it. The
House was adjourned most of November, so the quartering bill
was not passed until December 3. Denny promptly returned the
bill unsigned, with a message reminding the legislators that the
Privy Council had recently rejected a similar act. This one was
equally unacceptable, for it also contained a statement that
would have allowed citizens to refuse to quarter soldiers. The
objectionable passage was omitted when the bill was reconsi-
dered by the Assembly on December 8, but so too was any
reference to quartering in private houses. The new act outlined
a procedure providing lodging for soldiers only in public
houses.[12]

Governor Denny immediately ordered a survey made to determine how many quarters were actually available in the city's public houses. There were supposedly quarters enough for 400 soldiers. But the mayor's survey revealed that this number was too high. The innkeepers, it seemed, had deliberately reported "more quarters than their Houses wou'd allow of, from a mistaken notion that they were to be paid a Shilling a day for every head. . . ."[13]

It was soon apparent, therefore, that there was a serious shortage of quarters. By December 15 the troops had arrived, and Denny reported to the Council that despite his orders to city officials and the Assembly, "the King's Forces still remained in a most miserable Condition, neither the Assembly, Commissioners, nor Magistrates, having done any thing to relieve them, tho' the weather grew more pinching, and the small Pox was encreasing [sic] among the Soldiers to such a Degree that the whole Town would soon become a Hospital. . . ."[14]

Colonel Henry Bouquet, the officer in command of British troops in Pennsylvania, had orders from Loudoun to take whatever public or private quarters he needed by force and "if the Battalion there is not Sufficient, I have Order'd Mr. Webb, to March in as many more, as are necessary and Quarter the whole on them." Bouquet was loathe to take such a drastic step. Instead, he asked Denny to issue a warrant authorizing him to quarter soldiers in private homes. The governor deliberately left the warrant blank, so that Bouquet could have a free hand.[15]

The Assembly was outraged; it "did not think it possible your Honour could be prevailed with to issue Orders so diametrically opposite to an express Law passed by yourself but a few Days before. . . ." The legislators insisted that Denny compel the city officials to reconsider their earlier estimate of the number of troops that could be quartered in public houses. Denny's terse reply was delivered to the Assembly on December 18: "The King's Troops must be quartered."[16]

For the first time in the colony's history, the Assembly met on a Sunday. A reply was drafted to the governor's demands, and carried to him "when the Streets were full of People going to their respective Places of Worship." The Assembly's reply reviewed the whole dispute and concluded by placing the blame for the present difficulties squarely on Denny and

Loudoun. Neither had given the House specific information
about exactly what should be provided, nor had they indicated
how many troops were to be quartered. The Assembly's
confusion was evident: "We thought we had by the late Law
provided well for their Quartering in this Province; especially
as we had exactly followed the Act of Parliament made for the
same Purpose."[17]

Although Denny found the message "a long Narrative filled
with Abuses," he agreed to meet with a committee from the
Assembly the following day in order that the dispute between
them might be resolved. Benjamin Franklin opened the
conference by assuring the governor that the House was also
greatly concerned about the well-being of the army. At the
same time, however, the House believed that Denny "had
unnecessarily . . . issued orders for Quartering them on private
Houses by Force, and contrary to Law." Franklin reiterated the
position the Assembly had taken earlier: the public housekeep-
ers were able to provide enough quarters and if they refused,
the magistrates "should do their Duty and fine them as the
Law directed."[18] Denny remarked that he was not concerned
with where the fault lay. He simply wanted the troops
quartered. To this, the committee replied that it was the
governor's duty to execute the law as it was enacted.

When the committee suggested that soldiers might be
quartered in public houses in the suburbs, or in the
neighboring towns, Denny answered that the commander in
chief had demanded quarters in Philadelphia. If the people
were unhappy about this arrangement, they should complain to
Lord Loudoun. At this, the committee retorted that they
"wished the Governor would consider himself somewhat more
in his civil Capacity as Governor of the Province." He should
protect the people, and if a matter needed to be brought before
Loudoun, the governor should present it.[19] In other words, the
committeemen wanted Denny to help them protect the
constitutional rights of the people.

The committee then posed a question that struck at the heart
of the controversy. "What was to be understood," the
committeemen asked, "by Quartering being extended farther in
Time of War, than in Time of Peace"? Denny said he did not
know, "unless it was Quartering on private Houses." That
would be permissible, the committee said, only if the people
voluntarily offered quarters, but certainly no one should be

forced to provide for soldiers. The governor replied that the general would decide if troops were to be forcibly quartered. One committeeman angrily reminded Denny what might happen if generals were allowed such arbitrary power. A military officer "might say it was necessary to quarter the whole Army, not only in one City but in one Square or one Street; and thereby harass the Inhabitants excessively." At this point, the governor ended the conference, declaring he was interested only in facts.[20]

This uproarious conference did much more than raise tempers. It served as concrete evidence to Pennsylvania's political leaders that Loudoun's demand for quarters was a clear threat to American liberty. Indeed, Franklin summed up this fear when he called Denny — who was nothing more than the general's go-between — "a meer Bashaw or worse." To Americans like Franklin who were familiar with the writings of England's Real Whigs, there was no worse example of despotism than those Turkish bashaws whose armies allowed them to rule without the consent of the people.[21]

The following day the Assembly invoked the spirit, if not the rhetoric, of Franklin's charge. When Denny told the legislators that the mayor of Philadelphia was certain there was not enough public housing to quarter Loudoun's soldiers, the Assembly insisted that the governor could not violate existing law. That was all any Englishman concerned with the preservation of liberty could do. Of this the House was confident. "We are contented," the Assemblymen declared, "that the King's Ministers should judge of these Proceedings and that the World should judge of the Decency of our last Message."[22]

When Loudoun heard that his troops still had not been adequately housed in Philadelphia, he sent a message reiterating his demand that his soldiers be quartered. If Pennsylvania did not comply immediately he intended to seize quarters; to "instantly march a Number sufficient for that purpose and find Quarters for the whole." With that sword dangling over their heads, Franklin and the other provincial commissioners quickly agreed to rent additional housing and to make hospital space available for soldiers suffering from smallpox.[23]

The bitter, raucous quarrel between the Pennsylvania Assembly and the governor and Lord Loudoun was more than just another dispute between the legislature and the executive, or the Crown. It was more than a simple struggle for political power. It was a contest for political liberty, which in the case of quartering had been clearly defined in Britain by Parliamentary statute and the charters of rights issued in 1628 and 1689. But during the winter of 1756, Pennsylvania's leaders learned that they did not have the same rights as other Englishmen. They saw that British bayonets, or the threat of them, would be used to dictate solutions and enforce measures which were resisted by local governments.[24]

Wherever the British army violated what the colonists believed to be the rights of Englishmen as to quartering, local political agencies reacted with hostility. The city officials of Albany, New York, clashed first with the army during the summer of 1756. For although the New York Assembly had appropriated £1,000 to build barracks in Albany, nothing actually had been built when the troops arrived.[25] Without the barracks, troops would have to be quartered in private houses, for there were not nearly enough public houses in Albany to house two regiments. But the Assembly had not enacted legislation to cover this situation. Therefore, the mayor of Albany refused to quarter Loudoun's troops. He told the general that "he understood the Law that [Loudoun] had no right to Quarters or Storehouses, or anything else from them; and that [Albany] would give none." Loudoun promptly labeled the mayor "a fool" and thereafter communicated only with one of the mayor's staff, tersely informing him that as a military officer he "must Follow the Custom of Armies and help myself [to quarters]." When the mayor and his council remained adamant, Loudoun ordered his quartermasters to forcibly place soldiers into homes.[26]

Loudoun forced the residents of Albany to meet his demands, but he could not make them accept the arguments he used to justify his highhanded actions. In September 1756 the New York Assembly framed a bill which it hoped would protect homeowners from further forcible quartering. At first, Governor Charles Hardy demanded that the bill be amended to allow the military authorities more latitude. After a month of debate, however, Hardy swung over to the Assemblymen's position. He had become convinced, he told Loudoun in November, that it would be an enormous hardship for many families to have soldiers thrust into their homes. Loudoun was not sympathetic. He simply repeated his dogmatic contention that in wartime "no house has been exempt from Quartering the Troops the General thought Proper to have in any Place for carrying on the Service. . . ."[27]

Once again, therefore, in the winter of 1756, Loudoun threatened to send additional soldiers to Albany in order to compel the people there to house his troops. The mayor of that city told Loudoun that the people were opposed to such an illegal act. But, faced with British bayonets and political pressure from Lieutenant Governor James De Lancey, the mayor's resistance collapsed. By the end of the day British soldiers were quartered in every house in Albany.[28]

Just as in Philadelphia, the opposition to forced quartering in Albany came from political leaders committed to the defense of the rights of Englishmen.[29] Abraham Yates, sheriff of Albany during the war years, shared his angry thoughts about the conduct of the British army with his political ally William Livingston, with the governor, the city council, and his constituents. Yates argued that the military's claim to superior authority was "Inconsistent with the Constitution of England." He believed that all governmental power was limited by a man's "Fixed fundamental Rights Born with him. . . ." Obviously, Yates contended, the military's action posed a grave threat to "Freedom of his Person and Property . . . ," freedom that all Englishmen can constitutionally claim.[30]

The Albany city council agreed with Yates's analysis. "We conceive," the council resolved in June 1758, that "all kind of . . . the most Iniquitous and tirannical Violations . . . the most abominable Crimes have been committed, some of them under Coulour and Sanction of advancing His majesties Service. . . ." The practice of quartering soldiers in private homes against the wishes of the people has "assumed a Power over us Very inconsistent with the Liberties of a free and Loyal People. . . ." "Upon the Whole," the council concluded, "we conceive that his Majesties Paternal Cares to Release us [from the threat of France] have in a Great measure been Made use of to oppress us."[31]

The implications to be drawn from the Albany city council's resolution seem unmistakable: New York's political leaders had a clear perception of the rights and liberties of an English subject, and when one of those rights was threatened or violated, as was the right not to have troops quartered in private homes against the owners' consent, the colony's politicans vigorously and publicly protested that infringement. Therefore, the clash between the British army and the people of Albany was not merely a petty local dispute, but the thin edge of the wedge that was being driven between the colonies and the home country.

Governor Thomas Pownall of Massachusetts was one of the first English officials to grasp this fact. By the end of 1758 he had concluded that Loudoun's behavior was alienating the American people from the British Empire. He condemned Loudoun's aggressive methods as repulsive and unconstitutional. No military man had a right to interfere in civilian affairs, according to Pownall.[32] A number of other Massachusetts politicians, including Thomas Hutchinson and a substantial part of the lower house, were also disturbed by Loudoun's methods.

In January 1757 a committee from the House was sent to talk with Loudoun to determine precisely what he expected from Massachusetts. He told them that they should provide the soldiers who were quartered in the barracks on Castle William with bedding, candles, and firewood. Although the committeemen did not mention the subject, Loudoun ominously offered the information that in England during a war troops were quartered in private homes.[33]

The House quickly complied with Loudoun's request for supplies for the soldiers on Castle William.[34] His dark threat about quartering soldiers in private homes, however, touched off a display of political fireworks in the House. Several members demanded an investigation into the army's right to take quarters. Only a clever move by Jeremiah Gridley, a distinguished lawyer and representative from Brookline, prevented a full debate on the matter. Gridley asked that a joint committee be formed to consider the problem. Such a move, Gridley hoped, would not only win time for those who supported the army but would also put the question in safer, more conservative hands.

For awhile at least, Gridley's careful maneuver seemed likely to be upset by Thomas Hutchinson. When the joint committee to discuss quartering met, Hutchinson read a prepared statement which asserted that only civil authorities had the right to determine what should be done to meet the army's needs. "With great warmth and Sputter," Hutchinson, according to Gridley's biased account, "began to catachise . . . about

English rights." Gridley countered by pointing out that Loudoun had not demanded, but had asked the Massachusetts legislature to make quarters available.[35] In this particular instance, Gridley was correct; but Hutchinson must have known that Loudoun had threatened to seize quarters in Philadelphia and Albany when those governments refused to comply with his demands. Still, this was Massachusetts and so far Loudoun had abided by local law. Therefore, first Hutchinson and then the other members of the committee backed off from their hostile positions and recommended that the House implement Loudoun's requests.

It soon became apparent how unimportant words were, for whether he "demanded" or "requested" the fact was that Loudoun held a powerful hand. Early in August he asked Pownall to quarter a regiment of soldiers. Realizing the situation, Pownall urged the House to pass a bill empowering Boston officials to assign quarters, thus maintaining local governmental control over the army. The governor warned the legislators that if this were not done, the army would "plead necessity and provide for themselves." The threat worked: on August 27 the House appropriated money to build additional barracks for 1,000 men on Castle William. Although this was an expensive solution, it allowed the legislators to prohibit any quartering in towns in Massachusetts. Then Pownall tried to convince Loudoun to play along. He pleaded with the general to work through local officials as the law stipulated, reminding him that this was constitutional procedure.[36]

Loudoun did not react kindly to Pownall's advice. He vented his anger against Pownall in a lengthy letter to his friend the Duke of Cumberland. The general was especially irritated by Pownall's insistence that a military man had no right to violate civil law. According to Loudoun, the governor believed "every act of a General is an Infringement on the Liberty of the People, and if the Civil Magistrate . . . does not give Quarters, the Troops must perish in the Streets."[37]

In November the private quarrel between Loudoun and Pownall burst into the open. Two recruiting officers came to the governor complaining that local officials had refused them quarters in Boston. Pownall promptly communicated with the city's selectmen. They were sympathetic, but they reminded the governor that Massachusetts law prohibited any quartering in public or private houses. As an immediate and temporary solution to the problem, Pownall suggested that the recruiters use the barracks on Castle William. At the same time, he sent Loudoun a detailed report outlining the steps he had taken and explaining the Massachusetts quartering law. The law was designed to safeguard "an Essential right of the Subject that no one cou'd be quartered upon, unless by Law and there was no Law. . . ."[38]

Under almost any circumstances, Loudoun would have been angered at this situation, but Pownall's letter reached the general at an especially bad time. He faced a frontier crisis in northern New York: French and Indians had overrun that colony's defense perimeter. According to Loudoun's view, therefore, the military situation was too serious to allow civilian authorities to obstruct military activities. There was no excuse for disobedience, he stated in his letter to Pownall. Loudoun insisted that he had a right to quarters which superseded any provincial law. He promised to march three regiments into the city unless the recruiters were granted housing in Boston within forty-eight hours.[39]

Loudoun's ultimatum arrived in Boston on the evening of November 25. Early the next day, Pownall sent a brief message to the General Court. He told the legislature that "His Majesty's service, the protection and defence of his colonies very much depended upon a compliance with [Loudoun's demand]"[40] The House remained in session well into the night and reconvened on Sunday in order to hammer out a bill that would satisfy their principles, their constituents, and Loudoun. On Monday afternoon the bill was presented to the governor for his signature. The act made it clear that the legislators believed a colonial law was the prerequisite to any quartering. Moreover, although it provided for quartering in public houses, the law allowed innkeepers to complain to a justice of the peace if they thought too many soldiers had been quartered upon them.[41] In this way, the legislators preserved at least a modicum of the essential right of Englishmen to refuse to billet soldiers.

Neither the new law nor Pownall's explanation of his reasons for signing it pleased Loudoun. He renewed his threat to march troops into Boston and force the people to acknowledge his right to quarters wherever he chose them. Indeed, the Massachusetts legislature had no business even debating the matter; the army's absolute right to quarters "is settled and regulated by an Act of the British Parliament, which no Act of theirs can infringe or diminish."[42]

When Loudoun's latest condemnation of civil government became known, there was an outburst of public indignation. Much of the abuse was directed toward Pownall, who was seen as a supporter of Loudoun. Pownall was accused of leading a military faction bent on subverting the Massachusetts constitution. "Were this Government [by] Elections as Rhode Island is," Pownall stated, "I shou'd next year be turn'd out. . . ."[43] Similarly, a House committee reminded the general that "the Inhabitants of this Province are intitled to the Natural Rights of English born Subjects. . . ."[44] The rest of the committee's report was more conciliatory, though it recommended that the law remain unchanged.

While the General Court debated the committee's report, Pownall drafted his own reply to Loudoun. It was a clear, forceful statement of the governor's political philosophy. "In a Free Government where there is a Public Legislature and People Act by their Representatives," he wrote, "a Governor must endeavor *to lead* those People for he cannot *drive* them and he must lead them Step by Step as he can *gett footing.*" He concluded by questioning Loudoun's uncontrolled power. The use of such power not only caused the assembly to block other military legislation, but it alienated the people of Massachusetts from the royal government.[45]

By the end of December, Loudoun's temper had cooled and he accepted the assembly's report as sufficient evidence of its acquiescence to his demands. He boasted that while the other colonies watched, he had settled the Massachusetts controversy in the army's favor. In fact, Massachusetts was the clear winner. Despite Loudoun's bluster, the quartering of troops was still technically dependent upon an act of the Massachusetts legislature. Thus, Massachusetts had effectually upheld the procedural political forms that allowed the colonists to continue to lay claim to the rights of Englishmen in regard to quartering.[46]

After 1758, quartering was no longer an omnipresent problem. The focus of the war had shifted north to Canada and most colonies had built barracks to house the troops when they were not fighting. This should not obscure the fact, however, that neither the British generals nor the colonists changed their theoretical positions. The former still insisted it was their prerogative to seize quarters whenever and wherever they thought it necessary and the latter were equally insistent that forced quartering was a violation of an Englishman's constitutionally guaranteed rights.[47]

The quartering problem in America could have been resolved with tactful negotiation. There were English officials sympathetic to the arguments advanced by the colonists during the Great War for Empire. Welbore Ellis, Secretary of War in 1765 when Parliament finally began consideration of a quartering act for America, remarked: "It will certainly be useful and necessary for the magistrates there to have power given them to quarter upon private houses," but, he added, "the principal Objections are well founded." George Grenville agreed with Ellis that as it then stood the quartering act was likely to create a commotion in the colonies, "especially as the quartering of soldiers upon the people against their wills is declared by the petition of right to be contrary to law."[48] Grenville's dilemma seemed to be resolved when Thomas Pownall, now an advisor to the ministry on American affairs, offered to draft a bill palatable to the colonists.

Pownall's suggestions were incorporated into the final version of the Quartering Act and passed by Parliament on May 3, 1765. The act stipulated that soldiers were to be quartered in barracks; if there were not enough barrack space, they were to be billeted in public houses and inns. If these accommodations were insufficient, the governor and council were to hire vacant buildings.[49] Quartering in private houses was scrupulously avoided. In this way, Pownall thought to quiet American complaints. But he forgot something he should have remembered from his experience as governor of Massachusetts. Namely, that Americans had insisted only their own legislatures could enact such laws. For this reason the New York Assembly initially refused to acknowledge the Quartering Act. This was the assumption underlying the resistance to the Quartering Act that developed in Massachusetts, New York, New Jersey, South Carolina, and Georgia. About a decade later the First Continental Congress reiterated this same position when it listed the Quartering Act as one of those arbitrary laws "which demonstrate a system formed to enslave America." In short, as a result of their experience during the Great War for Empire, many Americans had come to believe that British imperialism presented a real danger to the preservation of liberty.[50]

The controversy between the British army and colonial governments over quartering helped to create a lasting resentment and a hardening of political attitudes which contributed to the alienation of the colonies from Great Britain. American political leaders would not quickly forget that the threat of military power had been used to force them to comply with what they conceived as an unconstitutional procedure, a practice that posed a grave danger to political liberty in America. Indeed, those who observed how British generals settled the quartering problem by threatening to use or actually using the King's soldiers against recalcitrant colonials could scarcely avoid the conclusion that in the event of future serious differences with Great Britain the colonies would either have to submit to royal demands or devise a resistance in kind.

CHAPTER VIII

WARTIME RESTRICTIONS
ON COLONIAL TRADE

During most of the eighteenth century American merchants carried on trade with the French West Indies. The French islands were the best available market for fish, grain, timber, horses, and other colonial products. This trade was not contrary to the Navigation Acts. With the outbreak of the Great War for Empire, however, the Crown prohibited all American trade with the French and, in 1757, banned the export of provisions from America to neutral ports.[1]

The task of enforcing these special war regulations was given to the royal navy and, in America, to the commander in chief of the British forces. Naval officers had sweeping powers which allowed them to search and seize vessels at sea, and the commanding general was empowered to lay embargoes on colonial shipping.[2] Still, some colonial merchants were able on occasion to trade illegally. While Anglo-American officials focused their attention on these relatively few smugglers, a great number of law-abiding merchants were angered because their political rights and interests were disregarded by the Crown.[3] American merchants and their representatives claimed that embargoes initiated by military fiat and implemented by methods that violated their rights as Englishmen were clear and dangerous manifestations of a trend toward a new assertive imperialism.

This inclination on the part of the Crown began rather inauspiciously. When General Edward Braddock met with a group of colonial governors in Alexandria, Virginia in the spring of 1755, he simply asked them to cooperate with the Crown to stamp out smuggling. Braddock's secret instructions included a specific warning about the people of New York and

Pennsylvania, "who are reported to be most Notoriously guilty of Supplying the French with Provisions." Still, the general decided to allow the colonies to handle the problem themselves. Pennsylvania, New York, Connecticut, and Massachusetts subsequently passed laws requiring a shipmaster to post a £1,000 bond to ensure that he would land only in British ports.[4]

As the war effort increased, however, some Anglo-American officials came to believe that these regulations were not preventing American goods from reaching the French.[5] Governor Robert Morris of Pennsylvania therefore urged his legislature to lay a general embargo on provisions, but the Assembly adjourned without taking action on his request. The legislators recognized neither the need nor the legal justification for prohibiting merchants from trading with other Englishmen or neutrals. Morris thought otherwise, and on July 3, 1755, the governor acted on his own, imposing a ban on the exportation of war materials and foodstuffs for one month.[6]

When the month was nearly up, Morris asked the Assembly to approve and extend his general embargo. The House again refused, pointing out that it had already enacted adequate legislation to prohibit goods from reaching the French which would be in effect until June 1756. Once again, Morris simply acted alone. He instructed customs officials late in August to continue the general embargo until further notice.[7]

Philadelphia's merchants complained loudly, but at the same time they seem to have honored the governor's embargo. "Our Markets are at a stand," lamented Thomas Willing in September 1755, "no Purchaser's appearing; the greatest Number of Vessells in our Harbour yet I have seen at this Time of Year."[8] Prices for corn, flour, and wheat reached their low points in the months during which the embargo was in effect.[9]

As the second year of the war against France began, Sir Charles Hardy, recently appointed governor of New York, convinced his Assembly that a general embargo should be laid. The legislators agreed, but they stipulated that Pennsylvania must duplicate New York's effort.[10] The Pennsylvania Assembly responded almost immediately. In mid-May 1756 it adopted a law patterned after New York's. The Pennsylvania legislators warned Governor Morris that their continued cooperation was dependent upon what New Jersey and Delaware did. Within a few weeks these two Delaware River provinces also agreed to impose a general embargo.[11]

This bit of colonial cooperation caused a sharp economic decline in Pennsylvania, where a bumper crop of grain had been harvested. After only a few weeks, Thomas Wharton told a New York merchant that "everything here is Stagnated." In mid-June, Thomas Willing recorded a steady decline in prices for provisions, adding that large quantities of foodstuffs were spoiling because of the embargo.[12]

Merchant complaints burst to the surface on July 10, when a group of distressed traders petitioned the Assembly to end the embargo. They explained to the legislators the hardships it was causing in the British West Indies. They also stated that Pennsylvania merchants were suffering more than those of any other colony as a result of the prohibition. New York's merchants, their Philadelphia rivals complained, did not need to export provisions because they were supplying the British army with food. Massachusetts exported only fish, and that had been exempted. Finally, the frustrated Philadelphia merchants pointed out, the southern colonies had lifted their embargoes long ago.[13]

The Assembly seemed ready to end the embargo, but Governor Morris asked the Assemblymen to consider extending it. A prolonged and wide-ranging debate, highly critical of the governor's leadership, followed. But once again he got the upper hand, for he abruptly prorogued the Assembly and instructed the customs officials to continue the embargo indefinitely.[14]

It seems clear, judging from merchants' comments and a sharp decline in the prices that provisions brought on the Philadelphia market, that the embargo was very effective. Thomas Willing told one of his customers that only ships carrying goods to the army or navy could possibly get out of the harbor. There were "100 men on Gard every Night round the Town . . ." to prevent smuggling, according to Thomas Riché. Governor Morris himself prowled the waterfront searching for smuggled goods. On at least one occasion, he "broke Open a Store with his own hands . . ." because he suspected there were contraband goods hidden there.[15] Although there may have been scattered instances of smuggling, Morris's vigilance coupled with the honesty of most merchants all but eliminated the exportation of provisions from Pennsylvania during the embargo.

Pennsylvania's economy did not revive fully even after the

embargo was lifted in August 1756. The Philadelphia market was glutted with corn, wheat, and flour. Before the embargo a hundred pounds of flour sold for 15 shillings 8 pence; in December, three months after the lifting of the embargo, the price was only to 9 shillings 5 pence. Corn and wheat prices underwent similar sharp declines. The total volume of the colony's trade was directly affected: ship clearances in 1756 were almost 25 percent less than they had been in the prewar year of 1754. Pennsylvania's economic slump had a wide impact; sailors and shipwrights, among others, had less work and farmers less money to spend because of the embargo. When the war began, observed Thomas Riché, many people thought the colony would prosper; they had "Great Expectation of Profits, but Was Deceived. . . ."[16]

With the exception of New York, which was the headquarters for the victualing contractors supplying the British troops, most of the other colonies also experienced economic hardship in 1756 as a result of their self-imposed embargoes.[17] Virginia was the largest exporter of Indian corn, the most important agricultural export in the 1750s. In 1754 Virginia exported a total of 408,373 bushels of Indian corn, more than half of which went to the West Indies. During the first full year of the war, however, Virginia's exportation of Indian corn was down more than 50 percent. War conditions also had an adverse effect on grain-importing colonies such as Massachusetts. The Boston selectmen told Governor Morris of Pennsylvania that flour was critically short and high priced because of the embargo. In March 1756 the House received a petition from a large group of Boston voters, asking for tax relief because of "the very decayed State of their Trade, and the great Decrease of their Numbers, by Means whereof their ability to bear the same proportion of the Province Taxes . . . is very much weaken'd."[18]

Late in August 1756, after four long months, the embargo was lifted by Pennsylvania's new governor. One of William Denny's first official acts was to remove virtually all restrictions on trade.[19] But the merchants' rejoicing was short-lived. Lord Loudoun, who had recently arrived in America to assume the duties of commander in chief of the British forces, insisted upon a new embargo.[20] A group of Philadelphia merchants suggested an alternative. They promised to sell 20,000 barrels of flour to the army at the current low market price. In this way, the merchants argued, the army's food supply would be guaranteed and the hated embargo would no longer be necessary.[21] The plan was rebuffed, though the new embargo was not immediately imposed as Loudoun demanded.

The delay was attributable to local politics; Governor Denny decided not to impose an embargo by executive order, but rather to ask the Assembly to enact an embargo law. Denny was new to Pennsylvania and no doubt he was eager to establish good relations with both legislators and businessmen. It would have been unwise politically to ride roughshod over community sentiment. Besides, there was no particular hurry, for only a relatively few ships could get out of the harbor before the river froze. In addition, a host of French privateers lurking in the main shipping lanes prevented all but the most daring shipmasters from sailing to the West Indies.[22]

Meanwhile, during the early months of 1757, the Assembly debated what form the embargo should take. According to Loudoun's instructions, Denny was to impose a total embargo; but the Assembly refused to ban trade with neutral ports. Such a sweeping restriction would destroy the colony's commerce and seriously undermine the war effort. A complete embargo, the Assembly explained to Loudoun through Denny, would

> effectually disable the Merchant from purchasing or importing Wines from the Madeiras and Western Island. . . . No Provisions can be exported from hence to Lisbon or Cadiz, without which we cannot procure the Salt that is absolutely necessary for the Use of His Majesty's Troops. . . . And without Salt it will be impossible for the Merchants here to supply His Majesty's West Indian Colonies with Beef and Pork, upon which they in a great Measure depend for Subsistance.[23]

Finally, the Assembly pointed out that the Board of Trade had asked only for a ban on commerce with the French and those neutral powers which directly supplied them. The legislators were prepared to enact such a law, but they were not willing to block, as Loudoun demanded, the merchants who traded with the neutral ports of Europe. The Assembly's answer clearly implied that it thought the general's order constituted an unreasonable interference in Pennsylvania's commercial life.[24]

While Governor Denny and the Assembly argued, Lord Loudoun abruptly ordered an embargo on all shipping from Virginia northward. Governor Denny responded with alacrity;

two days after Loudoun had issued the order the port of Philadelphia was closed. There was surprisingly little complaint from the merchants. Most of them seem to have thought the embargo would be lifted as soon as Loudoun had impressed enough ships and men for his Louisbourg campaign.[25]

As the weeks rolled by, however, it became clear that Loudoun had no intention of removing the embargo until his scheduled attack on Louisbourg was actually underway. Philadelphia's tradesmen began to grumble. Several groups asked Governor Denny for permission to sail so they could fulfill army contracts. Denny passed these requests on to Loudoun, for the general obviously was making the decisions. The latter ruled that qualified trading ships had to travel in a convoy guarded by British men-of-war. And, to prevent any breaches in his security system, Loudoun sent a warship to patrol Philadelphia harbor.[26]

Thomas Willing probably spoke for most Philadelphia merchants when he complained bitterly. "I don't know when this tedious Embargo will be taken off," he said early in May, adding, "at present it Stagnates all Business."[27] Local markets were glutted, driving the prices for foodstuffs down. The price of corn dropped more than 30 percent below the average prewar price. Wheat prices were down nearly 25 percent over 1756.[28] The embargo was effective; whatever smuggling went on was so slight that it did not relieve the glut. Therefore, local market prices remained depressed.

After more than two months under Loudoun's embargo, merchants and politicians began to protest loudly. In Massachusetts the Council approved a request for an exemption made by spokesmen for the fishing fleet; but the House refused to give its assent, so the fleet was still prohibited from sailing. Politicians in the House saw the request in a broader context. They argued that if the legislature made exceptions to the rules, the people would then begin to suspect "the Justice and Authority of their Ruler . . . and thereby weaken all Orders and Acts of Government."[29] Apparently many people were not satisfied with this rationalization for, according to Thomas Hutchinson, there was "universal complaint of . . . the entire cessation of all trade."[30] Before long, public opinion had its effect. On May 20, 1757, the House reversed itself and voted with the Council to end Loudoun's embargo in Massachusetts.

In Virginia public pressure was put on Governor Dinwiddie
to end the embargo. Early in May he gave in; he informed the
general that the embargo would be enforced only one more
week. The House of Burgesses, the governor explained, "are
unanimous in their Opinion of the absolute Necessity of taking
off the Embargo, otherwise the People will not be able to pay
their Taxes. . . ."[31]

The business community in Philadelphia took its complaints
about the embargo to the legislature in June. "Words cannot
express, nor Thought conceive, the State of Adversity to which
the People of the Province must be reduced," began their
petition, "unless this [embargo] be expeditiously removed."
The embargo's purpose was no longer clear to the businessmen.
If Loudoun had imposed it in order to get sailors, he now had
them. If the purpose was to ensure cheap supplies for the army,
that too had been accomplished. If it was laid to keep
Loudoun's military operations secret, then why had some other
colonies been allowed to send ships to sea?[32]

The Assembly responded to the merchants' petition by
drafting a sharply worded message to Governor Denny, urging
him to lift the embargo on Pennsylvania's shipping immediately. Denny replied weakly that he would relay the Assembly's
message to Loudoun.[33] For several reasons, Loudoun was
moved neither by pleas of economic hardship nor by political
logic. First, he apparently failed to see any connection between
commercial prosperity and a colony's ability to support the
war. Second, the general never gave up the idea that most
American merchants managed somehow to smuggle provisions
to the enemy. Third, he firmly believed that the enormous
political power wielded by the lower houses of assembly
should be subordinate to military necessity, as he alone
interpreted this necessity.

All of Loudoun's basic assumptions ignored reality. Several
colonies hesitated about undertaking a new campaign in 1757
because they claimed their ability to finance it had been
impaired by the long embargo. And, despite Loudoun's biased
opinion, his embargo was effective. For example, in the first
few days following its removal, sixty-three ships cleared
Philadelphia harbor, as compared with the normal ten or
twelve. Similarly, in Virginia, ships loaded with 50,000 bushels
of wheat—roughly one-quarter of that colony's yearly export
total—sailed immediately *after* Dinwiddie lifted the embargo.[34]

Finally, at best, Loudoun's actions were impolitic. He tried to ignore over a half century of colonial political experience. Among other things, this led colonials to look to their local assemblies for relief rather than to the home government which they knew would always support the generals.[35] Of course, this was not a new development; but when British military policy rode roughshod over local economic interests this centrifugal tendency was accelerated.

Loudoun's embargo was lifted officially in June 1757 because of an acute food shortage in Ireland and England, but similar trade restrictions were imposed again in subsequent years. As in the past, the home government and its military representatives in America assumed American merchants regularly violated the trade bans. In fact, there is no more reason to accept this assumption uncritically for the years 1758 and 1759 than for 1756 and 1757.

The evidence that is usually mustered to support the contention that Americans disregarded imperial trade regulations in the years after 1757 may be divided into two general categories. The first category consists of vague accusations made by Anglo-American officials who appear to have been anxious to escape any personal blame for whatever examples or charges of smuggling might be called to their attention. For example, in reply to an inquiry about smuggling made by William Pitt in 1760, Governor Cadwallader Colden of New York suggested that New Englanders were the chief culprits. At the same time, Governor Benning Wentworth of New Hampshire accused all the "Southern Governments" of being deeply involved in illegal trading activities. Governor Robert Morris and his successors in the Pennsylvania government charged their political enemies, the Quakers, with supplying the French with provisions.[36] Although the Quakers were within Pennsylvania's jurisdiction, their general reputation for crafty business dealings and their avowed pacifism in the midst of an imperial war made them ideal scapegoats.

In fact, however, Quaker merchants — who controlled at least half of Philadelphia's trade — were especially careful to stay within the law. The Philadelphia Monthly Meeting took an active part in enforcing trade regulations. Each month Friends were asked if they had done anything to deprive the King of revenue. When members of the Meeting were suspected of illegal trading activities, others brought pressure to bear on

them. According to Professor Frederick Tolles, this method of
"corporate discipline" was so effective that "for the entire
colonial period there is little evidence that Quaker merchants or
shipowners were guilty of smuggling."[37] The Meeting was so
cautious that in 1759 it warned its members against carrying
any molasses — English or French — because they "might run
into snares and inconveniences by which we may be likely to
bring trouble and uneasiness on ourselves and the Church or
give the least Encouragement or connivance to the Enemies of
the Crown."[38] When the Quakers' system of corporate discipline
is added to the available statistical evidence and to the fact that
in nearly every colony numerous individual merchants and
commercial associations openly rejected illegal profits, the sum
is an important counterexample to the smuggling thesis and the
evidence supporting it.[39]

Another of the vague accusations made by colonial officials
and used as evidence to support the thesis that Americans
traded heavily with the enemy rests on the use of flags of truce.
A flag of truce allowed a shipmaster to sail to an enemy port
for the purpose of exchanging prisoners of war. According to
those who were eager to find a scapegoat to account for alleged
instances of illegal trading, the "real" reason for obtaining a
flag was to gain access to enemy contractors. Both Governor
William Denny of Pennsylvania and Governor Stephen Hopkins of Rhode Island were charged with making available vast
numbers of flags for such illegal purposes.

Allegedly, Governor Denny initially sold flags for £1,000
apiece. Within a few months' time, however, he was selling
blank permits for as little as £20, a price certainly within the
reach of any merchant who wanted to trade with the French.
This story rests solely on the testimony of Denny's successor
and political enemy, James Hamilton.[40]

Several factors cast serious doubt on Hamilton's accusation.
Because there would be no need to conceal a ship's destination
if the owner had a flag of truce, the vessel would, in all
probability, clear through customs as the law required.
Therefore, from May to November 1759, when Denny was
supposedly selling large numbers of flags, there should have
been an equally large number of ships clearing for French or
neutral ports in the West Indies. In fact, there were only two.[41]
Other evidence also leads to the conclusion that flags were not
as available as Hamilton charged. Thomas Riché, a wealthy

Philadelphia merchant, wrote to a New York business associate in mid-1759: "Our hopes of a Flagg here I am afraid is over. There is so many men of the first Rank pushing for it."[42] Obviously, Riché's use of the pronoun "it," coupled with the port records, severely undercuts Hamilton's testimony and renders its use very doubtful at best.

Unless the net of conspiracy is spread wide enough to catch a great many public officials, tales of large numbers of flags issued by the Rhode Island government must also be questioned. Up to the end of 1758, according to an Assembly committee appointed to investigate the matter, only nine flags had been granted. Two years later, Governor Hopkins told Pitt he had issued thirty flags. He explained that a local magistrate was required by law to examine every ship sailing with a flag to ensure that a sufficient number of French prisoners were on board and only enough food for the voyage. Hopkins swore that "no Provisions for Sale, or any Warlike Stores have gone from this Colony among the French during this War, by any Permission, or Connivance of my Authority, or Officer in it."[43] It is possible, of course, that Hopkins and the local officials who scrutinized outgoing flagships were part of the smuggling conspiracy; but there is no concrete evidence to substantiate such a viewpoint. Once again, therefore, it seems clear that another facet of the smuggling myth is based on very little solid evidence.

The second category of evidence generally used to support the thesis that American merchants ignored imperial trade restrictions during the Great War for Empire consists of unfounded charges and scattered, verified examples of smuggling, most of which took place after 1759 when the war in North America had been successfully concluded. To be sure, some illegal trading went on, but not all of that should be blamed on American adventurers. Englishmen in the West Indies, as well as Dutch and Irish merchants, traded with French and neutral ports contrary to British policy.[44]

Although Dutch merchant ships were officially treated as belligerents by the royal navy after 1756, they continued to get supplies to the French West Indies. The fact was, the British navy was unable to maintain a completely effective blockade. Late in 1758, for example, three fleets of Dutch merchant ships slipped through to Martinique. In the following year, Commodore John Moore told Pitt he did not have enough ships to keep the Dutch from St. Eustatius, a neutral island used by French buyers.[45]

Irish merchants also carried goods to neutral islands in the West Indies where contacts might be made with interested Frenchmen. Indeed, Irishmen were legally exempted from wartime trade restrictions, a fact that angered Americans. Governor Charles Hardy said he had difficulty convincing the New York Assembly to lay an embargo "while they can use the Argument, if we do not trade with those Islands the Irish will." Similarly, the Connecticut legislature argued that trade restrictions were useless because the French would be supplied "from Ireland by the way of St. Eustatius." Irish trade with the West Indies increased significantly while American merchants were barred from the Caribbean.[46]

The conclusion is unmistakable: there is not enough valid evidence to maintain the belief that American merchants were responsible for prolonging the Great War for Empire. Indeed, there are enough significant counterexamples to render the thesis useless.

Still, the belief that few, if any, American merchants were loyal to the Empire continued to shape the behavior of British officials. They armed their generals in America with the power to impose embargoes without even so much as consulting the colonial assemblies. This, together with the fact that English trade laws were often poorly defined and illegally enforced, angered colonials who jealously guarded their rights as Englishmen. It would be a mistake, therefore, to assume that American merchants were unaware of the political ramifications of British policy, or that colonial political agencies were unsympathetic to the merchants' claims that their rights were being violated by arbitrary wartime trade restrictions.

Early in the war, lawyers hired by American merchants argued that there was no specific English law preventing trade with either Frenchmen or neutrals. Edward Shippen, judge of the Vice-Admiralty Court at Philadelphia, agreed with this conclusion. He pointed out that commerce with the enemy was not illegal according to the British Constitution, but depended upon Parliament's enacting specific legislation. Laws had been passed during Queen Anne's reign "to prohibit all trade and Commerce with France during *that* war; which shows the Opinion of the English Parliament to be that contacts with the Enemy for merchandise were not void or unlawful before the making of that law."[47] Because no new law had been passed since the outbreak of war in 1755, trade with the French was not illegal.

The presiding judge of the New York Vice-Admiralty Court also supported the right of colonials to deal with Frenchmen and neutrals. If an Englishman had proof the goods he carried belonged to him, argued Judge Lewis Morris, those goods could not be seized, regardless of their national origin. An Englishman's property rights were inviolable. Most American lawyers agreed with this opinion. John Watts, a prosperous New York merchant, once observed that few, if any, "Lawyers of any Eminence" thought an Englishman's property rights could be abridged without violating his constitutional rights.[48]

Early in 1757 Parliament enacted a law intended to iron out some of the commercial problems raised by the war. The Flour Act was designed to stop trade with the enemy and neutrals — with the latter out of fear they would pass goods on to the French.[49] Considered from almost any angle, the Flour Act was offensive. First, in order to enforce the act, the British navy came to treat colonial ships suspected of carrying prohibited goods as enemy ships liable to seizure and condemnation. According to colonials, such procedures clearly violated their constitutional rights. The Admiralty Court in England supported this contention when it ruled that "British subjects have [an] Undoubted right of Trading at [the neutral port of] Monte Christo. . . ."[50] But the navy ignored the Court's ruling and so American merchants were not appeased.

The second shortcoming of the Flour Act, according to the colonials' view, was its indiscriminate inclusiveness. That is, colonials could see no reason for banning American trade in foodstuffs with all neutral ports. "I wish the Government at Home," Thomas Willing wrote angrily from his Philadelphia headquarters, "had considered the difference between Our shipg. Provisions to Lisbon and Madeira . . . and our sendg. them to the Neutral Islands in the West Indies. . . ."[51]

The Flour Act was unpopular also because it seemed to discriminate against American merchants. Other members of the empire were allowed to trade with any neutral port, even the very suspicious Spanish port of Monte Christo in the West Indies. Irish merchants, for example, were permitted to export corn, beef, butter, and pork to whomever they chose.[52] It must have appeared obvious to Americans who carefully considered the Flour Act that their rights and interests would be disregarded whenever they clashed with the ministry's current political goals.

This suspicion was strengthened when, upon the death of George II, a Boston customs official applied to the Massachusetts Superior Court for a writ of assistance.[53] A writ of assistance permitted customs officers to search for goods they suspected had entered the colony illegally. In other words, a writ made it possible for them to operate in much the same arbitrary fashion as the royal navy did on the high seas.

For this reason, among others, a large group of Boston merchants saw the writs as a threat to their constitutional rights and they retained James Otis and Oxenbridge Thacher to argue against their issuance. Although Otis's arguments are well known, they have rarely been interpreted in the light of earlier legal decisions or as a manifestation of a widely held political philosophy. A consideration of these factors is essential to understanding one reason for the colonists' growing political alienation from the home government during the Great War for Empire.

As we have seen, both colonial judges and the Admiralty Court in England had stated that an Englishman's property rights were inviolable. To colonial merchants this meant the constitution ruled out arbitrary seizures of their property, whether on the high seas or in a warehouse.[54] A writ of assistance seemed to jeopardize this constitutional guarantee by arming customs officers with almost unlimited power to carry out search operations.

Following this line of reasoning, Otis called the writs "a wanton exercise of arbitrary power." He declared: "I will to my dying day oppose . . . all such instruments of slavery on the one hand and villany on the other as this writ of Assistance is. . . . No acts of Parliament can establish such a writ; tho it should be made in the very words of the petition, it would be void. An act against the Constitution is void."[55] Otis's use of the word "slavery" was not merely a rhetorical exaggeration, for it had a precise and widely understood political definition. "It meant," Professor Bernard Bailyn tells us, "the inability to maintain one's just property in material things and abstract rights, rights and things which a proper constitution guaranteed a free people."[56] Therefore, by using the political vernacular,

Otis's arguments reached a receptive audience outside the courtroom.

As if to reinforce Otis's implied point that the merchants' grievances should be viewed as a general threat, an article appeared in the Boston *Gazette* outlining the dangers writs of assistance held for all Englishmen. If the writs were issued, the writer warned, all Americans would be enslaved. Property rights and political rights would be subject to the arbitrary interpretation of a petty government official. "Every house-holder in this province," the writer insisted, "will necessarily become *less secure* than he was before this writ had any existence among us; for by it, a *custom house officer or ANY OTHER PERSON has a power given him,* with the *assistance of a peace officer,* to *ENTER FORCEABLY* into a *DWELL-ING HOUSE, and rifle every part of it where he shall PLEASE to suspect uncustomed goods are lodged.*"[57] Obvious-ly, the writer concluded, the writs were contrary to the constitution and should not be issued.

It is, of course, difficult to measure precisely the impact of these grievances on the colonists outside the mercantile community, but it can be estimated by remarks made by political leaders and agencies. Thomas Hutchinson, for exam-ple, maintained that "the common people" were convinced the "writs were contrary to their liberties as Englishmen." In 1757, he told Lord Loudoun there was "Universal complaint" about wartime trade restrictions, including the embargoes that the general had imposed.[58] Likewise, in Pennsylvania, the Assem-bly responded to a petition from a group of merchants protesting an embargo by jumping to the political conclusion implied by the complaint. That is, the politicians charged the embargo had been "illegally imposed" because the Assembly had not been consulted. "Upon the whole," the House concluded, "we apprehend a People cannot be said to be free, or in the possession of their Rights and Properties, when their Rulers shall, by their sole authority, even during the Sitting of their Assemblys stop the Circulation of Commerce and Industry of the People and reduce them to the greatest distress."[59] In Pennsylvania, as elsewhere, it appears, some Americans believed that their political rights were endangered by British military policy.

Merchants active in the antiproprietary faction, as well as

those who supported the proprietors, were frustrated by imperial trade restrictions. John Watts, a member of the New York Council, was outraged at the way he was treated by the Earl of Albemarle, commander of the British forces at Havana in 1762. The prices Albemarle set for goods brought to Havana by New York merchants were considered ruinous by Watts. "The unprecedented oppressions we suffer'd . . ." at the hands of "Your Hyde Park Generals" made the "people of this Colony . . . stark mad . . . ," asserted Watts to his English friends. Further, British policy angered both those men who dabbled in illegal adventures and those who carefully avoided illicit trading activities. Too often, it seemed to the public spirited merchant, the "burdens of patriotism were imposed by England and the West Indies but borne by Ireland and North America. . . ." At the same time, traders who had been tempted by quick illegal profits found that by 1762 the British navy was able to catch all but the luckiest adventurers.[60]

Because British officials clung dogmatically to the idea that American merchants as a group were disloyal to the empire, they were led to formulate a disruptive and ultimately destructive commercial policy. British war policy began with trade restrictions and enforcement measures of at least doubtful legality, then added embargoes imposed by military fiat, and ended by violating what important segments of American society considered their basic constitutional rights. The net result was an important contribution to America's growing political alienation from the empire.

CHAPTER IX

MILITARY POLICY AND THE
LOWER HOUSES OF ASSEMBLY

The failure to adopt a plan of union for the American colonies created serious problems during the Great War for Empire. Without the political machinery necessary to achieve a consensus, each colony seemed to have been left free to decide what contribution — if any — it would make to the war against France. This was the best possible arrangement as far as the colonies were concerned. The British generals who were sent to America, however, were not sympathetic with the politics of pluralism. They attempted to override provincial autonomy, insisting that it was their prerogative to say where, when, and how many men should fight.

The lower houses of assembly stoutly resisted the British military's attempt to assume these vital decisions. In doing so, Americans were primarily motivated by the belief that the army had to be controlled by local political agencies. They contended it was their right to determine the size and objectives of the provincial army and how it was to be financed.[1] The first two contentions brought the lower houses into direct conflict with the military commanders appointed by the Crown, and the latter with the royal or proprietary governors. In both cases the lower houses emerged victorious. By the end of the Great War for Empire the lower houses had achieved not only a position of political dominance in the colonies, but also the stature to speak for America in the conflict with the imperial government which ensued after 1763.[2]

The struggle of the colonial assemblies against imperial control of the war effort began as soon as the first British commander in chief arrived in America. Although the Crown had decided in 1754 not to encourage a political union in America, it did make a half-hearted attempt to establish an economic partnership with the colonies. Major General Edward Braddock was directed to ask the governors, who met with him in April 1755, if their colonies would contribute to a common defense fund which would be used to finance operations by both regular and provincial troops. Because the governors knew very well their assemblies would not approve such a plan, they gave "as their unanimous opinion that such a Fund can never be established in the Colonies without the aid of Parliament."[3] The Crown apparently had anticipated such an unfavorable response, for Braddock's secret instructions assured him that the royal exchequer would finance his campaign if the colonies would not.[4]

Braddock was also secretly told to allow the northern colonial army, commanded by Governor William Shirley of Massachusetts, to carry out its planned attack on Crown Point providing the colonists paid for the operation themselves. While most New Englanders were displeased because they had to assume the costs of the Crown Point expedition, they were delighted that their plan for independent action had won Crown approval. A correspondent to *Read's Weekly Journal* manifested the buoyant spirit of New England when he boasted: "the chief things we want here are money and a liberty to act. [If] these things are granted . . . there would not be a Frenchman or an Indian in America near enough to annoy us."[5]

Despite the prevalence of such an auspicious attitude, the administration of the Crown Point campaign presented Shirley with every one of the major difficulties faced by subsequent British commanders. His attempts to foster military cooperation among the colonies were opposed by the lower houses. This meant he had to conduct separate negotiations with each government in order to determine how many men each colony would contribute to the provincial army. He was forced to grapple with problems created by local jealousies; no one colony wanted to give more than its self-determined "just" share to the war against France. Further, Shirley had to contend with the lower houses of those colonies that insisted that their soldiers could only be used against Crown Point — the French fortress which New Englanders had decided was the single most important objective in North America.[6]

Shirley and his successors were faced with a very difficult situation. There was no widely accepted framework within which American politicians and the British army could work peaceably. As the need for new political procedures to cope with the special problems arising from the war was recognized, military leaders and the lower houses sought ways in which more cooperation between civilians and soldiers might be achieved.[7]

General Shirley first turned to the Crown for help in solving the problems of civil-military relations. Shortly after he assumed command of the British forces in North America, he submitted a plan urging several important, but limited administrative reforms. His proposal attempted to balance the Crown's prerogative and colonial political power by carefully integrating the new American military establishment into the existing imperial structure. He proposed that all governors be permitted to give royal commissions to provincial officers, a move obviously designed to tie the Americans more directly to the Crown and to strengthen the executive's political power. The lower houses of assembly were also to be made more dependent upon the Crown under Shirley's plan. They were to recruit, feed, and provide transportation for provincial soldiers, while the Crown would assume the costs of arming, clothing, and paying them. Since the colonies were being spared most of the expense of maintaining the army, Shirley believed the matter of the number of men each colony raised could be "left to the Discretion of the several Colonies concern'd. . . ."[8]

While Shirley waited for a response that never came, he summoned the governors of the northern colonies to a military planning conference. Meeting in New York in December 1755, the governors and the general agreed to follow the quota system originally worked out at the 1754 Albany Conference, and to launch attacks against Forts Niagara, Frontenac, Duquesne, and Crown Point.[9] This meant, of course, that the size and objectives of the provincial army were determined without the approval of the lower houses. Not surprisingly, therefore, the lower houses in Massachusetts, Connecticut, and New York rejected the conclusions reached by the governors.

When told by Governor Charles Hardy that it had to raise one thousand soldiers to fulfill its quota, the New York Assembly balked. A study committee reported that £40,000 would be required to finance a thousand troops. Such a sum, the committee told the House, could only be raised if new property taxes were laid. The assemblymen immediately rejected the idea of new taxes, claiming that their constituents thought their taxes were already too high.[10] After more than a week of dilatory debate, the House decided to adjourn until the other northern colonies made their plans known.

Hardy reported to the House early in March that Massachusetts and Connecticut "have far exceeded the Proportions alloted to them. . . ." Still the Assembly delayed. Finally, in mid-March, it voted to recruit 715 men, 400 of whom, however, had to be used for an "Offensive War against the Indians who almost daily ravage the Western Frontiers of this Colony." Despite pleas from Governor Hardy and General Shirley, the House insisted that 715 men were the absolute maximum it could support. Indeed, as late as July 1756, the Assembly resolved "that this colony has stretched its Strength and Substance to the greatest Pitch: and . . . is not in a Condition to enter into heavier Expenses. . . ."[11]

In Massachusetts there was the same conflict between an executive bent on fulfilling the Crown's expectations and an implacable lower house interested in maintaining its control over military policy. To begin with, the House stipulated that the Massachusetts troops could not be used south of Albany or west of Schenectady or to the eastward. In effect, this meant they could be utilized only against Crown Point. Next, after prolonged debate, the House decided not to increase the number of men it had originally voted to muster until Rhode Island and New Hampshire made proportionate increases in their quotas.[12]

Moreover, the legislators asked the Crown to subsidize the provincial army. The people of Massachusetts, the House told Shirley, "are ready to sink under the Burden of Taxes hereby brought upon them, and the Government have so stretched their Credit, that they even despair of borrowing Money sufficient to pay off their Troops. . . ."[13] Apparently, the legislators had heard a rumor that led them to believe Shirley was authorized to assume some of the financial burden of colonial mobilization. Although Shirley insisted he did not have the right to use military funds in this way, the House persisted in its demands. The general was then forced to decide whether a violation of his military instructions outweighed the value of substantial contributions from Massachusetts to the provincial army. Early in February he unwillingly granted the lower house's request to draw £30,000 from the commander in chief's funds.[14] Thus, in less than a year, Massachusetts had reversed the direction of imperial policy. Rather than contributing to a common fund designed to help finance the total war effort, Massachusetts and several of her immediate neighbors were receiving at least partial support from the Crown for colonial military operations of their own design.

Lord Loudoun, Shirley's successor as commander in chief, was highly critical of Shirley's concessions to the colonial assemblies. Loudoun was determined to get the colonies to do what he wanted, though he soon discovered how difficult that was. When the French captured Oswego in the summer of 1756, for example, Loudoun ordered the northern colonies to send reinforcements to help defend the New York frontiers. The response by Connecticut's lower house was typical of many of the northern colonies. Connecticut would like to help, the Assembly told Loudoun, but "as we are not acquainted with the Operations designed, it is attended with Difficulty to come to a determinate Resolution. . . ."[15] Reluctantly, Loudoun explained that his information led him to believe the French were massing troops in order to drive into the heart of New York. Beyond this, he would not go. He maintained that the decision to attack or simply to defend certain outposts belonged solely to the commander in chief. Loudoun did add somewhat defensively that if he told every lower house "the Services for which the Troops are destined, the Enemy must always be Appraised where to prepare to defeat that Attack."[16]

Again, Connecticut politicians were sympathetic, but still they refused to increase the size of the provincial army without a full and close examination of its objectives. Because Loudoun would not provide additional information, the Assembly voted not to send him more soldiers. Instead, the lower house empowered Governor Thomas Fitch to call up militiamen if and when he determined reinforcements were necessary. By way of explanation, Fitch gave Loudoun a quick lesson in American political procedures. "As Men are raised in this Colony as well as others by and in Consequence of the Votes, Acts, or Orders of the General Assembly," the governor instructed the general, "they must know at least the General

Service the Men are raised for . . . otherwise it will be
Extremely difficult to prevail on an Assembly to make
provisions for that purpose. . . ."[17]

Late in October Loudoun tacitly conceded defeat. He wrote
the northern governors that he was no longer interested in
reinforcements. He was plainly discouraged. "I believe you
will agree with me," he commented glumly to Governor
Charles Hardy of New York, "that the King must trust in this
Country to himself."[18] That, of course, was impossible.

Therefore, in November 1756, Loudoun tried to bring the
colonies into line by crudely applying economic pressure. He
warned a group of commissioners from New England that the
Crown would not pay for the provisions used by provincial
troops until the lower houses stopped interfering in military
affairs.[19] But the general's maneuver failed to achieve the
desired effect. In fact, it served only to further alienate some
New Englanders. One provincial colonel, for example, expressed his anger over the use of such inducements in a letter
to Joseph Dwight, an influential western Massachusetts
politician: "The Advantage of having our Provisions and
Warlike stores paid for by ye Crown weighs nothing with me,
the Nation ought to pay that and much more whether we
comply with ye proposal or not and the making of it with ye
Conditions . . . fills me with Indignation . . . we of New
England have deserv'd better treatment and every New
England breast will be fir'd with resentment. . . ."[20] Finally,
after both cajolery and compulsion had failed to gain colonial
cooperation, Loudoun decided to meet with the governors and
representatives of the northern colonies in order to discuss the
1757 campaign. From the outset it was obvious that Loudoun
was going to have to concede much more than he wanted to.
Each of the lower houses had sent their representatives to the
conference with explicit instructions, including those points
which were considered negotiable.[21] In other words, they
conceived of the conference as providing a framework within
which imperial military policy might be formulated.

Loudoun's opening speech dashed any such optimistic
hopes, however. He appeared to be far more anxious to assign
blame for the failure of the 1756 campaign than he was to
ensure that the same problems would not occur in 1757. He
began by ticking off what he considered to be the most serious
failings of the lower houses and concluded by lecturing the

delegates as to their subordinate role in the formulation of military planning.[22]

Unruffled, the delegates to the conference confronted Loudoun with a series of questions designed to force him to respond directly to the issues that had been raised by the lower houses in past years. That is, the commissioners wanted to know where the provincial troops were going to be used; how long they would be needed; and who would pay their expenses.[23] The question of the number of men each colony should raise was not mentioned because the lower houses considered that a matter to be explored independently by their representatives to the conference.

At this point, Loudoun's resistance to the demands made by the lower houses collapsed. He assured the commissioners that New England soldiers would not be sent "out of the Limits I know they are willing to go and that you will approve of their being led into." Further, he agreed to provision colonial troops when they acted in conjunction with regular forces and to limit the terms of provincial soldiers to one year.[24] He also resolved not to interfere in the determination of how many men each colony would contribute to the provincial army.

While Loudoun's abstention probably made the negotiations over quotas less divisive, there was still some friction among the commissioners. To begin with, there was no universally satisfactory formula. Some commissioners argued in favor of population as the basis for establishing quotas, others for earlier contributions, and others for a solution that would take into consideration local frontier exigencies. After some discussion, it was decided that population was the best guide to how many men each colony might contribute; but the commissioners could not agree on the figures.

The problem was that the commissioners' power to commit their colonies to raise a specified number of men was in all cases restricted to some ·degree. Theodore Atkinson, the secretary of New Hampshire, was empowered only to observe the proceedings and report to the legislature. The Rhode Island commissioners were fully authorized to make the quota decision for their colony, but while in Boston they were convinced by Atkinson that each assembly should decide upon its own quota.[25] Connecticut's representatives had been instructed by their assembly not to approve a quota of more than 1,250 men, the number agreed upon at Albany in 1754. The

Massachusetts legislature gave its delegates the widest latitude, with only the restriction that the quotas be equitably distributed.[26]

When the limits placed upon the commissioners by their assemblies caused a deadlock, Loudoun tried to play the part of the honest broker. He reminded the commissioners of the political consequences of their failure to devise a satisfactory quota system. "I showed them," he remarked candidly, "that the effect of not agreeing among themselves must have the effect of my dealing with them separately, which was not my plan, for I chose to sement [sic] their union and not to divide them.[27] Despite the general's warning, the commissioners still were unable to agree on a quota for each colony. Loudoun then tried assigning quotas; but at this point the commissioners despaired of achieving unity and decided to put the matter before the lower houses.[28]

Although a greater number of men than expected were eventually raised by the legislatures, many Anglo-American leaders expressed disappointment at the lack of political unity among the northern colonies. Early in 1758, for example, Governor Thomas Pownall of Massachusetts asked the other New England governments to "appoint Commissioners to consult a Plan of mutuall Defence." The governor's proposal quickly won support among Massachusetts and Connecticut politicians, although Rhode Island's leaders flatly rejected it, claiming they feared Loudoun would react angrily to being excluded from any discussions about military affairs.[29]

In fact, Loudoun was angry and he did try to prevent the conference from meeting.[30] Still, delegates from Massachusetts and Connecticut decided to meet in Boston early in February 1758 to consider a plan of common defense. After only brief discussion the delegates agreed on a mutual defense pact. If one colony were attacked, or threatened, troops from the other colony would immediately march to the aid of the besieged. Careful arrangements were made about who would command the combined force and how it would be supplied. Further, the two colonies decided upon a formula to be used in order to determine the number of troops each would contribute. Finally, it was resolved to invite Rhode Island and New Hampshire to join the proposed military league.[31]

Without the participation of all of the New England colonies and with Loudoun's active efforts to undermine any union independent of imperial authority, a military league such as that formed by Massachusetts and Connecticut was doomed to failure. Although joint ventures of this kind were largely unsuccessful, the drive for control of military affairs continued to be a preoccupation of the lower houses.

The announced goal of the Massachusetts legislature, for example, was "by a due Exercise of the Powers of Civil Government . . . to remove as much as may be all pretence of necessity of Military Government."[32] In practice, this meant scrutinizing each of the commander in chief's requests for troops very carefully. The House flatly refused to raise 360 rangers in the winter of 1758. A majority of the representatives argued that the quota assigned to Massachusetts by Loudoun did not take into consideration the colony's special frontier problems. Loudoun replied in a way that only could have provided additional evidence for those who feared the growth of military power in America. He threatened to use an "Act of Power" to keep 360 Massachusetts soldiers in the army. Still, the House would not alter its position and according to a British officer on the scene the "four Companies of the Massachusetts Rangers are resolved to walk home at the expiration of their term. . . ."[33] Faced with the unhappy prospect of subduing men in the field as well as in the legislature, Loudoun acquiesced and permitted the soldiers to return to Massachusetts at the expiration of their original terms of service.

A month later, in March 1758, Loudoun went to Boston in an attempt to prevent a full debate on the question of providing troops. The best efforts of his active supporters in the legislature had been unsuccessful, and the outcome of such a debate was not at all certain.[34] Indeed, Governor Pownall warned the general that unless he answered the questions put to him by the House "in such a manner to ease the Minds not only of the House but of the Body of the People they Represent," there might not be any troops from Massachusetts. Loudoun was apprehensive enough to ask Pownall to review his answers before they were submitted to the House. Pownall deleted two passages, explaining to Loudoun that they would "throw things into Confusion and Prevent the Letting of the Troops from the Province."[35] Although Loudoun greatly disliked modifying his position to please the House, he agreed to make the changes suggested by Pownall. The general

realized what was at stake. If the lower house of Massachusetts
— or any other colony — were permitted to decide whether or
not it would provide men, the Crown's prerogative would be
badly undermined.

Just as the Massachusetts Assembly prepared to debate the
question of providing troops, a letter arrived from William Pitt,
the new minister of war, urging the colony to recruit as many
men as it could, promising full payment for whatever war
expenses the colony incurred, and recalling Loudoun. Pitt's
new policy implied that the Crown supported the colonies'
argument for local control of the military. The lower houses
were now officially encouraged to raise only as many soldiers
as they decided were needed.[36]

Freed from the fear of arbitrary military power and with the
promise that specie payments from England would increase in
direct ratio to the amounts they spent, the lower houses rallied
to support the war as they never had before. Massachusetts
raised 6,500 men, more than twice the number that colony had
raised in previous years; Connecticut sent 4,450 soldiers into
the field by mid-1758; and although New York fell short of its
quota, three times as many soldiers were recruited in 1758 as in
1756. Although the number of men raised by the northern
colonies rapidly decreased after 1758, nearly 55,000 colonials
served in the five campaigns after that date.[37]

To be sure, the colonists welcomed and responded to Pitt's
economic incentives, but the political impact of the policy far
outweighed the economic relief. Pitt's new approach seemed to
be based on the assumption that the colonial assemblies simply
could not be constricted politically if they were going to
cooperate fully in the war effort. Pitt permitted each of the
lower houses to decide how many men they would contribute
to the provincial army, and he left unresolved the problem of
whether the governors or lower houses should control the
dispersal of public money. As a result, some lower houses
gained more power over matters usually reserved for executive
authority. In this way, the lower houses' sense of self-
determination was strengthened. Pitt's new policy did not
reverse the political direction in which the colonies had long
been moving. It was not intended to, of course. Pitt was
primarily motivated by a desire to win the war. In that — and
only that as far as American affairs were concerned — did he
succeed.

Imperial largess, by solving the problem of troop quotas, did make General Jeffery Amherst's tenure as commander in chief much easier than that of his predecessors. But the lower houses continued to assert their authority in other military matters. They still insisted, for example, that they must have a part in formulating military policy. Specifically, the lower houses told Amherst they must know where and for how long provincial troops were going to be used. Amherst's first reaction was that all the colonies needed to know was that Great Britain was at war. But, like his predecessors, Amherst soon capitulated and provided the lower houses with the information they had requested. By permitting the lower houses to share in making military policy — even in this rather prosaic manner — Amherst too aided the drive of the lower houses to acquire executive authority as well as legislative privileges.[38]

The lower houses also made significant inroads into executive authority in the realm of finance. By the end of the Great War for Empire the lower houses had imposed their authority over every phase of raising and distributing public revenue.[39] The basic forces at work in each colony were the same, but local circumstances gave particular shape to the resulting politics.

Pennsylvania's history during the war years provides an excellent example of the political struggles that took place wherever the lower houses of assembly sought to capture total control of financial matters. Of course, the attempt by the lower houses to extend their authority began long before George Washington's capitulation at Fort Necessity in the summer of 1754. But there can be no doubt that the war accelerated the trend toward the domination of colonial finances by the lower houses.[40]

When news of Washington's defeat reached Philadelphia, Lieutenant Governor James Hamilton asked the Assembly to appropriate money to help Virginia defend the western frontiers. The House passed a bill providing for £10,000 in bills of credit to be sunk, or amortized, in ten years by extension of the excise tax on liquor. The governor refused to approve the measure because it violated his secret instructions from Thomas Penn, the proprietor of the colony. Penn had stipulated in November 1753 that Hamilton should veto any money bill that did not allow the proprietor to have a voice in the expenditure of the income raised by taxes over and above what was needed to amortize bills of credit. To cloak the fact that he was acting according to secret instructions, Hamilton amended the Assembly's bill, reducing the life of the excise tax from ten to four years. To explain his action he referred the Assembly to the Currency Act of 1751, which limited the paper money issued by the New England colonies to a life of five years.[41]

The Assembly was not fooled. Angrily, the legislators resolved that "whatever ill Consequences ensue from Supplies not having been granted at this critical juncture, must lie at the governor's door." Before Robert Morris, the colony's new lieutenant governor, could reply, the Assembly adjourned.[42] 2

On March 17, 1755, Morris summoned the House into session, urging it to contribute to General Braddock's campaign against Fort Duquesne. Within a few days the Assembly demonstrated that its views about how money should be raised and who should control its expenditure were unchanged. The appropriation, or supply bill, as it was called, provided for £20,000 in bills of credit to be distributed by a committee of the Assembly. The paper money was to be sunk by an extension of the excise tax for ten years. As usual the tax rates had been set to provide the Assembly with an annual income (beyond that needed to sink the £20,000) of about £2,000. Morris's secret instructions prohibited such an arrangement. He told the Assembly that he could not approve the bill unless it contained a suspending clause, a provision that postponed legislative action until the Privy Council had reviewed the bill.[43]

Without revealing that it knew Morris was operating under secret instructions, the Assembly argued that binding instructions were intolerable in a government where the people had been guaranteed a role in making laws. The guiding assumption of the Assembly's charge was that in a democratic government laws should be the product of consultation between the people's representatives and the executive. Binding the executive with specific instructions before this process began challenged that fundamental tenet of a free government. To proceed in such a manner, the House complained, would render its meetings "useless." It seemed that the Assembly was merely to discover the proprietor's "Will and to obey." This would not only deny the lower house "the Privileges of an

English Constitution, but would, as far as in his [the proprietor's] Power, introduce a French one, by reducing our Assemblies to the insignificance of their Parliaments, incapable of making Laws, but by Direction . . . and only allowed to register his Edicts."[44]

This impasse was temporarily broken when the Assembly decided to use its own good credit to borrow £15,000, a procedure that did not require Morris's approval.[45] In this way, the Assembly won Braddock's favor and embarrassed the governor, but the scheme did little to help the House toward its goal of complete control of Pennsylvania's financial affairs. Therefore, that action would be staged again.

Braddock's defeat and death in July led everyone to look closely at the role they were playing in the political drama that was unfolding in Pennsylvania. Morris urged immediate passage of a military supply bill. The House responded with a £50,000 appropriation which was to be funded by a tax on all estates in the colony, including, for the first time, the proprietor's. Governor Morris refused to accept the bill because it violated his commission from Penn.[46]

Penn's desire to exclude his estates from taxation infuriated Benjamin Franklin. As an Assembly leader he had played a moderating role up to this point. His position was clear: he believed the Assembly had a "natural Exclusive Right" to design money bills and to dispose of the people's money without executive interference. Franklin argued his position quietly until Penn tried to evade taxation. As soon as that became public, Franklin bombarded Morris and Penn. He used the strongest language in the Real Whig arsenal.[47] He labeled the governor the "hateful instrument of reducing a free People to the abject State of Vassalage." Penn, Franklin declared on August 19, 1755, was "taking Advantage of Publick Calamity and Distress, and [the people's] Tenderness for their bleeding Country, to force down their Throats Laws of imposition, abhorent to common Justice and common Reason." "Our Lord Proprietary," Franklin fumed, "though a Subject like ourselves, would send us out to fight for him, while he keeps a thousand Leagues remote from danger! . . . This is not merely Vassalage, it is worse than any Vassalage we have heard of; it is something we have no adequate Name for; it is even more slavish than Slavery itself."[48] Clearly, Franklin and the

Assembly saw the machinations of Penn and Lieutenant Governor Morris as both odious and dangerous to the liberty of the people.

In October a newly elected Assembly passed a £60,000 supply bill, again taxing the proprietary estates, which Morris again vetoed. A few weeks later, however, after news reached Philadelphia that hundreds of angry frontiersmen were marching on the city and a letter arrived from Penn pledging £5,000 to frontier defense, the House appropriated £55,000. Although the House put aside its insistence upon taxing the proprietary estates, it did get the governor to agree that the funds would be spent under the direction of commissioners appointed by the Assembly—a practice that greatly extended the authority of the lower house.[49]

In July 1756 the House passed another bill that renewed its effort to tax the proprietary estates. But, as one of his last official acts, Morris bluntly rejected the bill. Likewise, his successor, Governor William Denny, vetoed a similar bill in September. The House protested strongly against Denny's instructions, which required him to act in such a manner, and voted to send Benjamin Franklin to England to persuade the Crown to curb the proprietor's power.[50] The Assembly then adjourned for the Christmas holidays.

When the House reconvened, it first rejected the Council's limitations on its bill and then voted to appropriate £100,000 for defense. Although this latest bill exempted the proprietor's estates from taxation, it did insist that the tax assessors be elected in each county and that an Assembly committee be empowered to distribute the money.[51] But on January 25, 1757, a committee of the Council condemned this new bill as "repugnant," and Denny rejected it. The following day the Assembly adopted a sharply worded remonstrance which its members, marching through the streets of Philadelphia, delivered en masse to the governor.[52] Denny again disapproved of the bill, but at the same time he sought advice from Lord Loudoun, the commander in chief of the British forces.

Loudoun arrived in Philadelphia on March 14, 1757, eager to settle the dispute between the Assembly and Denny. After consulting with Franklin, Loudoun recognized that concessions had to be made to the lower house. He therefore asked Denny to reconsider his proprietary instructions to determine "which of the instructions could be given up." When the Council hesitated, Loudoun applied more pressure; he wrote Denny, expressing his deep concern for the dangerous situation that existed. Once again, Loudoun urged the governor to "wave your instructions for the present and pass the [Assembly's] Bill. . . . "[53] At this point, Denny informed the Assembly he would pass the bill, which became law March 23, 1757.

The cast of contending politicians in Pennsylvania was slightly different after 1757: General Jeffery Amherst replaced Loudoun and Franklin was in England; but the plot — the lower house and the governor struggling for control of financial matters — was the same as it had been since the war began. In March 1759 the Assembly decided to raise £100,000 in bills of credit to be funded by a tax on all property, including the proprietor's. On the advice of his Council, Denny refused to sign the bill unless it exempted the Penns. But at this point General Amherst stepped into the dispute and convinced Denny he should approve the bill. Although the Council adamantly disagreed with the commander in chief, Denny signed the bill in April 1759.[54] Thus, for the first time in Pennsylvania history, the proprietor's property was subject to a tax regulated by the lower house. Even though the Privy Council eventually forced the Assembly to modify its tax schedule, as it applied to the proprietor, the Assembly had gained a firm control over the spending of tax money.[55]

The politics of finance in Pennsylvania were paralleled with only minor variations in the other colonies. In New York there was the same conflict between the governor and the lower house over control of public expenditures. Governors James De Lancy, Charles Hardy, and Cadwallader Colden (1753-1761) sought to deprive the lower house of several of its most important powers. The governors labored mightily to curb the assembly's power to determine annually the salaries of royal officials; to frame all money bills, denying the right of both the governor and the council either to initiate such measures or to propose amendments; to appoint committees to supervise the expenditure of particular sums; and to refuse to add suspending clauses stipulating that bills were subject to review by the Crown before they became law.[56] The Massachusetts lower house had established its mastery over financial affairs before the Great War for Empire began. But it did strengthen its hold by refusing to allow the Council either to initiate or amend its appropriation bills.[57] In Virginia, the House of Burgesses refused to appropriate money unless commissioners appointed by the lower house controlled the application of funds. Governor Robert Dinwiddie and the Board of Trade objected, but to no avail. By 1763 most of the lower houses, north and south, had more power over how public money was spent than did the British House of Commons.[58]

Even though the lower houses were concerned largely with practical political considerations, such as their insistence upon directing the provincial troops and controlling the funds raised to support them, they found it necessary to work out a rationale to support their claims to more political power. In chartered colonies, the lower houses used the charters as their first line of defense, arguing that they were inviolable. The Pennsylvania Assembly, for example, asserted in 1755 that the colony's charter guaranteed it a number of specific rights, plus "all other Powers and Privileges of an Assembly. . . ."[59] A more basic premise which was equally applicable to all colonies was that Americans were entitled to all of the rights of Englishmen. A New York assemblyman observed in 1757 that representatives and voters alike were "tenacious in their opinion, that the inhabitants of this colony are entitled to all the privileges of Englishmen; that they have a right to participate in the legislative power, and that the session of assemblies here, is wisely substituted instead of a representation in parliament, which, all things considered, would, at this remote distance, be extremely inconvenient and dangerous."[60] The corollary to this argument was that the lower houses in America were equivalent to the British House of Commons and therefore, within their limited sphere, American assemblies had the same rights and privileges as the Commons.[61]

As long as the war in America lasted, imperial officials made no concerted effort to challenge either the theoretical arguments for, or the practical manifestations of, the extension of authority by the lower houses in America.[62] For this reason, the war marked a significant decrease in the efficacy of the royal prerogative. Indeed, by 1763 the lower houses of assembly had become the most important centers of political power in America. To protect this dynamic structure from the challenge of an assertive English imperialism, Americans ultimately concluded that they had to be independent from Great Britain.

CHAPTER X

AMERICAN POLITICS AFTER THE GREAT WAR FOR EMPIRE

The problems and benefits of administering the British Empire in North America began long before 1763. In the decades before the Great War for Empire, Englishmen had given considerable thought to the imperatives and assumptions of empire. Thomas Mun's dictum provided the matrix for popular economic thought. "The ordinary means," Mun wrote in 1664, "to increase our wealth and treasure is by *Foreign Trade* where-in wee must ever observe this rule: to sell more to strangers than we consume of theirs in value."[1] The role of the colonies, of course, was to contribute what Britain needed in order to better equip her for international commercial competition. Wealth and power — the two "engines" of policy, according to Adam Smith — had the same objective: the balance of trade. The efficacy of the entire commercial system was measured by the condition of the balance. Not surprisingly, therefore, English merchants and their spokesmen became increasingly influential in the formation of government policy during the 1740s. In the years before the War of the Austrian Succession, the various economic interest groups seeking to shape public measures became larger and better organized. Of these groups, Professor Klaus Knorr concludes, "There is little, if any exaggeration in the judgment of Adam Smith who asserted that 'of the greater part of the regulations concerning the colony trade, the merchants who carry it on, it must be observed, have been the principal advisors.' "[2] Knorr adds, however, that the imperial policies pursued by the merchants were supported generally by those who held political power whether Tories or Whigs. "As a whole," he concludes, "the influential in England stood for Empire as a good business proposition and for laws that, in their eyes, appeared to make this business as profitable and secure as possible."[3]

An anonymous pamphleteer, commenting upon the impact of the Peace of Aix-la-Chapelle, excitedly summed up the change in Britain's perception of the role of the colonies: "Good God! what an immense Profit would it have been to us to have supply'd all North America with British Manufactures, and in return to have received their rich Furs?"[4] To a large degree, this kind of ecstatic dream was becoming real. Before 1750 the American colonies had exported more than they had imported from Great Britain. The dramatic changes that were transforming England's economy reversed this situation after 1750. Manufactured goods poured into the colonies at a rate that far exceeded America's exports.[5]

Because it was widely recognized that Britain's power was dependent upon the colonies, this change in the economic relationship between America and Great Britain had to be resolved. As early as 1751 Matthew Decker, a popular mercantilist writer, realized that something would have to be done to make it possible for Americans to consume ever-increasing quantities of English manufactured goods in the face of declining American exports. Decker proposed that the colonists be permitted to sell their goods in any market in the world. With more capital, and tighter prohibitions against manufacturing, "our colonies in America . . . might be made ten times more advantageous to us than they now are, by consuming most of our Manufactures, and by turning the general Balance of Trade with Europe greatly in favour of their Mother Country. . . ."[6] The idea of free trade for the colonies was too radical a departure from past mercantilist practices, however, and Decker's proposal died for lack of political advocates.

Restrictive proposals were received more favorably. Malachi Postlethwayt, an assiduous collector of data and advice for commercial interests, touched a responsive chord when, during the height of the Great War for Empire, he suggested that "all the colonies . . . be united under a legal, regular and firm establishment, settled and determined by the wisdom of a British legislature. . . ."[7] Among others, William Knox, a colonial official who had returned from Georgia to England in 1761, concurred with the need for regularizing the management

of the American colonies. Knox assumed that the purpose of the
colonies was to increase the wealth and power of England. To
best achieve this, he argued, the colonists should be confined
to the eastern seaboard by treaty with the Indians and British
army garrisons should be located in the principal port cities in
order to enforce the treaties, protect the colonists, and reinforce
their subordination to Great Britain.[8] A tax on all colonial
exports would raise the funds to support the troops.

Writing anonymously and in the guise of an Englishman,
Benjamin Franklin countered schemes like Knox's by arguing
that the risk of American rebellion would not be lessened if the
colonists were confined to the Atlantic seaboard. If they were
restricted to the coast, Franklin contended, Americans would
soon turn to manufacturing their own goods because there
would not be enough land to farm. Moreover, if they were not
allowed to expand beyond the Appalachian Mountains, it
would be impossible to protect the colonists from savage
Indian attacks regardless of how many men and forts England
committed to their defense. Franklin claimed that territorial
expansion would both ensure America's continued economic
dependence upon Great Britain and relieve England of "the
responsibility for the murder of our own people."[9]

Although these differences over the means of ensuring the
loyalty and dependence of the American colonies were not
finally resolved until the Peace of Paris, it is clear that before
the Great War for Empire was concluded there was widespread
agreement that it was time to create a more rational, more
efficient, more profitable empire.[10] William Pitt's policy during
the Great War for Empire was based on this new ideology.
From the outset of his administration, "commercial aims were a
powerful component in Pitt's strategic thinking. . . ."[11] He
sought both to deprive France of an empire and to tie the
colonies more closely to Britain's new economic needs.
Realizing that British exports to America had increased five
times during the first half of the eighteenth century, Pitt acted
on the premise that English prosperity depended on tighter
imperial controls. Temporary British war measures designed to
suppress American trade with the French West Indies became a
permanent policy. In 1763 Parliament authorized the royal
navy to enforce the Acts of Trade and Navigation and all
customs officers were ordered to their American posts. Colonial

officials happily reported progress in curbing illegal trade, but American merchants, already dejected by a deepening postwar economic slump, grew bitter over the new restrictive policies.[12]

The impact of the economic depression, which most northern colonies felt by 1760, was especially severe because the war had altered "normal" trading patterns. Thus, the sharp plunge in American commodity prices after 1760 was a tangible manifestation of a more serious and long-range problem; namely, where were Americans to market their goods so that they could purchase British manufactures, when neither England nor the British West Indies offered markets of sufficient capacity for American products.[13] Thomas Pownall, one of the few members of Parliament with colonial experience and knowledge, saw the problem clearly: "It is the singular disadvantage of the Northern British colonies," he wrote shortly after the Great War, "that while they stand in need of vast quantities of the manufactures of Great Britain, the country is productive of very little which affords a direct remittance thither in payment; and from that necessity therefore, the inhabitants have been driven to seek a market for their produce, where it could be vended, and by a course of traffic, to acquire either money or such merchandize as would answer the purpose of a remittance, and enable them to sustain their credit with the mother country."[14] The market to which Americans had been driven was the French West Indies. While those Caribbean islands had long provided a source of income for American merchants, Parliament's wartime prohibition against shipping provisions to neutral ports made the northern colonies far more dependent upon the West Indies than they had been before 1755. Specifically, when trade with southern Europe was closed off, northern merchants were forced to market more of their goods in the West Indies. Before the war an average of thirty ships each year left Boston for southern European ports; during 1760-1762, the average dropped to twelve. To make up this difference, twice as many ships left Boston for the West Indies after the war than before 1755. The same situation characterized the middle colonies. A major Philadelphia firm estimated that more than one-third of the grain shipments from that city were diverted from southern Europe to the West Indies. The difficulty inherent in this new trading pattern was apparent. "The islands, which are the [legal] market for flour," noted the *Pennsylvania Gazette*, "are too small to take off the quantity we can spare."[15] Traditionally, this problem had been resolved by trading goods for French West Indian sugar and then smuggling it into the colonies to avoid paying the prohibitively high duty. It has been estimated that more than ten times more illegal French sugar was brought into the colonies than legal English sugar.[16] During the war, as we have seen, this illegal trade was sharply curtailed by a series of embargoes and a naval blockade of the French West Indies. Although many merchants suffered serious financial setbacks as a result, some of the pressure was alleviated by lucrative military contracts. The decline in military purchases coupled with the British navy's vigilant pursuit of smugglers heightened the dilemma confronting colonial merchants.

To make matters worse, the postwar depression was not restricted to the American colonies. Business in England also fell off sharply. The number of bankruptcies in 1763 was higher than in any single year since 1728, which prompted English merchants to call in their American loans and drastically restrict credit. To aid British commercial interests, Parliament passed the Revenue Act, which further impeded the West Indian trade and the flow of specie to the American colonies. The Sugar Act, as it was usually called, did not prohibit the exportation of provisions and lumber (the chief American exports) to the French West Indies. It did place such a high duty on the importation of foreign sugars that this vital trade became almost useless for Americans who wanted to accumulate credits so that they could buy British manufactured goods. Squeezed between rising prices for imports and the falling prices of exports, Americans trading with the West Indies were outraged at a tax that cut further into their profits. In New York, John Watts commented crisply and darkly, "the weak must go to the wall."[17]

Nearly all American merchants—weak and strong, fair traders and smugglers—realized that they had a stake in preventing the destruction of the West Indies trade. By their own admission, northern colonial merchants could not obey the Sugar Act and stay in business. Nor, without nearly unrestricted access to foreign sugar, would they be able to buy anywhere near the quantities of English manufactures they needed. This would mean, Governor Stephen Hopkins of Rhode Island argued early in 1764, that "the quantity of fish, flour, lumber, horses, etc. produced in the northern colonies, [would] be lessened much more than one half, until they dwindle down into the diminutive size of these markets."[18] Remonstrances making these same points were sent to Parliament from the New York House of Representatives and the Massachusetts Assembly.[19]

Other segments of the northern colonial population were already feeling the dire economic consequences predicted for merchants if the West Indian trade were substantially reduced. Lawyers, who had generally prospered during the Great War and as a result had become important in provincial politics, found their case loads much reduced because of the decline in trading.[20] Residents of Boston likewise felt an economic pinch, complaining they were being forced by a rural-dominated legislature to bear an excessive proportion of the province's tax bill. With less than 6 percent of the colony's population, Boston paid 17 percent of the taxes in 1756. Not surprisingly, this inequitable distribution of the tax burden came to a head in 1765. In that year, heeding the anguished cries of Boston's mercantile community, the General Court finally cut the city's share of the provincial tax by a fourth, largely at the expense of the far western towns.[21]

Segments of the northern colonial population with less access to political power did not fare as well as the Bostonians. Imperial trade restrictions meant that American seamen were at best underemployed. This was a marked change from the wartime situation, when thousands of seamen worked on colonial privateers which preyed successfully on French shipping in the Caribbean. When the war concluded and these seamen came ashore to find work, they found a constricted labor market often glutted with off-duty British soldiers willing to work for less than the going wage. Likewise, the number of poor people in small New England towns increased sharply as a result of declining economic opportunity after 1760.[22]

Underemployment and constricted commercial activity dampened the enthusiasm with which Americans hailed the defeat of France, especially when they faced the high cost of that victory. In order to pay for the extraordinary effort that was necessary to drive France from North America, the colonists had gone deeply in debt. Taxes had skyrocketed. Whereas the tax bill for Massachusetts residents in 1753 was £15,000, in 1759 it amounted to over £100,000. Inhabitants of Connecticut and Pennsylvania often did not have to pay any taxes before the Great War for Empire. During that struggle, the per capita

rate for Connecticut residents rose as high as 25 pence, and for
Pennsylvanians as high as 18 pence. To be sure, the subsidies
received from Parliament paid off much of the colonies'
indebtedness and reduced taxation far below the per capita rate
Englishmen were paying. Still, the rates must have seemed
excessive to Americans accustomed to paying low taxes or none
at all. Moreover, a policy of rapid currency contraction in
colonies such as Connecticut and Rhode Island probably
sharpened the impact of taxation and the general economic
distress.[23] Clearly, for small commercial farmers, merchants,
underemployed seamen, ship carpenters, and many others, the
idea that England would demand that the colonists assume a
larger share of the imperial burden was outrageous. "What are
the people of England now doing with us?" asked Tench
Francis, a Rhode Island merchant. "Nothing but Ruine seems
to hang over our heads."[24]

Expressions of anxiety by American merchants cannot be
dismissed as simply reactions to a temporary postwar slump. In
fact, economic difficulties in the 1760s were caused by
fundamental structural changes in the Atlantic economy which
had been accelerated by the Great War for Empire. Specifically, during the war British firms had extended their business
operations so widely that by 1763 they were bypassing
established American importers and retailers. Together with the
effort by British merchants to reduce the American share of
trans-Atlantic shipping, the postwar depression can be seen as a
direct challenge to American economic sovereignty.[25]

The threat of economic collapse led Americans from both
sides of local political factions, merchants and seamen alike, to
look to the colonial assemblies for help against British
imperialism. In each of the northern colonies, politicians
increasingly dependent upon the support of a large percentage
of the population eagerly took up the fight for increased
economic independence. As seen by some the issue was
whether Americans' "signal services in war" had been forgotten
by a corrupt ministry bent on subverting liberty.[26]

The Stamp Act was viewed as a more dangerous sign of this
process than the Sugar Act. Surely, Americans reasoned, the
strenuous effort made by the colonies to defeat the French
should be rewarded, not dismissed. "Several thousands of the
hardiest and most able young men," Governor Thomas Fitch of
Connecticut pointed out, "the hope and strength of the farmers,

have been destroyed, lost and enervated in the many arduous distant campaigns during the course of this terrible war."[27] Who benefited most from this noble sacrifice? To be sure, the American colonies were free from the menace of Indian attack. But the heavy war debts, the decline in the value of real estate due to the opening up of a vast new territory, and most importantly, the loss of the basic right to be consulted before being taxed caused many Americans to agree with Daniel Dulany's conclusion that Great Britain "protected the colonies to preserve *herself*."[28] The logical extension of Dulany's conclusion was evident: If Great Britain acted out of narrow self-interest in 1755, it followed that she would be unconcerned about American rights after the war when they conflicted with the pursuit of revenue to benefit British taxpayers. The right of an Englishman not to be taxed unless represented was, of course, fundamental to the preservation of liberty. Lose the part and the whole was sure to follow.

Thus, as early as 1765, the obvious question to ask given the colonists' political perspective was posed by Stephen Johnson, a Connecticut clergyman: Is it to be slavery or independence for America?[29] The final answer, of course, was more than a decade in the making; but when the Stamp Act was imposed, as Edmund Morgan has made so clear, a great many Americans saw the question to be "whether they would be men and not English or whether they would be English and not men."[30]

As the tactics for independence were unknowingly rehearsed during those turbulent years immediately following the Great War for Empire, the conflicts became sharper. There was nothing novel about the manner of resistance; the courts, the lower houses of representatives, crowds protesting in the streets, were, by 1765, familiar parts of American politics. The issues were at least a decade old. The war had given rise to the problems of quartering, trade regulations, impressment, and the need to raise revenue to administer a vast empire. Moreover, the war had accelerated those social and political trends that caused Americans to believe they were morally and politically superior to Englishmen. Coupled with the development of the lower houses of assembly as centers of political power—also largely a wartime phenomenon—the conflicts between Americans and Englishmen became contests for political autonomy. Nowhere, perhaps, was the impact of the issues raised by the Great War more evident than in New York, where the problems of trade with the French West Indies, currency, and the presence of British troops combined to precipitate a direct confrontation between Englishmen and Americans.

In the summer of 1766 the New York Assembly refused to appropriate money to provide British soldiers in the colony's barracks with "fire, candles, vinegar, salt, beer, cider or rum." Ostensibly, the assemblymen refused to comply because these extras were not required by law when troops were quartered in England. It seems probable that the Assembly was acting to represent the interests of several of its constituencies by refusing to comply with all the provisions of the Quartering Act. On the one hand the assemblymen apparently hoped that they could use the promise of eventual and full compliance with the act to win Governor Henry Moore's approval of a new issue of currency to relieve the dismal economic situation.[31] On the other hand, the assemblymen knew they had popular support for twisting the tail of the British lion.

Governor Moore noted shortly after his arrival in New York City that "no means has been left untried by the Populace to make their [the two British regiments stationed in New York] situation uneasy to them and to excite them to committ [sic] some action, for which public censure might be drawn on them."[32] The people's hatred of the British soldiers was militantly demonstrated in the summer of 1766 when several thousand New Yorkers poured into the streets to protest a foray by some soldiers against the "Liberty Pole." Both General Thomas Gage, commander in chief of the British army, and Moore saw clearly what was at stake in the struggle between soldiers and civilians. "The Populace," Gage concluded, "are not willing to part with the Power and Authority they have so long usurped, to which they think the Soldiers may give some obstructions."[33]

In Albany, the scene of numerous disputes between civilians and British soldiers, the city council flatly refused when requested to provide for the troops.[34] At least one member of the council, Abraham Yates, a shoemaker who became a lawyer and a member of the Livingston faction during the Great War, was especially hostile toward the British army. In 1757, when Yates was sheriff of Albany, Lord Loudoun, then commander in chief of the British Forces in North America, rudely and threateningly brushed aside Yates's objection to Loudoun's demands for quarters for his troops. At one point in the

controversy, Loudoun told Yates that during a war "the army
were to have the Administration and those who would oppose
it ought to be hanged. . . ."[35] Yates was shocked; he poured out
his rage and his political beliefs in his private journal,
intending to use the charges as the basis for a civil suit against
Loudoun. The idea that the army took precedence over the civil
authority during a war Yates branded "against the Law of God,
the Law of England, and the Law of Nature." The English
constitution "is no arbitrary tyranny Like the Turkish Grand
Seignor or the French Kings whose wills or rather Lusts
dispose of the Lives and fortunes of their unhappy Subject . . .
But a most Excellently . . . Qualified monarchy. . . ." The
King's actions are restricted by the law, "each man having a
Fixed foundamental Right Born with him as to Freedom of his
Person and Property in his estate which he cannot be deprived
of but either by his Consent or Some Crime for which the Law
has imposed such a Penalty. . . ."[36] Clearly, this was not the
case when Loudoun came to Albany and demanded quarters
for his soldiers, briskly disregarding the right of a citizen,
guaranteed since 1629 by the Petition of Rights, to refuse to
accept soldiers into his home. Although Yates's entries in his
journal stopped before coming to the logical conclusion — that
Loudoun should be removed by the King—William Livingston,
Yates's political mentor, had seen enough. Livingston advised
Yates not to press his case. A court would not believe,
Livingston cautioned, that Loudoun actually believed the
military superior to civil authority, for that would be "high
treason."[37] The youthful Yates accepted Livingston's wise
advice; he decided not to pursue his "case" against Loudoun.

Yates's hostility toward the British army had roots other than
his dispute with Loudoun. In 1761 Yates ran for election to the
New York Assembly. Despite Livingston's help—he sent
several of his sons to round up voters—Yates finished third
behind two De Lancey candidates. Livingston's pessimistic
preelection analysis had proved to be accurate. Yates's
opponents not only had "great interest" on their side, but they
also used the army to intimidate the voters. In particular, Yates
discovered that an officer in the British army, Colonel John
Bradstreet, had done everything he could to persuade Albany
voters not to elect him. Bradstreet, according to Yates,
"Treatned [sic] some that he would Never pay their accounts
Others that he would take their horses some People have Kings

horses on fodder from them, and Others he woud Declare war against them, and more of the Like wild Expressions."[38]

Yates's defeat in Albany was one of the few losses the Livingston faction suffered in the elections of 1761. Elsewhere in the province the Livingston faction routed the De Lancey group, winning nearly absolute control of the lower house, which they retained until 1768. While they dominated the Assembly, the Livingston faction initially took the lead in opposing Grenville's program of imperial legislation. While the Livingston group was not ready in 1765-1766 to embrace radical politics, they were quite willing to resist encroachments on their rights as Englishmen in the manner of traditional Whigs.[39] Therefore, they refused to comply fully with the Quartering Act in 1766 and 1769.

Further, it seems clear that the Livingston faction's opposition to providing for the troops was motivated also by the popular dislike of the British army and the aggressive imperialism it symbolized. Certainly, the Livingstons were well aware that their noncompliance would be cheered in Albany and New York City.[40] This small, tentative step in the direction of popular politics placed the Livingstons far short of the goal set by the radicals. After the struggle against the Stamp Act, Professor Bernard Friedman argues, "the radicals made adherence to the American cause in the Constitutional crisis, rather than the customary family, financial, and denominational ties, the principal test of popularity."[41] Still, the Livingston faction's opposition to providing for the British troops — a position with which they felt comfortable because of their experience during the Great War for Empire — provided the bridge for many of them to move to the left in their political thinking.[42] In Albany, for example, the man who had been most outspoken in his opposition to the demands of the British army, Abraham Yates, transformed the nature of politics in that city. He and other nonpatricians built a party largely of groups that had previously been left out of Albany politics, the Dutch lower class and the non-Dutch immigrants.[43] Because they took positions on imperial questions, Yates and his group stimulated a dynamic interplay between local and imperial politics that was certainly related to the coming of the Revolution. One of the first actions of the Albany Committee of Correspondence, chaired by Yates, was to send a letter of commiseration to the people of Boston. The people of Albany "have experienced the

brutal insolence of the Military during the last war," the
committee wrote. "They can, from a retrospective View of their
conduct *then,* easily form an idea of their oppressive measures
now carried on against [Boston's] Inhabitants."[44]

While the emergence of a distinctively American politics,
initially stimulated by issues and events that emerged from the
Great War for Empire, is most clearly seen in New York, the
same phenomenon can be seen in all of the northern colonies.
During the 1750s and 1760s the old social-political order
crumbled. Launched by local controversies that were made
more significant by the Great War and the economic distress
and aggressive imperial legislation that followed it, a new
political ideology and practice took final form in the 1770s.
Led by a desire for a new, virtuous order that allowed men to
determine and realize their self-interest, the American people
took an irrevocable step into the future in 1776.

EPILOGUE

Great Britain expended huge amounts of blood and treasure to drive the French from North America. Whatever the motive most important to the Crown, the empire was protected and extended. It was a magnificent accomplishment that elicited enthusiastic praise from some Americans. But other Americans were not grateful, not even appreciative. Their wartime experiences had stimulated the development of attitudes that led them to take an anti-imperialist stance and to encourage active popular resistance, a combination that gave rise to the question of whether empire and liberty were compatible. This is not to say that American experience during the Great War for empire was determinative, but it certainly gave concrete meaning to the opposition thought that Bernard Bailyn claims was "devoured by Americans." In short, it seems very unlikely that the outburst over the Stamp Act would have been so intense if it had not been preceded by seven or eight years of experience with an assertive imperialism that had rudely touched the lives of many Americans.

It was not that British goals changed after 1763. The difference was that beginning in 1755 the British ministry determined to enforce those goals. This drive to rationalize the Empire alienated some and angered many important segments of American society. American merchants learned during the Great War that their interests were largely ignored. Thus, James Otis complained that "the late acquisitions in America, as glorious as they have been, and as beneficial as they are to Great Britain, are only a security to these colonies against the ravages of the French and Indians. Our trade upon the whole, is not, I believe, benefited by them one groat."[1] American merchants soon went beyond Otis. They began to perceive in British policy a direct assault on the prosperity they had created. As they had during the war, merchants turned to the lower houses of assembly to translate their economic grievances into political protests.

By 1763 the assemblies were powerful enough to speak for the colonies on imperial questions. The war had accelerated the lower houses' drive for more authority. Waged by astute political leaders, contests with governors and imperial officials led to the assumption of numerous powers previously held by the executive. For this reason the trend toward rationalization of the empire was viewed by the lower houses as a direct challenge to American political autonomy.

Earlier manifestations of British imperialism were bitterly recalled in the years after 1763. With an obvious reference to American experience during the Great War for Empire, John Adams asked rhetorically in 1765, "Have we not been treated . . . with abominable insolence, by officers of the British navy. . . . Have not some generals from England treated us like servants, nay more like slaves than Britons?" Adams urged Americans not to be as timid as they had been in resisting impressment and expressions of arrogant military power. Likewise, John Dickinson's influential *Letters from a Farmer in Pennsylvania* warned Americans that the suspension of the New York Assembly for refusing to comply with the Quartering Act was "as much a violation of the liberty of the people of that province, and consequently of all these colonies, as if the Parliament had sent a number of regiments to be quartered upon them till they should comply."[2] Lord Loudoun's arrogance had not been forgotten.

As the imperial crisis deepened more Americans came to believe that Great Britain fought against the French from 1755-1763 simply for the "sake of her trade and dominion. . . . She did not protect us from *our enemies on our account,* but from *her enemies on her account.* . . ."[3] This view of the past had its origins in American experience with British imperialism during the Great War for Empire.

NOTES

CHAPTER I

1. Lewis Namier, *England in the Age of the American Revolution* (London, 1930), for the nature of English politics; Charles Wilson, *England's Apprenticeship* (New York, 1965), for English commercial development; A. H. John, "War and the English Economy, 1700-1763," *Economic History Review*, 2d ser., VII (1955), 329-339; Michael Kammen, *Empire and Interest: The American Colonies and the Politics of Mercantilism* (New York, 1970), p. 53. Some men, Kammen tells us, were anxious about the development of special commercial-political interests (pp. 91-92).

2. Benjamin Franklin, "Observations Concerning the Increase of Mankind" (Boston, 1755) in *Franklin Papers*, IV, 229.

3. Stanley N. Katz, *Newcastle's New York: Anglo-American Politics, 1732-1753* (Cambridge, 1968), pp. 23-28.

4. John A. Schutz, *William Shirley: King's Governor of Massachusetts* (Chapel Hill, 1961), pp. 8-12, 12-16, 23-25, 42. Katz *(Newcastle's New York,* pp. 35-36) comments on the adverse affects of patronage politics. Governors William Cosby and George Clinton, for example, "shared . . . a lack of political finesse, undisguised avariciousness, subservience to their wives and political advisors and a general slothful, unintelligent approach to their official duties."

5. Schutz, *Shirley,* pp. 62-84; Katz, *Newcastle's New York,* pp. 55-58.

6. Cadwallader Colden to John Catherwood, Nov. 21, 1749, New York Historical Society, *Collections,* 1920, p. 159, as quoted in Katz, *Newcastle's New York,* p. 57.

7. *Acts and Resolves, Public and Private, of the Province of Massachusetts Bay* (Boston, 1869-1922), III, 70. Bernard Bailyn, "The Origins of American Politics," in *Perspectives in American History,* I (1967), 60-68, discusses the structural differences between politics in America and in England in the eighteenth century. While Robert E. Brown makes claims about "democracy" which are misleading, he does establish that the franchise in Massachusetts was widespread; see his *Middle-Class Democracy and the Revolution in Massachusetts* (Ithaca, N.Y., 1955). Chilton Williamson (*American Suffrage from Property to Democracy, 1760-1860* [Princeton, 1960]) comes to similar, if less idealistic, conclusions about the extent of the suffrage in colonial America.

8. Robert Zemsky, *Merchants, Farmers, and River Gods: An Essay on*

Eighteenth-Century American Politics (Boston, 1971), p. 225, quoting Representative Samuel Fish. Zemsky demonstrates convincingly the accuracy of this contemporary estimate; see, in particular, pp. 285-311.

9. *Ibid.,* p. 249.

10. Political developments in Rhode Island are discussed by David S. Lovejoy, *Rhode Island Politics and the American Revolution, 1760-1776* (Providence, 1958), and analyzed by Mack E. Thompson, "The Ward-Hopkins Controversy and the American Revolution in Rhode Island: An Interpretation," *William and Mary Quarterly,* 3d ser., XVI (1959), 363-375. One of the best books on Pennsylvania politics is William S. Hanna, *Benjamin Franklin and Pennsylvania Politics* (Palo Alto, 1964), especially pp. 7-12, for the Assembly's growth and development. See also Katz, *Newcastle's New York,* p. 42.

11. English politics in the mid-eighteenth century are fully treated in Namier, *England in the Age of the American Revolution.*

12. Caroline Robbins, *The Eighteenth-Century Commonwealthman: Studies in the Transmission, Development and Circumstance of English Liberal Thought from the Restoration of Charles II until the War with the Thirteen Colonies* (Cambridge, 1961), pp. 8-16.

13. James Alexander, *A Brief Narrative of the Case and Trial of John Peter Zenger,* ed. Stanley N. Katz (Cambridge, 1963), p. 9.

14. New York *Weekly Journal,* Nov. 12, 1733, as quoted in *ibid.,* p. 114.

15. I disagree with Professor Katz's analysis on the point (*ibid.,* pp. 6-11); Patricia U. Bonomi (*A Factious People: Politics and Society in Colonial New York* [New York, 1971] pp. 104-105, 112) contends that Morris was a political man, convinced that "moving in the midst of things and making some difference there was worthwhile." Indeed, even if Morris was initially simply playing a role, this often leads to behavioral change.

16. *Weekly Journal,* Sept. 23, 1734, in Katz, *A Brief Narrative,* p. 122.

17. *Ibid.,* p. 128.

18. *Ibid.,* p. 133.

19. Bonomi, *Factious People,* pp. 124-125, 138. See also, Beverly McAnear, "Politics in Provincial New York, 1689-1761" (unpublished Ph.D. dissertation, Stanford University, 1935) pp. 754-755.

20. Katz, *Newcastle's New York,* pp. 111-113, 207-213; Bonomi, *Factious People,* pp. 140-178.

21. William Livingston and others, *The Independent Reflector . . . ,* ed. Milton Klein (Cambridge, 1963), p. 56.

22. *Ibid.,* pp. 61-67; 69-75; 89-94; 111-117; 142-148; 171-214; 282.

23. William Smith, *The History of the Late Province of New York, from Its Discovery to the Appointment of Governor Colden in 1762* (New York, 1829), p. 40; *Votes and Proceedings of the General Assembly of the Colony of New York,* for 1752 (New York, 1752), p. 21; Klein, ed., *Independent Reflector,* pp. 419-425.

24. Early Pennsylvania politics are analyzed by Gary B. Nash, *Quakers and Politics: Pennsylvania, 1681-1726* (Princeton, 1968). For the early years of the eighteenth century, see Roy Lokken, *David Lloyd, Colonial Lawmaker* (Seattle, 1959).

25. *Ibid.,* p. 146.

26. *Ibid.,* pp. 194-196.

27. David Lloyd, *A Vindication of the Legislative Power* (Philadelphia, 1724-1725), p. 3, as quoted in *ibid.,* p. 223.

28. James Hutson, "Benjamin Franklin and Pennsylvania Politics, 1751-1755: A Reappraisal," *Pennsylvania Magazine of History and Biography,* XCIII (1969), 303-371. An opposite point of view is argued by Hanna, *Benjamin Franklin and Pennsylvania Politics.*

29. Ralph Ketcham, ed., *The Political Thought of Benjamin Franklin* (Indianapolis, 1965), p. xxi.

30. Hutson ("Franklin and Pennsylvania Politics," pp. 316-317) argues convincingly that the Isaac Norris group of Quakers approached Franklin in 1751 because they knew he shared their Whig values; Ketcham, *Political Thought of Franklin,* pp. xxxii, xxxvii.

31. Benjamin Franklin to Peter Collinson, May 28, 1754, *Franklin Papers,* V, 332-333. It is Hutson's contention that Franklin wrote Collinson about this matter knowing he would put the letter before Penn ("Franklin and Pennsylvania Politics," p. 334).

32. Morris to William Shirley, June 16, 1755, *Pennsylvania Archives,* 1st. ser., II, 362.

33. Klein, ed., *Independent Reflector,* p. 290; election sermons in Massachusetts and Connecticut abound with many of these same beliefs. See, for example, Samuel Checkly, *A Day of Darkness . . .* (Boston, 1755); Ebenezer Pemberton, *A Sermon . . .* (Boston, 1757); Moses Dickinson, *A Sermon . . .* (New London, Conn., 1755); and Joseph Fish, *Christ Jesus the Physician . . .* (New London, 1760).

CHAPTER II

1. Lords of Trade to Sir Danvers Osborne, Sept. 18, 1753, *New York Colonial Documents,* VI, 800-802. When the instructions reached New York, Osborne was dead; therefore, Lieutenant Governor James De Lancey assumed the responsibility for arranging the conference. Although I disagree with some of its conclusions, Robert C. Newbold's *The Albany Congress and Plan of Union of 1754* (New York, 1955) is a reliable survey.

2. Indian affairs are discussed in Chapter III.

3. Shirley to the Massachusetts House of Representatives, April 2, 1754, *Shirley Correspondence,* II, 40-46. Shirley was apparently responsible for inviting Connecticut and Rhode Island to the Albany conference, although the Board of Trade had not included either of those colonies in its original summons; see "Massachusetts Archives," IV, 442-444 (Massachusetts State Archives). Shirley's role in the conference is discussed briefly by John A. Schutz, *William Shirley, King's Governor of Massachusetts* (Chapel Hill, 1961), pp. 180-182.

4. *Pennsylvania Gazette,* May 9, 1754. Franklin's cartoon and article were reprinted in the *Boston Gazette,* May 21, 1754, among other colonial newspapers.

5. Franklin to James Parker, March 20, 1751, *Franklin Papers,* IV, 117. The letter was printed as an appendix to Archibald Kennedy's pamphlet, *The Importance of Gaining and Preserving the Friendship of the Indians to the British Interest Considered* (New York, 1751).

6. *Pennsylvania Archives,* 8th ser., V, 3694-3697.

7. *Ibid.,* pp. 3708, 3717-3718. In addition to Franklin, Pennsylvania sent the

Speaker of the Assembly, Isaac Norris, and John Penn and Richard Peters, members of the Provincial Council.

8. Massachusetts delegates to the conference were empowered to enter "into articles of Union and Confederation with the aforesaid Governments for the general defence of His Majesty's subjects and interests in North America, as well in time of peace as of war" (Massachusetts Historical Society, *Collections* [7 ser., 71 vols.; Boston, 1792], 3d ser., V, 9-10).

9. *Ibid.*, 3d ser., V, 11-17. See Lawrence Henry Gipson, *The British Empire before the American Revolution: Zones of International Friction,* (15 vols., New York, 1936-1970), V, 116-117. Theodore Atkinson of New Hampshire noted that most of the delegates' commissions "began with the Stile of the Governrs, not the King. . . ." (Beverly McAnear, ed., "Personal Accounts of the Albany Congress of 1754," *Mississippi Valley Historical Review,* XXXIX [1953], 731). De Lancey had been an early advocate of a colonial union but his enthusiasm waned as his political squabble with Governor Shirley was intensified; see, Patricia U. Bonomi, *A Factious People: Politics and Society in Colonial New York* (New York, 1971), pp. 175-176.

10. *New York Colonial Documents,* VI, 860. The men chosen to serve on the committee were: Thomas Hutchinson, Massachusetts; Theodore Atkinson, New Hampshire; William Pitkin, Connecticut; Stephen Hopkins, Rhode Island; Benjamin Franklin, Pennsylvania; Benjamin Trasker, Maryland; William Smith, New York.

11. Benjamin Franklin, *Autobiography* (New York, 1964), p. 134.

12. *Franklin Papers,* V, 337-338.

13. "Reasons and Motives on Which the Plan of Union Was Formed [July 1754] *Franklin Papers,* V, 400.

14. Gipson maintains that Thomas Hutchinson deserves much of the credit for authoring what ultimately became the Albany Plan of Union. Gipson's arguments for this hypothesis are put forth in vol. V of his *British Empire,* pp. 128-130; in "Thomas Hutchinson and the Framing of the Albany Plan of Union, 1754," *Pennsylvania Magazine of History and Biography,* LXXIV (1950), 5-35; in "The Drafting of the Albany Plan of Union: A Problem in Semantics," *Pennsylvania History,* XXVI (1959), 291-316; and in "Massachusetts Bay and American Colonial Union, 1754," *Proceedings* of the American Antiquarian Society, LXXI/I (1961), 63-92. Professor Verner W. Crane has been an outspoken critic of Gipson's thesis; see Crane's "Letters to the Editor on the Albany Congress Plan of Union, 1754," *Pennsylvania Magazine of History and Biography,* LXXV (1951), 350-362, and "Letters to the Editor on the Drafting of the Albany Plan of Union," *Pennsylvania History,* XXVII (1960), 126-136. My own judgment is that the plan which was reported out by the committee on union was based initially on Franklin's "Short Hints"; that it was undoubtedly modified in some aspects by the views of other delegates, including Thomas Hutchinson; and that the plan was put in final form by Franklin.

15. The Albany Plan may be found in the *Franklin Papers,* V, 387-392; and Franklin's "Short Hints" in *ibid.,* pp. 337-338.

16. *Ibid.* Franklin later supported all of these provisions ("Reasons and Motives on Which the Plan of Union Was Formed," *ibid.,* V, 415-416).

17. For development of the statements in this and the following paragraph, see Bernard Bailyn, *The Ideological Origins of the American Revolution* (Cambridge, 1967), pp. 55-70.

18. "Short Hints towards a Scheme for a General Union of the British Colonies on the Continent," (June 28, 1754) *Franklin Papers*, V, 361.

19. "Reasons and Motives on Which the Plan of Union Was Formed, [July 1754] *ibid*, V, 403.

20. *Ibid*. Franklin suggested that in order to be perfectly balanced the governors and councilors who were appointed by the Crown should choose the President General. He — and presumably others — rejected this solution as impracticable.

21. This is the contention of Gipson (*British Empire*, V, 131-135).

22. At least one writer criticized the ratification procedure for being too vague; see *A Short Reply to Mr. Hopkin's Vindication by Philolethes* (Providence, R.I., 1754). And Governor Horatio Sharpe of Maryland was surprised to discover that Governor De Lancey had sent the Plan of Union to England before the colonies had an opportunity to amend it; W. H. Browne et al., eds., *Archives of Maryland* (65 vols.; Baltimore, 1883-1952), VI, 79.

23. "Richard Peters: Rough Notes on a Debate at Albany," [July 1, 1754] *Franklin Papers*, V, 365.

24. R. R. Palmer, *The Age of the Democratic Revolution: A Political History of Europe and America, 1760-1800* (2 vols.; Princeton, N.J., 1959), I, 214-216.

25. *Pennsylvania Archives*, 8th ser., V, 3733; Franklin, *Autobiography*, p. 135. The "certain member" was probably Isaac Norris, Speaker of the Assembly and a commissioner to the Albany Congress. While at the Congress Norris apparently had opposed the military features of the Plan and this probably accounted for his rejection when it was before the Quaker-dominated Pennsylvania Assembly; see McAnear, ed., "Personal Accounts of the Albany Congress of 1754," p. 744.

26. The committee's report appears in Massachusetts Historical Society, *Collections*, VII, 207-209; Benjamin Trumbull, *A Complete History of Connecticut* (2 vols., New London, Conn., 1898), II, 357.

27. Massachusetts Historical Society, *Collections*, VII, 207-209. William Smith of New York later wrote that Connecticut's delegates to the Albany conference were "too jealous of the powers of the President." See his *History of the Late Province of New York* (Albany, 1757), II, 183-185.

28. *Ibid.*

29. *Ibid.*

30. *Connecticut Colonial Records*, X, 293. The Assembly also instructed the governor to "give attention to all the steps taken by the several governments on this continent relating to the plan of the proposed union of the several Colonies in North America for their mutual defence, and use means, as he shall judge prudent, to prevent any further proceedings thereon" (*Ibid.*, pp. 293-294).

31. *A Short Reply to Mr. Stephen Hopkins's Vindication, and False Reflections against the Governor and Council of the Colony of Rhode Island* (Providence, 1755).

32. *Rhode Island Colonial Records*, V, 394.

33. *Ibid.*, V, 424. Herbert L. Osgood (*The American Colonies in the Eighteenth Century* [4 vols., New York, 1925], IV, 321) mistakenly writes that Rhode Island flatly opposed the Plan of Union.

34. Massachusetts Archives, LXXXIII, 231-232, 239, 246-247.

35. The members of the committee from the House were James Russell, William Brattle, John Choate, and James Otis; from the Council, Samuel Watts,

Ezekiel Cheever, Andrew Oliver, and Stephen Sewall; *Journals, Massachusetts House,* XXXI, 152-153.

36. *Ibid.,* Dec. 3, 1754, p. 137.

37. Massachusetts Archives, Dec. 4, 1754, VI, 169; pp. 169-183 for the committee's plan for a partial union.

38. *Journals, Massachusetts House,* XXXI, 152-153, Dec. 14, 1754; p. 182, Dec. 27, 1754.

39. Josiah Willard, Secretary for the General Court to William Bollan, Dec. 31, 1754, in Albert B. Hart, *The Commonwealth History of Massachusetts* (5 vols.; New York, 1927-1930), II, 461. The lower house's defeat of the Albany Plan appears to be a good example of the lack of what Robert Zemsky terms "leadership influence" (*Merchants, Farmers, and River Gods: An Essay on Eighteenth-Century American Politics* [Boston, 1971], pp. 303-308). Despite the support of Governor Shirley and, initially, such leaders as William Brattle, John Choate, James Allen, and Nathaniel Sparhawk, the "backbenchers" were able, it would seem, to have the Plan of Union referred back to committee, modified substantially, and then, with the leadership deserting Shirley's cause, the House voted to consult their constituents before any further consideration of intercolonial union.

40. Thomas Hutchinson, *The History of the Colony and Province of Massachusetts Bay* (3 vols.; Cambridge, Mass., 1936), III, 23.

41. Shirley to Thomas Robinson, Dec. 24, 1754, *Shirley Correspondence,* II, 112.

42. Shirley's plan must be reconstructed from Franklin's criticism of it; see Franklin to Shirley, Dec. 4 and Dec. 22, 1754, *Franklin Papers,* V, 443-447, 449-451; Schutz, *Shirley,* p. 184.

43. *Ibid.,* p. 444.

44. *Ibid.*

45. *Ibid.,* p. 445. Franklin remarked that it would be putting the American people on the same footing as the French to allow the governors to "march Inhabitants from one End of the British and French Colonies to the other . . . without the Approbation or Consent of their Representatives first obtain'd to such Expeditions. . . ."

46. *Ibid.,* pp. 446, 449.

47. "Remark, Feb. 9, 1789," *ibid.,* p. 417.

CHAPTER III

1. Lawrence Henry Gipson, *The British Empire before the American Revolution: The Great War for the Empire. The Years of Defeat, 1754-1757* (15 vols.; New York, 1936-1970), VI, 71.

2. William Johnson to James De Lancey, July 30, 1755, *Johnson Papers,* I, 794-797; John C. Fitzpatrick, ed., *The Writings of George Washington from the Original Manuscript Sources, 1745-1799* (39 vols.; Washington, D.C., 1931-1944), II, 39-42.

3. *Wilderness Politics and Indian Gifts: The Northern Colonial Frontier, 1748-1763* (Lincoln, Nebr., 1966), pp. 29-34. The gifts were not simply a form of bribery; the Indians had become absolutely dependent upon the white man's goods.

4. *New York Colonial Documents,* X, 154, 237-238, for reports by Abbe Piquet about his success in recruiting warriors in 1760.

5. Boston *Evening Post,* April 18, 1757.

6. *The Importance of Gaining and Preserving the Friendship of the Indians to the British Interest Considered* (New York, 1751).

7. Colden was the author of *The History of the Five Indian Nations,* originally published in 1727.

8. "The Present state of Indian affairs, with the British and French colonies in North America, with some observations thereon for securing the Fidelity of the Indians to the Crown of Great Britain and promoting Trade among them," *New York Colonial Documents,* VI, 738-747.

9. Wilbur R. Jacobs, ed., *The Appalachian Frontier: The Edmond Atkin Report and Plan of 1755* (Lincoln, Nebr., 1967). Atkin was a member of the South Carolina Council and a merchant.

10. *Ibid.,* pp. 14-37.

11. *Ibid.,* p. 37.

12. The journals of the Congress are printed in *New York Colonial Documents,* VI, 870 ff.

13. John R. Alden, "The Albany Congress and the Creation of the Indian Superintendencies," *Mississippi Valley Historical Review,* XXVII (1940), 198-200.

14. *Ibid.,* p. 199. Alden strongly implies that Johnson prompted the Indians who appeared before the Congress in his behalf.

15. The text of the Albany Plan of Union may be found in *Franklin Papers,* V, 361-364.

16. Alison Gilbert Olson, "The British Government and Colonial Union," *William and Mary Quarterly,* 3d ser., XVII (1960), 22.

17. Alden, "Indian Superintendencies," p. 200.

18. *Johnson Papers,* I, 465-466.

19. *Votes and Proceedings of the Pennsylvania Assembly,* for 1753-1754 (Philadelphia, 1754), p. 65; Robert C. Newbold, *The Albany Congress and Plan of Union in the Colonies* (New York, 1955), pp. 136-140, 170-171.

20. For a general discussion of this trend, see Jack P. Greene, "The Role of the Lower Houses of Assembly in Eighteenth-Century Politics," *Journal of Southern History,* XXVII (1961), 451-474.

21. Massachusetts voted £600 as its share of the expenses incurred by Johnson (Vote of the General Assembly of Massachusetts, May 7, 1755, *Johnson Papers,* I, 491-493); New Hampshire debated the matter and decided they would not contribute anything until they saw what the other colonies were going to do (Governor Benning Wentworth to Johnson, May 23, 1755, *ibid.,* I, 536-538); New York's Assembly considered the probable cost of the gifts that were to be given to the Indians, but failed to appropriate any money.

22. Shirley to Johnson, March 26, 1755, *Johnson Papers,* I, 462-463; and the same, *Shirley Correspondence,* II, 175.

23. Johnson to Shirley, Dec. 17, 1754, *Johnson Papers,* I, 430; and the same, May 16, 1755, *ibid.,* I, 505. "For me . . . to wait the future discussions of Colony proportions [Johnson wrote] to risque my Fortune upon a repayment from the respective Assemblies, is a dependence which neither my Judgment nor my Experience will suffer me to trust to."

24. Scholars have taken either Johnson's or Shirley's side in this controversy based largely upon their interpretation of Braddock's vague instructions to the

two men. John Schutz supports Shirley in his biography, *William Shirley: King's Governor of Massachusetts* (Chapel Hill, N.C., 1961), pp. 201-202, 205-207, 217, 223, as does Gipson, *British Empire*, VI, 143-147. On the other hand, Francis Parkman *(Montcalm and Wolfe* [New York: Collier Books, 1962], p. 233) and Jacobs *(Wilderness Politics and Indian Gifts,* pp. 148-151) put Johnson in a favorable light.

25. Braddock to Johnson, April 15, 1755, *Johnson Papers,* I, 465-466. Minutes of the Alexandria Conference, April 14, 1755, PRO/CO, 5/46.

26. Shirley to Johnson, April 16, 1755, *Johnson Papers,* I, 472-477.

27. The New York group included: Goldsbrow Banyar, secretary to the Provincial Council of New York and deputy clerk to the Supreme Court of New York; the De Lancey brothers, James and Oliver, one of whom (James) was lieutenant governor in 1755; Thomas Pownall, an ambitious young man whose brother was secretary to the Board of Trade; and Peter Wraxall, Johnson's personal secretary and publicist; and later, for a time, Governor Charles Hardy. See Schutz, *Shirley,* pp. 198-199, for a brief description of the relationship between Livingston, Governor Robert Morris of Pennsylvania, and Shirley. Johnson's relationship with the De Lancey faction is discussed in Beverly McAnear, "Politics in Provincial New York, 1689-1761" (unpublished Ph.D. dissertation, Stanford University, 1935), pp. 706-708, 872-875.

28. Johnson to Shirley, June 19, 1755, *Johnson Papers,* I, 614; Johnson to Oliver De Lancey, June 16, 1755, *ibid.,* I, 601.

29. Johnson to Braddock, May 17, 1755, *ibid.,* I, 514, and Johnson to Robert Orme (Braddock's aide-de-camp), May 19, 1755, *ibid.,* I, 522. Orme was asked to help "prepare" the home government to accept Johnson's position.

30. Johnson to Braddock, June 27, 1755, *ibid.,* I, 664-665. Johnson's position was that the Six Nations were supreme among all the tribes of the Ohio Valley; therefore, negotiations with any tribe had to be approved by the Six Nations. Acceptance of this argument meant, of course, acceptance of Johnson's complete control of Indian affairs, for he was acknowledged by everyone concerned to be in control of the Six Nations (Ralph L. Ketcham, "Conscience, War and Politics in Pennsylvania, 1755-1757," *William and Mary Quarterly,* 3d ser., XX [1963], 429).

31. Johnson to Shirley, July 15, 1755, *Johnson Papers,* I, 721-722.

32. "Notes on Indian Affairs at Mount Johnson," July 4, 1755, *New York Colonial Documents,* VI, 984-988. Wraxall was, of course, one of the most active members of the New York clique promoting Johnson's drive for an independent position at Governor Shirley's expense. Shortly after the conference ended, Wraxall urged Johnson to step up his attack on Shirley despite the fact that Shirley—with the death of Braddock—had become commander in chief *(Johnson Papers,* July 20, 1755, I, 757. Johnson to Pownall, July 31, 1755, *ibid.,* I, 804-806; and Johnson to Robert Orme, Aug. 1, 1755, *ibid.,* I, 813-816). Boasting about his role in the conference, Orme replied (Sept. 2, 1755, *ibid.,* I, 896) that he would by happy to speak to his friends in London about Johnson's negotiating skills, which was just what Johnson wanted, of course.

33. Pownall to Johnson, Aug. 16, 1755, *ibid.,* I, 853. Goldsbrow Banyar earlier had urged Johnson to contact Pownall, writing, "he [Pownall] can do you great Services if he goes home and I am fully convinced will warmly espouse your interest" *(ibid.,* Aug. 6, 1755, I, 834; James De Lancey to Johnson, Sept. 21, 1755, *ibid.,* II, 68).

34. Johnson to Lords of Trade, Sept. 5, 1755, *Shirley Correspondence, II,* 247-248.

35. "Commission from George II," Feb. 17, 1756, *Johnson Papers,* II, 434-435. Johnson was also made a baronet at this time. Johnson's victory at Lake George in 1755 — one of only two British victories in that dark year — obviously helped his claim to the superintendency. Some Americans believed Johnson did not deserve any or all of the credit he received from the crown. William Livingston commented, "Sir William is Certenly a luckey man, has gott himself Immortal Honours by mear accidents" (Livingston to Abraham Yates, Aug. 30, 1759, Yates Papers [New York Public Library]). In May 1756, Atkin was made southern superintendent of Indian affairs (Jacobs, ed., *Atkin Report,* p. xxii).

36. Bernard Bailyn, "The Origins of American Politics," *Perspectives in American History,* I (1967), 80.

37. Wraxall to Johnson, Oct. 3, 1755, *Johnson Papers,* II, 136. Hardy also probably realized that Johnson's appointment meant that his lieutenant governor, James De Lancey, was out to undermine the governor's authority.

38. Alexander Colden to George Harison, Dec. 18, 1755, Richard Harison Papers (New York Historical Society). The Presbyterian party was led by William Livingston, John Morin Scott, and William Smith, Jr.; their later activities are detailed in Dorothy R. Dillon's, *The New York Triumvirate: A Study of the Legal and Political Careers of William Livingston, John Morin Scott, and William Smith, Jr.* (New York, 1949).

39. Hardy to the Lords of Trade, Jan. 16, 1756, *New York Colonial Documents,* VII, 3. Hardy showed his political naiveté once again by recommending Johnson for this new, lesser job!

40. On the democratization of New York politics before 1765, see Milton M. Klein, "Democracy and Politics in Colonial New York," *New York History,* XL (1959), 221-246.

41. The Assembly could only take a verbal jab at Johnson's shady land schemes; it could not prevent him from acquiring thousands of acres of choice lands at *very* low prices. The Assembly's thrust at Johnson can be found in the New York Historical Society, *Collections,* 1876, p. 378; Johnson's arrogant response in a letter to Cadwallader Colden, Nov. 3, 1764, *Johnson Papers,* IV, 576-577.

42. *Pennsylvania Colonial Records,* VII, 88-90. The proclamation specifically exempted those Indians who left their tribe and put themselves into protective custody.

43. *Pennsylvania Archives,* 1st ser., II, 619. The members of this committee were: Isaac Norris, the Speaker of the House, James Hamilton, John Mifflin, Joseph Fox, John Hughes, Evan Morgan, and Benjamin Franklin; Mifflin and Fox were Quakers.

44. Johnson to the Lords of Trade, May 28, 1756, *New York Colonial Documents,* VII, 88. Shirley to Morris, April 15, 1756, *Pennsylvania Colonial Records,* VII, 92-93.

45. *Ibid.,* VII, 144. The Assembly's message to the governor stressed the need for passage of its Indian trade bill; the Quaker party blamed much of the current Indian trouble on the rapacity of Indian traders acting under proprietary authority.

46. Johnson to the Lords of Trade, July 17, 1756, *New York Colonial Documents,* VII, 118-119.

47. Aug. 19, 1756, *Franklin Papers*, VI, 487. Franklin believed that peace would not be achieved until the Indians had been "well drubb'd."

48. Peters to Shirley, May 6, 1756, *Pennsylvania Archives*, 1st ser., II, 651.

49. Loudoun to Denny, Sept. 22, 1756, *Pennsylvania Colonial Records*, VII, 270. Interestingly enough, Loudoun himself had some reservations about Johnson's ability to "manage those Indians that lie at such a distance and in that Situation." Loudoun wondered if "it might not be reasonable if they [Pennsylvania] could settle with the Indians in their Neighborhood, for their own preservation . . . without giving them any permanent Rights, to intermeddle in Indian affairs" (Loudoun to Johnson, Sept. 10, 1756, LO 1760).

50. Council Meeting, Oct. 29, 1756, *Pennsylvania Colonial Records*, VII, 305-308.

51. Governor Morris did know about Johnson's commission as superintendent of Indian affairs before he met the Delaware at Easton in July 1756 (*Pennsylvania Colonial Records*, VII, 192-194; *ibid.*, Pennsylvania Assembly: Reply to the Governor, Oct. 29, 1756, VII, 307-308).

52. Johnson warned the Board of Trade that Pennsylvania's negotiations "will throw all Indian politics left to their management into confusion and perhaps into a Flame which may not be easily quenched" (Sept. 28, 1757, *New York Colonial Documents*, VII, 279). The Indian superintendent made similar statements to Lord Loudoun and General Abercromby (Loudoun to Denny, Jan. 28, 1758, *Pennsylvania Archives*, 1st ser., III, 338; and Johnson to Abercromby, June 21, 1758, *Johnson Papers*, II, 850).

53. The Penns told Richard Peters that the Board of Trade had requested they give up all of their western claims, Nov. 7, 1757 (Massachusetts Historical Society; the Easton conference records, *Pennsylvania Colonial Records*, VII, 199 ff.). Johnson refused to attend the Easton conference (Johnson to Abercromby, Sept. 10, 1758, AB 638).

54. *Pennsylvania Colonial Records*, VIII, 240, Dec. 23, 1758.

55. Amherst to Colonel Henry Bouquet, May 2, 1762, and June 6, 1763 (Bouquet Papers [Canadian Archives]).

56. Amherst's pattern of thought on the Indian question emerges clearly from his correspondence. See, for example, his letters to Bouquet, Jan. 16, 1762, July 25, 1762, and Bouquet to Amherst, Oct. 9, 1762 (ibid.).

57. Amherst to Johnson, May 7, 1761, *Johnson Papers*, III, 387; the Crown's ban on settlement, Nov. 23, 1761, *New York Colonial Documents*, VII, 473; and Lords of Trade to Governors, Dec. 2, 1761, *ibid.*, p. 478. A group of Albany merchants had protested to the Crown about Amherst's Niagara settlement (Jan. 28, 1762, *ibid.*, VII, 488-489). Amherst's disclaimer may be found, among other places, in his letter to Governor Horatio Sharpe, Oct. 20, 1762, *ibid.*, VII, 508.

58. Assembly to Governor Denny, Dec. 23, 1758, *Pennsylvania Archives*, 8th ser., VI, 4913; "The regaining the Indian affections, which we always expected the most natural Barrier and Security of the extended western Boundary of this Colony, has been and will still continue the Object of our strictest Attention. . . ."

59. Amherst ordered that the Indians be given ammunition "very Sparingly." This idea failed to take into account how dependent the Indians were on firearms for their survival (Amherst to Bouquet, May 2, 1762, Bouquet Papers). Johnson warned Amherst that this was a dangerous policy (June 12, 1761, *Johnson Papers*, X, 286-287; Aug. 18, 1761, *ibid.*, III, 520).

60. Francis Parkman's *History of the Conspiracy of Pontiac* (2 vols.; Boston, 1851) should be compared with Howard Peckham's revisionist account, *Pontiac and the Indian Uprising* (Princeton, 1947), and with Wilbur R. Jacobs, "Was the Pontiac Uprising a Conspiracy?" *Ohio Archeological and Historical Society Quarterly,* LIX (1950), 26-37.

61. Feb. 24, 1764, *Johnson Papers,* IV, 341.

62. Jan. 14, 1764, Stanislaus M. Hamilton, ed., *Letters to Washington and Accompanying Papers* (5 vols.; New York, 1898-1902, III, 265).

63. The Earl of Halifax to Gage, Jan. 14, 1764, Clarence E. Carter, ed., *The Correspondence of General Thomas Gage . . . 1763-1775* (2 vols.; New Haven, 1931-1933), II, 10.

64. Livingston to Eleazer Wheelock, March 22, 1764, Wheelock Papers, quoted in Bernhard Knollenberg, *Origin of the American Revolution: 1759-1766* (New York: Free Press, 1965), p. 111; Morris to his nephew, Samuel Powell, July 4, 1763, in the *Pennsylvania Magazine of History and Biography,* XV (1891), 378-380; letter in the *London Chronicle,* Jan. 14, 1764, reprinted in the *Pennsylvania Journal,* April 19, 1764, and the Newport *Mercury,* Dec. 31, 1764. The *Virginia Gazette,* Nov. 4, 1763, observed that "the ministry are greatly embarrassed by the Indian war. . . . "

65. John Shy (*Toward Lexington: The Role of the British Army in the Coming of the American Revolution* [Princeton, 1965], pp. 142-143) argues that the complaints of Americans at this time were a cover for their unwillingness to pay taxes to maintain the troops. I think this argument underestimates the depth of Americans' hostility toward the army and overestimates the healing power of victory. Knollenberg (*Origin of the American Revolution,* pp. 110-111) also disagrees with Shy's analysis.

66. June 13, 1764, HM 2587.

67. Oct. 5, 1765, as quoted by William A. Whitehead, *Contributions to the Early History of Perth Amboy* (New York, 1856), p. 103n, in Shy, *Toward Lexington,* p. 142. Charles Thomson, Pennsylvania politician and author of a pamphlet attacking imperial Indian policy ("An Enquiry into the Alienation of the Delaware and Shawanese Indians from the British Interest," London, 1758), also agreed with the Massachusetts legislature: "While we were surrounded by the French, we had no army to defend us: but now they are removed . . . we are burthened with a standing army and subjected to insufferable Insults from any petty officer. . . ." (Thomson to Cook, Lawrence & Co., Nov. 9, 1765, New York Historical Society, *Collections,* 1878 [New York, 1879], p. 7).

68. PRO/CO, 5/403. For a fuller statement of the idea that British policy after about 1750 was motivated by a concern for rationality, see John Shy, "Thomas Pownall, Henry Ellis, and the Spectrum of Possibilities, 1763-1775," in Alison Gilbert Olson and Richard Maxwell Brown, *Anglo-American Political Relations, 1675-1775* (New Brunswick, N.J., 1970), pp. 183-186. '

69. Intercolonial rivalry is discussed by W. Neil Franklin, "Pennsylvania-Virginia Rivalry for the Indian Trade of the Ohio Valley," *Mississippi Valley Historical Review,* XX (1934), 463-480, and by Jacobs, *Wilderness Politics and Indian Gifts,* pp. 120-122. Factionalism within Pennsylvania is analyzed by Nicholas B. Wainwright, *George Croghan, Wilderness Diplomat* (Chapel Hill, 1959), pp. 163-189.

70. Loudoun to Henry Fox, Aug. 9, 1756, LO 1522. Two lower houses of assembly proposed regional cooperation as an alternative to imperial control of

Indian affairs; see Massachusetts House of Representatives to Jasper Mauduit, June 13, 1764, HM 2587, and the Pennsylvania Assembly's response to Amherst contained in its message to Governor James Hamilton, Oct. 22, 1763, *Pennsylvania Archives,* 8th ser., VI, 5484-5485. For the demise of the effort to centralize authority, see Peter Marshall, "Colonial Protest and Imperial Retrenchment; Indian Policy, 1764-1768," *Journal of American Studies,* V (1971), 1-17.

CHAPTER IV

1. Compare Lord Loudoun's instructions for recruiting, Nov. 15, 1756, LO 2221, with those issued later by Colonel Henry Bouquet, July 15, 1757, *Papers of Colonel Bouquet,* ser. 21631, 1, 33, and by General John Forbes, March 20, 1758, *Pennsylvania Colonial Records,* VIII, 59-60. Henry Fox, Secretary of State for the Southern Department, told the colonial governors on March 13, 1756, that each man who enlisted in the regular army for the duration of the war would receive 200 acres of land, free from the payment of quitrents for ten years, in either Nova Scotia, New Hampshire, or New York (LO 924). The Connecticut Assembly gave a counterfeiter who was in a Hartford jail the opportunity to enlist in the royal navy (*Connecticut Colonial Records,* X, 535-536). Governor Robert Dinwiddie asked the Virginia House of Burgesses to pass a law that would put all vagrants into the regular army (*Dinwiddie Papers,* p. 628). The Burgesses subsequently excluded all men from the service who "hath any vote in the election of Burgess or Burgesses. . . ." (W. W. Henning, ed., *The Statutes at Large, Being a Collection of All the Laws of Virginia* [13 vols.; Richmond, 1809-1823], V, 94-96).

2. Governor William Shirley to the Lords of Trade, Dec. 1, 1747, *Shirley Correspondence,* I, 406-419; Lawrence Henry Gipson, *The British Empire before the American Revolution* (15 vols.; New York, 1936-1970), VII, 70.

3. Carl Bridenbaugh, *Cities in Revolt: Urban Life in America, 1743-1776* (New York, 1955), p. 114.

4. Rudé (New York, 1964). Some of Rudé's other works include: *The Crowd in the French Revolution* (Oxford, 1959), *Wilkes and Liberty: A Social Study of 1763 to 1774* (Oxford, 1962). See also, Gordon S. Wood, "A Note on Mobs in the American Revolution," *William and Mary Quarterly,* 3d ser., XXIII (1966), 635-642. Wood points out that Rude's descriptions of European mobs are remarkably like those descriptions of the American Revolutionary crowds. Several other studies of the eighteenth-century crowd are of special interest: E. P. Thompson, "The Moral Economy of the English Crowd in the Eighteenth Century," *Past and Present,* 50 (1971), 76-136; Pauline Maier, "Popular Uprisings and Civil Authority in Eighteenth-Century America," *William and Mary Quarterly,* 3d ser., XXVII (1970), 3-35.

5. Rudé, *The Crowd in History,* pp. 253-254; *ibid.,* p. 205.

6. *Ibid.,* pp. 254-255.

7. William A. Smith points out that England had a tradition of crowd demonstrations. "Since concern for English rights and liberties was a concept deeply imbedded in the society, it came to be tacitly accepted by that society that mob violence in defense of those rights or in protest against some major grievance was in itself a legitimate, if not a legal right of freeborn English

subjects" ("Anglo-Colonial Society and the Mob, 1740-1775" [Ph.D. dissertation, Claremont Graduate School, 1965], p.1). The difference between England and America in regard to crowd demonstrations was profound: in America official political agencies often supported the demands of the demonstrators.

8. The foregoing description is based on Shirley's report to the Lords of Trade, Dec. 1, 1747 (*Shirley Correspondence,* I, 406-419, and John A. Schutz, *William Shirley, King's Governor of Massachusetts* (Chapel Hill, 1961), pp. 127-130. Boston presented a petition to the Council denouncing the practice of impressment and begging that it be stopped. The "Behaviour of the [British] officers, who with their lawless Rabble like Russians enter the Houses of the Inhabitants in the Night" certainly was a "Breach of Magna Carta, and the Charter of this Province, and an Act of Parliament" stated the petition. The Council rejected it (John J. Waters, Jr., *The Otis Family in Provincial and Revolutionary Massachusetts* [Chapel Hill, 1968], p. 90).

9. Bridenbaugh, *Cities in Revolt,* p. 116. Commodore Knowles had a different explanation for the impressment riot. He believed that the law exempting the West Indies from impressment had "fill'd the Minds of the Common People ashore as well as Sailors in all the Northern Collonies (but more especially in New England) with not only a Hatred for the King's Service but a Spirit of Rebellion. . . ." (PRO/Admiralty, 1/234, Jan. 18, 1748, as quoted in Daniel A. Baugh, *British Naval Administration in the Age of Walpole* [Princeton, 1965], p. 221). Both Shirley's and Knowles's explanations credit the people of New England with considerable knowledge of English laws and the rights of citizens.

10. Bridenbaugh, *Cities in Revolt,* p. 116. Maier, "Popular Uprisings," pp. 13, 24.

11. *Journals, Massachusetts House,* XXXIII, pt. 2, 434, April 15, 1757. Earlier the House had declared that impressment was "impracticable," "exclusively burthensome" and had a tendency to "depopulate" the colony (*ibid.,* p. 18, May 28, 1756).

12. Thomas Hutchinson to William Bollan, Sept. 11, 1756, Hutchinson, Msc. Bound, XII (Massachusetts Historical Society). Governor Thomas Pownall told William Pitt (May 16, 1759) that the people of Massachusetts had an "Almost unconquerable Aversion . . . to go on Board King's Ships. . . ." (*Pitt Correspondence,* II, 91-92).

13. The Pennsylvania Assembly first simply ignored Commodore Spry's request for permission to impress (*Pennsylvania Colonial Records.* VII, 132, May 23, 1756). Later the Assembly stated it could not comply with Admiral Boscowen's demand (*ibid.,* VII, 164-165); Governor Jonathan Belcher laid a request for permission to impress before the New Jersey Council asking only that it "do what you think most for the Kings Service and for the interest of this Colony." The Council refused to allow an impress (W.A. Whitehead et al., eds., *Archives of the State of New Jersey* [30 vols.; Newark, 1880-1906], XVII, 114-115, 206). Maryland also refused to allow an impress (Governor Sharpe to Pitt, Oct. 22, 1757, *Pitt Correspondence,* I, 123). Admiral Moore was so desperate that he convinced General Barrington to impress three hundred soldiers from the troops stationed in Guadeloupe (Barrington to Pitt, May 9, 1759, *ibid.,* II, 95).

14. Loudoun to Lord Colville, March 4, 1758, LO 5696.

15. "Jack Tar in the Streets: Merchant Seamen in the Politics of Revolutionary America," *William and Mary Quarterly,* 3d ser., XXV (1968), 383.

The action is described in the journal of Colonel James Montresor, New York Historial Society, *Collections,* 1881, pp. 150-151; my estimate (1,100) as to the number of men rounded up comes from Joseph Shippen to Major Burd, May 31, 1757, Papers of the Shippen Family (Historical Society of Pennsylvania).

16. New York *Gazette* or *Weekly Post-Boy,* Aug. 12, 1754; the law referred to by Americans was 6 Anne, 1708, which exempted Americans from impressment. The Admiralty argued that the law was only meant to apply during the War of the Spanish Succession, which ended in 1713 (George W. Edwards, *New York as an Eighteenth Century Municipality* [Port Washington, N.Y., 1967], pp. 110-111).

17. Jesse Lemisch, "The American Revolution from the Bottom Up" in Barton Bernstein, ed., *Towards a New Past: Dissenting Essays in American History* (New York, 1968), pp. 47-49; Neil Stout, "The Royal Navy in American Waters, 1760-1779" (unpublished dissertation, University of Wisconsin, 1962), pp. 362-381; and Maier, "Popular Uprisings," p. 9.

18. Sharpe to Shirley, Feb. 2, 1756, PRO/CO, 5/46. Sharpe told Governor Morris of Pennsylvania that if Shirley did not order a stop to the enlistment of servants he, Sharpe, would have to use his power as governor to end the practice (*Pennsylvania Archives,* 1st ser., II, 573-574). Stanley M. Pargellis's *Lord Loudoun in North America* (New Haven, 1933) is a fine pioneer study of recruiting problems encountered by the British army during the early years of the war; see especially, pp. 104-110, 119-121.

19. Morris to Shirley, Feb. 16, 1756, *Shirley Correspondence,* II, 391-392, and Shirley to Morris, Feb. 20, 1756, *ibid.,* p. 392n.

20. *Votes and Proceedings of the Pennsylvania Assembly,* V, 4185-4186. At least part of the Assembly's argument against enlisting servants manifested racist tendencies. The lawmakers maintained that if white servants were taken from their owners by the army, they would be "driven to the Necessity of providing themselves with Negro Slaves, as the Property in them and their Service seems at present more secure" (*Pennsylvania Colonial Records,* VII, 37).

21. Morris to Assembly, Feb. 13, 1756, *ibid.,* VII, 40. It is interesting to note that at the same time Morris wrote General Shirley asking him to prohibit recruiters from enlisting any more servants (*Pennsylvania Archives,* II, 576).

22. Shirley to Morris, Feb. 29, 1756, *Shirley Correspondence,* II, 410-411.

23. Shirley to Fox, March 8, 1756, PRO/CO, 34/73; General Daniel Webb to Loudoun, April 10, 1756, LO 1034. Shirley to William Smith, Jr., and to William Livingston, March 1, 1756, William Alexander Papers (New York Historical Society). Shirley asked Smith and Livingston to post bond for and defend in court, if necessary, the officers who were arrested by colonial officials.

24. Fox to all governors, March 13, 1756, *New York Colonial Documents,* VII, 76; *Journals, Massachusetts House,* XXXIII, 82, July 3, 1756; for Maryland's refusal, see Pargellis, *Loudoun,* p. 120; *Votes . . . N.Y.,* July 2, 1756, PRO/CO 5/1216; George Washington to Dinwiddie, Sept. 8, 1756, *Dinwiddie Correspondence,* p. 1061; Governor Jonathan Belcher to the New Jersey Assembly, March 28, 1756, LO 3195.

25. *Pennsylvania Gazette,* Nov. 18, 1756; Loudoun thought the Assembly intended to pay the masters (Loudoun's Diary, March 26, 1757, HM 1717).

26. An Act for the better Recruiting of his Majesty's Forces on the Continent

of America, and for the better Regulation of the Army, and preventing of Desertion there (29 George II, c. 25 [1756]).

27. Franklin to Sir Everard Fawkener, July 27, 1756, *Franklin Papers,* VI, 474-475.

28. *Ibid.* Thomas Pownall told Loudoun that a group of Pennsylvania merchants proposed "that if their Servants shall be exempt from being enlisted they will pay the passage of all Recruits which can be raised in Germany" (LO 2002).

29. Corbin Lee to Governor Sharpe, April 30, 1757 (LO 3506); see also LO 5738 for a writ issued for the arrest of Arthur Browne, an officer in the British army.

30. Franklin to Loudoun, May 21, 1757, LO 3699.

31. Loudoun to Fox, Nov. 22, 1756, LO 2263. Recruiting Instructions, 1757, LO 6761.

32. In Massachusetts, for example, justices entertained actions for false debts in order to obtain the discharge of recruits who, according to one of the provisions of the Mutiny Act, could not be enlisted if they owed more than £10; see Sam Mackay to Colonel John Forbes, Feb. 6, 1758, LO 5549.

33. John Winslow to Governor William Shirley, Oct. 20, 1755, John Winslow's Journal and Correspondence (Massachusetts Historical Society).

34. Winslow to Governor Charles Lawrence, Oct. 27, 1755, *ibid.*

35. Winslow to Shirley, Dec. 19, 1755, *ibid.*

36. *Journals, Massachusetts House,* XXXII, pt. 2, 317-318, Feb. 4, 1756. *Ibid.,* pp. 331-332, Feb. 13, 1756; Shirley told Secretary Henry Fox on June 14, 1756, that he had "moderated" the demands of the Assembly in that he got it to agree that only men born in New England, or with families or relatives there, would be affected by his order (*Shirley Correspondence,* II, 464-465).

37. Gridley to Loudoun, June 6, 1757, LO 3797. There were also civil suits brought against recruits to prevent their enlistment. This method was used in other colonies; see, for example, *Connecticut Colonial Records,* XI, 293, 296 (May 1759); Charles Steltzers to Loudoun, March 30, 1757, from "The Philadelphia Gaol," and General Jeffery Amherst to Cadwallader Colden, Dec. 27, 1760, *Colden Papers,* V, 389-390.

38. Captain Harry Charteris to Loudoun, June 11, 1757, LO 3816.

39. Pownall to Loudoun, Feb. 6, 1758, LO 5547. On November 28, 1757, the Boston *Evening Post* commented bitterly in an article reprinted from a London newspaper which described how Englishmen had been beaten and forced into the army.

40. Governor Thomas Fitch to Loudoun, Jan. 17, 1758, LO 5417.

41. A series of letters in the Loudoun Papers describes this incident. LO 5058, 5155, 5325, 5348, 5356, 5359, 5417.

42. Loudoun's Diary, III, March 26, 1757, HM 1717; for similar complaints about how recruiters operated, see James Kenny, "Journal to ye Westward, 1758-1759," *Pennsylvania Magazine of History and Biography,* XXXVII (1913), 416, and Samuel Grubb, Orderly Book, June 26, 1759, HM 606.

43. Loudoun to Fox, Nov. 22, 1756, LO 2263; Lieutenant George Cottnam to Colonel John Forbes, Dec. 12, 1757, LO 5003. See also, John Watts to William Baker, May 12, 1762, *Watts Letter Book,* p. 48. Watts noted that despite a big bounty it was unlikely that colonials would enlist in the Regulars, for there was "an aversion to that Service. . . ."

44. Pargellis, *Loudoun,* pp. 109, 130. Pargellis suggests that because so few Americans volunteered, the ministry had to send greater numbers of British regiments to the colonies than they had originally planned. It was much less expensive to recruit men in the colonies than to transport soldiers from England. Pitt estimated in 1757 that raising 6,000 men in America would not cost the government as much as sending 1,000 English regulars to the colonies (George L. Beer, *British Colonial Policy,* 1754-1765 [New York, 1907], p. 57).

45. Loudoun, Diary, II, Oct. 2, 1757, HM 1717.

46. Mackay to Forbes, Dec. 16, 1757, LO 5023, 5073; Lieutenant William Cook to Governor Benning Wentworth, Dec. 31, 1757, LO 5165.

47. Lieutenant Robert Makinen told Colonel Forbes, Dec. 27, 1758, that a crowd attacked his party in New London, Connecticut (LO 5077; Pownall to Loudoun, Feb. 6, 1758, LO 5547; Captain Skey to Loudoun, March 5, 1758, LO 5703). Western Pennsylvanians, chiefly Germans, also attacked British recruiting parties (C. J. Shippen to his father, Sept. 17, 1760, Shippen Papers [Historical Society of Pennsylvania]). For the trouble in Philadelphia, PRO/WO 34/89 as cited in J.C. Long, *Lord Jeffery Amherst: A Soldier of the King* (New York, 1933); the New York clash was reported by the *Mercury,* Jan. 23, 1764.

48. Captain Samuel Mackay to Colonel Forbes, Dec. 23, 1757, LO 5073; Captain Harry Charteris to Loudoun, June 11, 1757, LO 3816; James Robertson to Loudoun, Jan. 6, 1758, LO 5348; *Pennsylvania Colonial Records,* VII, 37-40; Maier, "Popular Uprisings," p. 13.

49. Richard Merritt has calculated that the number of American symbols (American place-names used in several colonial newspapers) rose sharply in 1755, the year of Braddock's defeat ("The Colonists Discover America: Attention Patterns in the Colonial Press, 1735-1775," *William and Mary Quarterly,* 3d ser., XXI [1964], 272-273; Pargellis, Loudoun, p. 125).

50. Archibald Kennedy, *Serious Advice to the Inhabitants of the Northern Colonies on the Present Situation of Affairs* (New York, 1755), pp. 5-6, 14.

51. Charles Chauncey, *A Letter to a Friend, Giving a Concise, but Just Account . . . of the Ohio Defeat* (Boston, 1755), pp. 8-9; in a second pamphlet Chauncey pointed with obvious pride to the colonials' victory at Lake George, commenting that this removed the stigma of defeat from Englishmen (*A Second Letter to a Friend Giving a More Particular Narrative of the Defeat of the French army at Lake George by the New England Troops* (1755), pp. 14-15).

52. William Vinal, *A Sermon on the Accursed Thing That Hinders Success and Victory in War, Occasioned by the Defeat of the Hon. Edward Braddock Esq. . . .* (Philadelphia, 1755), p. 14.

53. Boston *Evening Post,* Nov. 15, 1755. The editor reprinted some excerpts from an old military tactics manual which stressed the need for flankers; he then commented: "It would have been much to the Advantage of North America if these Excellent Rules had been observed by the Commander in some late important Expeditions" (*ibid.,* Dec. 15, 1755).

54. New York *Mercury,* Aug. 11, 1755; *Pennsylvania Gazette,* July 31, 1755. Governor Charles Hardy had ordered the printers in New York not to publish anything about Braddock's defeat, according to a letter from Alexander Colden to James Parker, July 28, 1755, *Franklin Papers,* VI, 113-114.

55. Dinwiddie to Shirley, July 29, 1755, *Shirley Correspondence,* II, 212-213;

Dinwiddie to James Abercromby, Aug. 7, 1755, *Dinwiddie Papers*, p. 144; House of Burgesses to Dinwiddie, PRO/CO 5/16.

56. Pennsylvania Assembly to Governor Robert Morris, *Votes and Proceedings of the Pennsylvania Assembly*, for 1754-1755, (Philadelphia, 1755), p. 117. The New York Council wanted Dunbar's army sent to Albany so that it could help General Shirley or General Johnson (Aug. 1, 1755, LO 620; Morris to Shirley, July 30, 1755, *Pennsylvania Colonial Records*, VI, 513).

CHAPTER V

1. "Queries of George Chalmers, with the Answers of General Gage, in relation to Braddock's Expedition—the Stamp Act—and Gage's Administration of the Government in Massachusetts Bay," Massachusetts Historical Society, *Collections* (Boston, 1858), IV, 367-368.

2. Pownall presented his views on colonial government in a pamphlet entitled *The Administration of the Colonies* (London, 1774). His specific comment on impressment may be found in the Earl of Loudoun's letter to the Duke of Cumberland, Oct. 17, 1757, LO 4653.

3. Lawrence Henry Gipson, *The British Empire before the American Revolution* (15 vols.; New York, 1936-1970), VI, 75-77; VII, 266-268; Theodore Thayer, *Pennsylvania Politics and the Growth of Democracy, 1740-1776* (Harrisburg, 1953), pp. 67-68. John Shy (*Toward Lexington: The Role of the British Army in the Coming of the American Revolution* (Princeton, 1965), pp. 171-172) supports the idea that a "fair price" and good business methods largely avoided conflict over impressment.

4. Thomas Robinson to William Shirley, Oct. 26, 1754, *Shirley Correspondence*, II, 100-101. The Mutiny Act, passed annually by Parliament, governed the British army whenever it left its barracks. It stipulated that the army had to work through local civil officials in order to obtain supplies.

5. Braddock to Robinson, April 19, 1755, PRO/CO, 5/46. The arrangements that had been made in advance were very loose. Governor Horatio Sharpe of Maryland, for example, told Governor Robert Dinwiddie of Virginia on December 26, 1754, that he had been unable to get enough wagons for Braddock because "I have no acquaintance near that part of the country [Will's Creek, Virginia] whom I could desire to make purchases for me. . . ." (*Dinwiddie Papers*, p. 647).

6. "Letter from the Commissioners in charge of running the Road" to Governor James Hamilton, April 16, 1755, *Pennsylvania Colonial Records*, VI, 368.

7. Franklin, *Autobiography* (New York, 1964), p. 139.

8. *Franklin Papers*, VI, 19-22. See also Whitfield Bell and Leonard W. Labaree, "Franklin and the Wagon Affair," American Philosophical Society, *Proceedings*, CI (1957), 551-558.

9. Braddock to Thomas Robinson, June 5, 1755, LO 581.

10. Morris to Braddock, June 6, 1755, *Pennsylvania Colonial Records*, VI, 415. Morris asked the Assembly to establish a price for hiring wagons, but it adjourned before a bill could be agreed upon; *Pennsylvania Archives*, 8th ser., V, 3908, 3916, 3925.

11. Morris to Edward Shippen, Samuel Morris, Alexander Stedman, and Samuel McCall, Jan. 31, 1756, *Pennsylvania Archives,* 1st ser., II, 598-599; Morris to Shirley, April 22, 1756, *ibid.,* 638-639; Charles Dick to Governor Robert Dinwiddie, Oct. 20, 1756, *Dinwiddie Correspondence,* p. 1115. Dick, who was an army contractor, commented that often the sum due a farmer was less than what it would cost him to travel to Philadelphia. He also noted that many of these people had brought suits against him.

12. Election returns for Cumberland, Lancaster, and York counties in the *Pennsylvania Gazette,* Oct. 9, 1755, and compared with those of 1754 (*Gazette,* Oct. 10, 1754) and 1753 (*Gazette,* Oct. 11, 1753).

13. *Votes . . . N.Y.,* April 26, 1756 *PRO/CO* 5/1216.

14. Hardy to [whoever is in command], July 19, 1756, LO 1319; Loudoun to Hardy, Sept. 19, 1756, LO 1669; Hardy to Loudoun, Sept. 20, 1756, LO 1856.

15. Loudoun to Hardy, Sept. 23, 1756, LO 1884.

16. Captain Gabriel Christie to Captain Cunningham, April 15, 1757, LO 3363. Abraham Yates, sheriff of Albany, noted that many people were determined to resist, and to suffer, rather than have their wagons and horses or themselves taken by the British army (Yates to William Livingston, Dec. 7, 1757, Yates Papers, Copy Book and Journal, June 1754-Sept. 1758 [New York Public Library]).

17. General James Abercromby to Lieutenant Governor James De Lancey, Oct. 10, 1758, AB 739. Abercromby told De Lancey that Captain Christie was "daily pestered with writs in Consequence of Actions lodged against him for the legal and faithful discharge of his trusts. . . ." For a petition received by the New York Assembly, see *Votes . . . N.Y.,* PRO/CO 5/1216. Some farmers "chose to drive the Waggons and Horses into the Woods . . ." to escape impressment (Loudoun to Hardy, Sept. 23, 1756, LO 1884). The British officer's comment on local politicians, Mar. 29, 1757, LO 3210.

18. Forbes to Richard Peters, Aug. 28, 1758, *Forbes, Writings,* p. 191.

19. Bouquet to Forbes, June 7, 1758, *Papers of Henry Bouquet,* II, 50. For examples of Bouquet's method, see Bouquet to George Stevenson, June 3, 1758 *ibid.,* p. 27; and Bouquet to Conrad Weiser, June 5, 1758, *ibid.,* p. 33; June 11, 1758, *ibid.,* p. 73; June 12, 1758, *ibid.,* pp. 121-122; Forbes to Bouquet, Sept. 17, 1758, *ibid.,* pp. 522-523.

20. St. Clair to Richard Peters, June 6, 1759, *Pennsylvania Archives,* 1st ser., III, 661; John Miller to Peters, Sept. 26, 1758, *ibid.,* p. 545. George Ross, a signatory of the Declaration of Independence, had a fight with an army officer sent to impress wagons in 1755. Ross had the officer arrested; see Bell and Labaree, "Wagon Affair," p. 555. Isaac Norris to Benjamin Franklin, Nov. 21, 1758, Letterbooks of Isaac Norris, II (Historical Society of Pennsylvania).

21. House to Governor William Denny, March 3, 1759, *Pennsylvania Colonial Records,* VIII, 282-283.

22. Amherst to Denny, March 7, 1759, *ibid.,* p. 285.

23. *Pennsylvania Archives,* 8th ser., VI, 4493. The general's bill established a rate schedule based on the weight each wagon carried, rather than a flat, per diem rate. The army believed the latter allowed the farmers to cheat by not carrying as much as they were supposed to (Bouquet to Conrad Weiser, May 31, 1759, *Papers of Henry Bouquet,* II, 172-173).

24. Assembly to Denny, July 7, 1759, *Pennsylvania Colonial Records,* VIII, 373-374.

25. Bouquet to Denny, July 12, 1759, *Pennsylvania Archives,* 1st ser., III,

670-671. Bouquet also remarked that sending soldiers with the sheriffs had not achieved better results. General Stanwix filed an equally gloomy report about Buck and Chester counties (Stanwix to Denny, Aug. 13, 1759, *Pennsylvania Colonial Records,* VIII, 376-377).

26. Hughes to Bouquet, Sept. 2, 1759, *Papers of Colonel Bouquet,* ser. 21644, IV, pt. 2, 68-69.

27. In 1759, the army in Pennsylvania obtained transport by buying wagons and horses in order to avoid dealing with recalcitrant colonials (Bouquet to Harry Gordon, July 23, 1759, *ibid.,* ser. 21652, XIX, 194, and Edward Shippen to Bouquet, Aug. 8, 1759, *ibid.,* ser. 21644, IV, pt. 2, 15-16).

CHAPTER VI

1. Minutes of the Alexandria Conference, April 14, 1755, PRO/CO 5/46. Technically, of course, Major General Edward Braddock was supreme commander, but nothing he said at Alexandria implied that he intended to use his authority.

2. John Shy, (*Toward Lexington: The Role of the British Army in the Coming of the American Revolution* [Princeton, 1965], p. 347) points out that to purchase all the steps to lieutenant colonel cost £3,500. See also James W. Hayes, "The Social and Professional Background of the Officers of the British Army, 1714-1763 (Unpublished thesis, University of London, 1956), pp 66-70.

3. Shy, *Toward Lexington,* p. 90.

4. Governor Robert Dinwiddie told James Abercromby (June 10, 1756) that the presence of foreign officers would be regarded unfavorably by most Americans. (*Dinwiddie Papers,* p. 35). A provincial officer, Lieutenant Colonel Hugh Mercer, however, had only praise for the Swiss officer, Colonel Henry Bouquet; (Mercer to James Burd, April 23, 1759, Thomas Balch, ed., *Letters and Papers Relating Chiefly to the Provincial History of Pennsylvania* [Philadelphia, 1855], p. 156).

5. These estimates are based on a sampling of twenty British officers who held these ranks while in America. For a complete table of years of service, Hayes, "Officers of the British Army," p. 221.

6. Boston *Evening Post,* Feb. 28, 1757.

7. Forbes to Pitt, Sept. 6, 1758, *Pitt Correspondence,* I, 342. See also Colonel Henry Bouquet to General John Forbes, Aug. 31, 1758, *Papers of Henry Bouquet,* II, 450-451; Colonel Hugh Mercer to Bouquet, March 21, 1759, *Papers of Colonel Bouquet,* IV, pt. 1, 92.

8. Again, these judgements are based on a sampling of twenty-five American officers, chiefly those who led troops raised in Massachusetts, Connecticut, Pennsylvania, and Virginia.

9. For example, see R. F. Wood, "Jesse Platt," *New York Genealogical and Biographical Record,* Oct. 1939, p. 7, for a description of a New York company. There were, among others, twenty weavers, twenty-five shoemakers, six tailors, five carpenters, and eleven blacksmiths who had enlisted in the company. Of the 863 privates who enlisted in several New York regiments in 1758, 303 men were listed as skilled workers of one kind or another, 200 men as farmers; all but 10 per cent of this sample were American-born (New York Historical Society, *Collections,* 1891, pp. 60-134); in 1759, 461 privates from New York,

King's, Queen's, Westchester, and Orange counties enlisted in the provincial army. Half this sample was foreign-born and more than half listed as unskilled, chiefly laborers, (ibid., pp. 135-213). The average age of privates in both samples was 24 years. A sample of 331 privates who enlisted in the Pennsylvania army in 1758 reveals that 34 percent were American-born and about 36 percent were skilled workmen, (Pennsylvania Archives, 2d ser., II, 472-494); in 1759 a sample of 285 privates showed 43 percent were American-born and 26 percent skilled. (ibid., pp. 500-514). Again the average age was about 24 years.

10. This was true for all the provincial armies, not only New England troops. See, for example, Stanislaus M. Hamilton, ed., Letters to Washington and Accompanying Papers (5 vols.; New York, 1898-1902), I, 332; and Captain Samual Grubb's Orderly Book, HM 606, as well as the Diary of Ebenezer Dibble of Cornwall, Connecticut (Connecticut State Library).

11. The Diary of Jabez Fitch, Jr. in the French and Indian War, 1757 (Rogers Island Historical Association, 1966), Oct. 1, 1757; Joseph Nichols, Diary, July 3, Sept. 10, 1758, HM 89.

12. Ezra Stiles to Jared Eliot, Sept. 24, 1759, as quoted in Lewis Namier, England in the Age of the American Revolution (London, 1961), p. 301. I disagree with John Shy's interpretation of this quote. Shy underestimates the generally hostile tone of the letter, as well as the existence of considerable evidence to support Stiles's opinion (Toward Lexington, pp. 143-144).

13. March 15, 1759; see also Pennsylvania Gazette, May 12, 1757, Jan. 14, 1759, Sept. 4, 1760, and Oct. 9, 1760, reporting incidents in several colonial cities; also, the Boston Evening Post, March 7, 1757, for an example of public punishment of redcoats.

14. "The Battle is not to the Strong nor the Race to the Swift, But Victory undoubtedly comes from the Lord . . ." wrote Joseph Nichols in his Diary, Aug. 25, 1758 after Abercromby's defeat at Ticonderoga.

15. Edward Shippen to his son Joseph, Sept. 15, 1758; Balch, ed., Letters and Papers Relating . . . Pennsylvania, p. 23.

16. Isaac Norris wrote to Charles Norris, April 28, 1755; "I cannot wonder that the Officers at least, Such as have been of note and Rank, Should in of their Military Duty arrive among us in a very ill Humour. An American expedition is at best a kind of transportation to such as these . . ." (Norris Letterbook [Historical Society of Pennsylvania]). Writing of the opinions of Englishmen and Americans during Queen Anne's War (1702-1713), W.S. Churchill wrote: "the British thought the colonists uncouth, narrow and hypocritical. The colonists thought the British haughty and incompetent" (Marlborough, IV, 396, as quoted in O.A. Sherrard, Lord Chatham: Pitt and the Seven Years War [London, 1935], p. 28). The difference between this earlier experience and that during the Great War for Empire was the extent — a larger number of people participated in the Great War for Empire.

17. F. E. Whetton, Wolfe and North America, p. 220, as quoted in J. C. Long, Lord Jeffery Amherst, King's Soldier (New York, 1933), p. 52.

18. Braddock to Secretary Thomas Robinson, June 5, 1755, LO 581.

19. Loudoun to Cumberland, Aug. 29, 1756, LO 1626.

20. Colonel Henry Bouquet, for example, hinted to General John Forbes on Aug. 20, 1758 that Abercromby's defeat was due to "the laxness of his provincials" (Papers of Henry Bouquet, II, 397). Abercromby himself tried to

lay a good part of the blame for his defeat upon the colonials' lack of discipline; see Governor James De Lancey's letter to Abercromby, Aug. 7, 1758, AB 513.

21. Dinwiddie to Lords of Trade, Feb. 23, 1756, *Dinwiddie Papers*, p. 345.

22. George Washington to Dinwiddie, Feb. 2, 1756, *Dinwiddie Correspondence*, p. 860. Washington to Loudoun, Jan. 10, 1757, LO 2659. George William Fairfax wrote to Dinwiddie, Sept. 4, 1755: "I wish our good countrymen were not so tenacious of their liberties at this time and put the soldiery during the expedition under martial law . . . " (*ibid.*, p. 792).

23. Loudoun to Duke of Cumberland, Aug. 20, 1756, Stanley Pargellis, ed., *Military Affairs in North America, 1748-1765* (New York, 1936), p. 223.

24. "My Plan for the Provincial Troops," he wrote the Duke of Cumberland on Nov. 22, 1756, "is not to take many of them" (LO 2262). Lieutenant Alexander Johnson suggested to Loudoun that the manual of arms be revised so that American soldiers could master it with a short period of training. Johnson's manual of arms reduced the number of movements from 184 to 48 and the number of commands from 64 to 19. This simplified procedure was not adopted. Johnson's proposed manual can be found in his letter to Loudoun, Dec. 20, 1756, LO 2371.

25. John Shy misses a point, I think, when he points out that the "better sort" of men were usually chosen as officers ("A New Look at Colonial Militia," *William and Mary Quarterly*, 3d ser., XX [1963], 176-177).

26. *Connecticut Colonial Records*, X, 344. For the equally high Massachusetts pay scale, see Journals, *Massachusetts House*, XXXI, 285; *Connecticut Colonial Records*, X, 424, 344; *Journals, Massachusetts House*, XXXII, 145, 152.

27. The Virginia House of Burgesses refused to pass a draft law (H. R. McIlawine, ed., *Journals of the House of Burgesses* of Virginia [13 vols., Richmond, 1905-1915], *Journal* for the year 1755, p. 284). Massachusetts refused to enact a law in 1756 (Governor William Phips to Loudoun, Oct. 13, 1756, LO 2019), though the Assembly did pass such a law later; Connecticut specifically refused in June 1760 (Amherst to Fitch, *Fitch Papers*, II, 73). New Jersey consistently refused to enact a draft law, (W. A. Whitehead et al., eds., *Archives of the State of New Jersey* [30 vols., Newark, 1880-1906], XVII, 91-94). See also *Connecticut Colonial Records*, X, 602-603; *Journals, Massachusetts House*, XXXII, 152; *Votes . . . N.Y.*, March 1, 1759, PRO/CO 5/1216.

28. Samuel Willard to Assembly, Oct. 12, 1757, Connecticut Archives, War, VI, 278; De Lancey to House, March 15, 1758, *Votes . . . N.Y.* PRO/CO 5/1216. The New York Assembly extended its draft law in 1759 only after a long debate and a very close vote, (De Lancey to Pitt, Feb. 28, 1759, *Pitt Correspondence*, II, 41). The *Pennsylvania Gazette* reported that men had fled Connecticut in 1758 and New York in 1759 to avoid the draft, (April 13, 1758, April 26, 1759). General Amherst urged Connecticut to raise its quota of troops by impressment. The Assembly debated the matter and concluded that impressment was bad because of the "very great Inquietudes attending such a Method of proceeding and the ill Success for former Attempts of that kind . . ." (Fitch to Amherst, May 23, 1760, *Fitch Papers*, II, 66).

29. Joseph Nichols, Diary, Aug. 8, Sept. 17, 1758, HM 89; Obadiah Harris, Regimental Journal, Oct. 2, 1758, HM 91.

30. See, for example, the Orderly book of John Grant, entries for Aug. 8 and

Sept. 13, 1761, HM 595. General John Forbes placed an ad in the *Pennsylvania Gazette,* June 1, 1758, warning that all people who had any dealings with deserters would be prosecuted, but a captain under his command later told Bouquet that "deserters appear openly on the plantations and in the villages where they are not interfered with until they are discovered by some [regular] soldier" *(Papers of Colonel Bouquet,* V, 84-85). A writer to the *Connecticut Gazette,* Aug. 16, 1755, urged people to capture deserters because they "are robbing the Public who are daily labouring to support them" (Governor Thomas Pownall to Loudoun, Sept. 14, 1757, LO 4465; and Thomas Hutchinson's letter to General James Abercromby reporting the success of Pownall's proclamation, July 29, 1758, AB 483.

31. Loudoun to Pitt, Aug. 16, Oct. 17, 1757, LO 4239; Loudoun to the Duke of Cumberland, Oct. 3, 1756, Pargellis, ed., *Military Affairs in North America,* pp. 239-240; Loudoun to Pitt, Feb. 14, 1758, LO 5598; James Otis, *The Rights of the British Colonies Asserted and Proved* (Boston, 1764); Colonel James Robertson to John Calcraft, June 22, 1760, LO 6251.

32. John Winslow repeatedly refused to order his Massachusetts troops to cut firewood for the regulars (Colonel Lawrence to John Winslow, Jan. 6, 1756, John Winslow's Journal and Correspondence [Massachusetts Historical Society]): and Joseph Nichols recorded in his Diary (HM 89) that when his regiment was used to unload bateaux there was much complaining.

33. Israel Williams to William Williams, Aug. 7, 1758, Israel Williams Letters and Papers (Massachusetts Historical Society).

34. Lawrence Henry Gipson (*The British Empire Before the American Revolution: The Years of Defeat, 1754-1757,* [15 vols., New York, 1936-1970], VI, 12-13) and Shy, (*Toward Lexington,* pp. 144-146) believe that the Great War for Empire was a unifying force.

35. Richard L. Merritt, *The Growth of American Community, 1735-1755* (New Haven, 1966); Ithiel de Sola Pool et al., *Symbols of Democracy* (Palo Alto, 1952).

36. Merritt, *Growth of American Community,* pp. 273-275.

37. De Sola Pool's formula for measuring the quality of usage of symbols is $F - U$ over $F + U + N$. F is the number of symbols appearing in favorable contexts, U the number appearing in unfavorable contexts, and N the number appearing in neutral contexts. For American symbols used in the pamphlet literature dealing with Braddock's defeat, the quality of usage was +.417; for British symbols it was - .200.

38. In 1757 there were only three pamphlets published in America dealing with the war. The quality of usage for British symbols in 1757 was still a -.500. For a slightly different interpretation, see Shy, *Toward Lexington,* pp. 146-147.

39. Johnson to Sir Thomas Robinson, Jan. 17, 1756, *Johnson Papers,* II, 420.

40. Lyman to Jonathan Trumble, Sept. 1, 1759, *Fitch Papers,* II, 27.

41. Pargellis, ed., *Military Affairs in North America,* pp. 43-44; Loudoun brought a modified version of this order with him in July 1756. The new pecking order gave colonial officers the status of *eldest* captain when joined with regulars (LO 1143). George L. Beer, (*British Colonial Policy, 1754-1763* [New York, 1907], pp. 174-178) suggests that this last provision solved the problem about rank. After King George's War a number of American provincial officers were angered because they had not received permanent commissions as they had been led to believe they would. This memory caused some Americans to be very reluctant to leave their businesses for an army post during the Great

War for Empire (Beverly McAnear, "Politics in Provincial New York, 1689-1761" [Ph.D. dissertation, Stanford University, 1935], p. 554).

42. On March 26, 1756, for example, Governor Fitch was asked by the Connecticut Assembly to commission Winslow as commander in chief of the forces raised by that colony (PRO/CO 5/47; Charles Hardy to Lord Halifax, May 7, 1756, Pargellis, ed., *Military Affairs in North America,* p. 172).

43. Winslow to Hardy, July 5, 1756, John Winslow's Journal and Correspondence, 11, 236-237 Massachusetts Historical Society . At the same time, Israel Williams wrote to Joseph Dwight, July 7, 1756, that if the provincials and regulars were joined together, "the Provincial Troops must do ye business and others will reap the honors and advantages" (Israel Williams Letters and Papers [Massachusetts Historical Society]).

44. "Council of War Held at Albany," July 6, 1756, LO 1314.

45. "Resolution of the Provincial Field Officers at Ford Edward," July 25, 1756, LO 1352.

46. Winslow to Abercromby, July 27, 1756, LO 1368.

47. Loudoun to Winslow, July 31, 1756, LO 1377A, and Loudoun to Shirley, Aug. 2, 1756, LO 1387.

48. Winslow to Shirley, Aug. 2, 1756, *Shirley Correspondence,* II, 497.

49. Shirley to Winslow, Aug. 10, 1756, LO 1456; Fitch to Winslow, Aug. 4, 1756, Winslow's Journal and Correspondence, III, 13-14.

50. Loudoun to Winslow, Aug. 9, 1756, LO 1450; Winslow to Loudoun, Aug. 10, 1756, LO 1452. Stanley Pargellis (*Lord Loudoun in North America* [New Haven, 1933], pp. 91-92) interprets this controversy as a "misunderstanding" which allowed "extremists in the provincial camp a chance to air their views."

51. Winslow to Secretary Fox, Dec. 30, 1756, PRO/CO 5/46.

52. William Williams to Israel Williams, July 11, 1758, Israel Williams Letters and Papers (Massachusetts Historical Society). George Washington came to a similar conclusion during his dispute over rank with Captain John Dagworthy (J. C. Fitzpatrick, ed., *Writings of George Washington* [39 vols.; Washington, D.C., 1931-1944], I, 289-290).

53. Thomas Hutchinson to Israel Williams, July 31, 1758, *ibid.*

54. William Cobbett, ed., *The Parlimentary History of England, from the Earliest Period to 1803* (36 vols.; London, 1806-1820), VIII, 446-447.

55. *Ibid.* See also, Verner W. Crane, ed., *Benjamin Franklin's Letters to the Press, 1758-1775* (Chapel Hill, 1950), pp. 279-282.

56. *Ibid.,* p. 281.

57. Albert H. Smyth, ed., *The Writings of Benjamin Franklin* (10 vols.; New York, 1905-1907), IX, 261.

58. Myles Cooper, *A Friendly Address to All Reasonable Americans* (New York, 1774).

59. Charles Lee, *Strictures upon a "Friendly Address to All Reasonable Men"* (Philadelphia, 1774).

60. Salem *Essex Gazette,* Jan. 17, 1775.

61. For a highly imaginative analysis of this phenomenon, see John Shy, "The American Military Experience: History and Learning" *Journal of Interdisciplinary History,* I (1971), 205-228. Shy applies contemporary learning theory to explain the way in which America's "remembered (military) past has always more or less constricted both action in the present and thinking about the future" (p. 210). He argues that military memory is a "strange and selective thing . . ." (p. 207).

CHAPTER VII

1. See, for example, Lawrence Henry Gipson, *The Coming of the Revolution* (New York, 1959), p. 128, and the more sympathetic, but similar treatment of the colonists' arguments in Stanley M. Pargellis, *Lord Loudoun in North American* (New Haven, 1933), p. 210; Theodore Thayer, *Pennsylvania Politics and the Growth of Democracy, 1740-1776* (Philadelphia, 1948), p. 60; John Zimmerman, "Governor Denny and the Quartering Act of 1756," *Pennsylvania Magazine of History and Biography*, LXXXXI (1967), 280-281; Nicholas 'B. Wainwright, "Governor William Denny in Pennsylvania," *ibid.*, LXXXI (1957), 178-179; Ralph L. Ketcham, "Conscience, War and Politics in Pennsylvania, 1755-1757," *William and Mary Quarterly*, 3d ser., XX (1963), 419.

2. Pargellis, *Loudoun*, p. 188.

3. Sir Thomas Robinson to Colonial Governors, Oct. 24, 1754, *New York Colonial Documents*, VI, 916. Robinson had informed the governors only that "you should use your utmost dilligence and authority in procuring an exact observance of such orders as shall be issued from time to time by the Commander in Chief, for quartering troops. . . ."

4. Bernard Bailyn *(The Ideological Origins of the American Revolution* [Cambridge, 1967], pp. 61-64) brilliantly demonstrates how much the political culture of America was shaped by the ideas and fears of England's radical whigs. In particular, they pointed out the dangers of arbitrary military power.

5. Edward Shippen to Joseph Shippen, March 19, 1755, "Military Letters of Captain Joseph Shippen of the Provincial Service, 1756-1758," *Pennsylvania Magazine of History and Biography*, XXXVI (1912), 35.

6. Colonel Thomas Dunbar to Governor Morris, July 14, 1755, LO 3483; Morris to Dunbar, July 31, 1755, *Pennsylvania Colonial Records*, VI, 515.

7. Morris to Mayor and Aldermen of Philadelphia, Aug. 1, 1755, *Pennsylvania Colonial Records*, VI, 516; their reply, Aug. 9, 1755, *ibid.*, p. 533; Morris to the Assembly, Aug. 11, 1755, *ibid.*, p. 535.

8. *Pennsylvania Archives*, 8th ser., V, 3951-3952, 3968. The bill was officially signed into law on August 16, 1755.

9. *Acts of the Privy Council: Colonial Series* (6 vols.; Hereford, Eng., 1908-1912), IV, 337-339. At the same session the Council vetoed Pennsylvania's militia law, branding it "improper and inadequate."

10. Loudoun to Colonel John Stanwix, Sept. 23, 1756, LO 1885. Loudoun had already received reports from John Rutherfurd that made it clear there was going to be trouble between the army and the Pennsylvania government; see Rutherfurd to Loudoun, Aug. 12, 14, 16, 1757, LO 1473, 1485, 1499.

11. Loudoun to Denny, Oct. 28, 1756, LO 2104.

12. *Ibid.*

13. *Pennsylvania Colonial Records*, VII, 349-350. The law provided four pence a day for lodging soldiers.

14. Minutes of the Council, Dec. 15, 1756, *Pennsylvania Colonial Records*, VII, 358-359. Doctor James Stevenson had asked Colonel Bouquet to see to it that a hospital was provided for those soldiers suffering from smallpox.

15. Loudoun to the Duke of Cumberland, Nov. 22, 1756, LO 2262; Minutes of the Council, Dec. 18, 1756, *Pennsylvania Colonial Records*, VII, 361-362.

16. Assembly to Denny, Dec. 17, 1756, *ibid.*, pp. 363-364. Pargellis (*Loudoun*, p. 201) states that the sheriff brought the blank warrant to the Assembly's attention.

17. Assembly to Denny, Dec. 20, 1756, *Pennsylvania Colonial Records,* VII, 364-369.

18. Conference Committee, Dec. 20, 1756, *ibid.,* p. 370.

19. *Ibid.,* p. 371.

20. *Ibid.,* pp. 373-374.

21. *Ibid.;* Richard Peters to Thomas Penn, Dec. 26, 1756, Penn Papers (Historical Society of Pennsylvania); Bailyn, *Ideological Origins,* pp. 63-64n.

22. *Ibid.,* p. 375.

23. Loudoun to Denny, Dec. 22, 1756, LO 2382. Richard Peters to Provincial Commissioners, Dec. 26, 1756, *Pennsylvania Colonial Records,* VII, 380.

24. Not all of Pennsylvania's political leaders were willing to press their claim to the rights of Englishmen, if it meant damaging the war effort. Joseph Shippen, for example, seemed to support the Assembly's position on quartering, but he was anxious that the quarrel should not persist. It was this concern for the well-being of the Empire, rather than any basic disagreement over the quartering issue, that was one of the key factors separating Pennsylvania's politicians (Joseph Shippen to Edward Shippen, Jan. 19, 1757, Shippen Family Papers [Historical Society of Pennsylvania], II, 99).

25. Governor Hardy to Assembly, July 6, 1756; Assembly to Hardy, July 8, 1756, *Votes . . . N.Y.,* PRO/CO 5/1216.

26. Loudoun to the Duke of Cumberland, Aug. 29, 1756, LO 1626. Abraham Yates, sheriff of Albany, recorded that this procedure resulted in the death of a pregnant woman (Yates Papers, Copy Book and Journal, June 1754-Sept. 1758 [New York Public Library]).

27. The Assembly's bill may be found in *Votes . . . N.Y.,* PRO/CO 5/1216, Oct. 9, 1756; Hardy's initial reaction to the bill is contained in his letter to the Lords of Trade, Oct. 13, 1756, *New York Colonial Documents,* VII, 163; Hardy's letter to Loudoun on Nov. 11, 1756, reveals his change (LO 2199; Loudoun to Hardy, Nov. 21, 1756, LO 2250).

28. Loudoun to the Duke of Cumberland, Nov. 22, 1756, LO 2262. In August 1757 a petition signed by a large number of Albany citizens was presented to the city council. All of the Aldermen signed the petition, intended for Governor De Lancey, but the mayor avoided doing so by leaving town. The petition was sent without the mayor's signature (Yates Papers, Copy Book and Journal). Captain Gabriel Christie wrote General Abercromby, Sept. 5, 1757, that the mayor was worried that he would be "turn'd out of his office" as a result of his refusal to sign the antimilitary petition. Christie believed, however, that De Lancey's support would be sufficient to defeat any challenger (LO 4404). According to a survey Loudoun ordered made, there were 329 households in Albany. He calculated that it would be possible in a pinch to quarter 190 officers and 2,082 soldiers in Albany's 329 homes. This meant there would be approximately seven soldiers to each home (LO 3515).

29. Loudoun observed that "opposition [in New York] seems not to come from the Lower People, but from the leading People who raise the dispute in order to have merit with the others, by defending their liberties, as they call them" (Loudoun to the Duke of Cumberland, Nov. 22, 1756, LO 2262).

30. Yates Papers, Copy Book and Journal.

31. *Ibid.*

32. Pownall's views on civil military relations are summed up in his *Administration of the Colonies* (London, 1764). See also John A. Schutz, *Thomas Pownall, British Defender of American Liberty* (Glendale, 1951).

33. Loudoun Diary, II, Jan. 26, 1757.

34. *Journals, Massachusetts House,* XXXIII, pt. 2, 336, Feb. 17, 1757. Governor Shirley had convinced the House it should build barracks on Castle William. "I am sensible," he said in December 1754, "that the Inhabitants of this Province who are unaccustomed to have Soldiers Quartered upon them, will be averse to such a Proceeding even under the Regulation of an Act of Parliament." On January 3, 1755 the House voted £800 to build barracks on Castle William. Shirley's recommendation is found in *ibid.,* XXXI, 179, Dec. 26, 1754; the House's bill, LO 540.

35. Jeremiah Gridley to McAdam, Feb. 26, 1757, LO 2929.

36. Loudoun to Pownall, Aug. 9, 1757, LO 4173; Pownall to the Massachusetts House of Representatives, Aug. 25, 1757, LO 4366; Massachusetts House of Representatives, Aug. 31, 1757, LO 4346; Pownall to Loudoun, Sept. 2, 1757, LO 4389.

37. Loudoun to the Duke of Cumberland, Oct. 17, 1757, LO 4642.

38. Captain Nicholas Cox to Colonel John Forbes, Nov. 4, 1757, LO 4760; Captain Samuel Mackay to Forbes, Nov. 4, 1757, LO 4755. The law to which the selectmen referred may be found in LO 4761; Pownall to Loudoun, Nov. 4, 1757, LO 4757.

39. Loudoun to Pownall, Nov. 15, 1757, LO 4838.

40. Pownall to General Court, Nov. 26, 1757, LO 4905.

41. An Act of the Massachusetts Assembly, Dec. 1, 1757, LO 4931.

42. Loudoun to Pownall, Dec. 6, 1757, LO 4955, LO 4958.

43. Pownall to Loudoun, Dec. 19, 1757, LO 5041.

44. Massachusetts Assembly to Pownall, Dec. 16, 1757, LO 5021. Schutz, *Pownall,* pp. 112-114, tends to underestimate the ideological importance of the quartering dispute.

45. Pownall to Loudoun, Dec. 15, 1757, LO 5014.

46. Loudoun to William Pitt, Feb. 14, 1758, LO 5598. Each year the Assembly passed a quartering act, without which it was legally impossible to quarter troops anywhere other than the barracks at Castle William. Pownall was in complete agreement with the Assembly's position. See, for example, Pownall to the General Court, March 1758, LO 5941; Abercromby to Amherst, Oct. 19, 1758, AB 778.

47. General Amherst expressed his views on quartering in a letter to Governor Denny, March 7, 1759, *Pennsylvania Colonial Records,* VIII, 285; for the Pennsylvania Assembly's reply, *ibid.,* pp. 330-331. Other lower houses held similar views: *Connecticut Colonial Records,* XI, 176-177; John Shy, "Quartering His Majesty's Troops in New Jersey," New Jersey Historical Society, *Proceedings,* 178 (1960), 82-94. The New Jersey Assembly had voted to pay people upon whom soldiers were quartered (Loudoun to Belcher, April 7, 1757, LO 3307). Still, Colonel James Montresor had to confront the magistrates of Bordentown with a company of his soldiers with fixed bayonets before they would allow quartering (Montresor, *Journal,* New York Historical Society, *Collections* [1881], p. 122). Ensign Richard Nickleson to Colonel John Forbes, Dec. 9, 1757, LO 4976, for New Hampshire's law. And for South Carolina, Jack P. Greene, "The South Carolina Quartering Dispute, 1757-1758," *South Carolina Historical and Genealogical Magazine,* L (1959), 193-204.

48. PRO, State Papers, 41/25, as quoted in John Shy, *Toward Lexington: The Role of the British Army in the Coming of the American Revolution* (Princeton, 1965), p. 185; George Grenville Papers, III, 11-12, *ibid.*

49. 5 George III, c. 33.

50. For a sampling of American hostility in regard to quartering, see the following: Colonel Henry Bouquet to Colonel John Stanwix, Aug. 25, 1757, *Papers of Colonel Bouquet*, I, 59, 112 (Bouquet wrote: "The Lawyers, Justices of the Peace, and in general the whole people are eternally against us. . . ."); Isaac Norris to Benjamin Franklin, Jan. 4, 1760, *Franklin Papers*, IX, II. New York's refusal to appropriate money for quartering in 1765 is revealed in *New York Colonial Documents*, VII, 845-846, 867-868; New York merchant John Watts insisted that the question was whether "People . . . had rather part with their Money, tho' rather unconstitutionally, than to have a parcel of Military Masters put by Act of Parliament a bed to their Wives and Daughters" (Watts to James Napier, June 1, 1765, *Watts Letter Book*, p. 355); Merrill Jensen, ed., *English Historical Documents* (London and New York, 1955), IX, 805-808.

CHAPTER VIII

1. The Molasses Act of 1733, for example, did not prohibit colonial trade with the French West Indies, but specifically legalized the importation of French sugar and molasses, provided certain export duties were paid. See Oliver M. Dickerson, *The Navigation Acts and the American Revolution* (New York, 1963), pp. 82-87; 30 George II, c. 9. On the eve of the war, American trade with the British and French West Indies was at a low point; in fact, there was a general economic depression (William S. Sachs, "The Business Outlook in the Northern Colonies, 1750-1775" [Ph.D. dissertation, Columbia University, 1957], pp. 33-34, 40-48).

2. Thomas Robinson to General Edward Braddock, April 16, 1755, LO 570.

3. Historians have differed sharply on the question of the extent and effect of illegal trade during the Great War for Empire. George L. Beer (*British Colonial Policy, 1754-1763* [New York, 1907], pp. 128-131), and Lawrence Henry Gipson (*The Coming of the Revolution, 1763-1775* [New York, 1954], pp. 28-33), and Virginia Harrington (*New York Merchants on the Eve of the Revolution* [New York, 1935], pp. 262 ff.) argue that American trade with the French was so extensive that it prolonged the war and, thus, are extremely critical of American merchants. Other historians, including Richard Pares (*War and Trade in the West Indies, 1739-1763* [New York, 1936], pp. 467-468) and Victor Johnson ("Fair Traders and Smugglers in Philadelphia, 1754-1763," *Pennsylvania Magazine of History and Biography*, LXXXIII [1959], 125-149) see the ideological importance of American complaints and contend that British enforcement tended to alienate many American merchants. I side with the latter group.

4. Robinson to Braddock, April 16, 1755, LO 570. Pennsylvania's law to prevent illegal trade may be found most easily in the *Pennsylvania Gazette*, April 10, 1755; Connecticut legislation on the matter is in Jonathan Trumbull, Sr., Papers, Trumbull to Joshua Mauger, April 2, 1755; the Massachusetts law in *Journals, Massachusetts House*, XXXI, 226, 229, 250.

5. *Ibid.*, XXXII, 61, 64, 87, 92-93, June 11, 12, 16, 18, 1755. In Pennsylvania, rumors that American goods were reaching the French were noted by John Stamper, who had an interest in a ship sent to the neutral port of Hispanola (Stamper Letter Book [1751-1770] [Historical Society of Pennsylvania]).

6. Governor Morris to Assembly, June 27, 1755, *Pennsylvania Colonial Records*, VI, 439; Morris to Shirley, July 6, 1755, *ibid.*, p. 463.

7. *Ibid.*, VI, 592.

8. For merchants' petitions to the Pennsylvania Council complaining about the embargo, see *ibid.*, p. 451; for comments to business associates which indicate that many merchants intended to abide by the embargo, see Thomas Willing Letter Book, especially Willing to Scott, Pringle and Scott, Sept. 5, 1755 (Historical Society of Pennsylvania); and Thomas Wharton Letter Book (Historical Society of Pennsylvania); and Wharton to John Sayre, July 30, 1755; and Thomas Riché Letter Book (Historical Society of Pennsylvania), particularly Riché to James Cowles, Aug. 13, 1755; Willing to Caddington Carrington, Sept. 22, 1755, Willing Letter Book.

9. Anne Bezanson, R. D. Gray, and Miriam Hussey, *Prices in Colonial Pennsylvania* (Philadelphia, 1935), p. 395.

10. *New York Colonial Documents*, VII, 81-90 (May 10, 1756).

11. Morris to Assembly, June 2, 1756, *Pennsylvania Colonial Records*, VII, 142; and Morris to Assembly, July 20, 1756, *ibid.*, p. 196. The Delaware legislature set July 7 as the expiration date for its embargo, while New Jersey decided on August 1.

12. Wharton to Gerrad Beckman, May 28, 1756, Wharton Letter Book; Willing to Philip Haughton, June 19, 1756, and to Weyler and Hall, July 16, 1756, Thomas Willing Letter Book.

13. "Petition from Sundry Merchants, Owners and Masters of Vessels now in the Port of Philadelphia . . ." July 10, 1756, *Pennsylvania Archives*, 8th ser., V, 4270-4271.

14. *Ibid.*, p. 4260; *Pennsylvania Colonial Records*, VII, 196 ff. (July 20, 1756).

15. Thomas Willing to Nat. Booth, Aug. 12, 1756, Thomas Willing Letter Book; Thomas Riché to Jacob Van Zandt, Aug. 19, 1756, Thomas Riché Letter Book; Thomas Wharton to John Waddel, Aug. 23, 1756, Thomas Wharton Letter Book.

16. Bezanson et al., *Prices in Colonial Pennsylvania*, pp. 396, 37. One of the reasons for imposing an embargo, of course, was to drive down the price of foodstuff needed by the British army (Sachs, "Business Outlook," p. 70; Thomas Willing to John Hobhouse, April 19, 1756, Thomas Willing Letter Book; Thomas Riché to [illegible], Dec. 29, 1756, Thomas Riché Letter Book; and John Stamper to John Williams, Dec. 31, 1756, John Stamper Letter Book).

17. Benjamin Franklin wrote to William Parsons (June 28, 1756) that "New York is growing immensely rich, by Money brought into it from all Quarters for the Pay and Subsistence of the Troops" (Timothy Horsfield Papers, Vol. I [American Philosophical Society]). Sachs, "Business Outlook," pp. 79-80, for a list of New York merchants and politicians who profited from war contracts.

18. Walton Bean, "War and the British Colonial Farmer: A Reevaluation in the Light of New Statistical Records," *Pacific Historical Review*, XI (1942), 442n. It should be noted, however, that the decline was not due solely to the war. Virginia did not have an especially good harvest in 1755 (Richard L. Morton, *Colonial Virginia* [2 vols.; Chapel Hill, 1960], II, 681; *Pennsylvania Archives*, 1st ser., II, 708 [July 29, 1756]). The price of flour in Boston remained high until 1759 (Arthur H. Cole, *Wholesale Commodity Prices in the United States, 1700-1861* [Cambridge, 1938], pp. 6-7; *Journals, Massachusetts House*, XXXII, pt. 2, 385 [March 3, 1756]).

19. Minutes of the Provincial Council, Aug. 20, 1756, *Pennsylvania Colonial Records,* VII, 220ff.

20. Loudoun to Denny, Sept. 22, 1756, *ibid.,* VII, 270.

21. Richard Peters to Thomas Penn, Penn Manuscripts, Official Correspondence, VIII (1756-1757). This idea may have been borrowed from the Irish merchants who often made guarantees to the British army for a certain amount of beef and then were free to sell the surplus wherever they chose to.

22. Thomas Willing to "cousin" Thomas Willing, Dec. 9, 1756, Willing Letter Book (1754-1761); the *Pennsylvania Gazette,* Dec. 9, 1756, also carried reports of the recent successes of French privateers.

23. Assembly to Denny, Feb. 18, 1757, *Pennsylvania Colonial Records,* VII, 418-419.

24. *Ibid.*

25. Loudoun to the governors of New York, New Jersey, Pennsylvania, Maryland, Virginia, Connecticut, Massachusetts, and Rhode Island, March 2, 1757, LO 2959. John Stamper to Gentlemen [Stamper's overseas representatives], March 5, 1757, John Stamper Letter Book. At one time, Loudoun *had* stated that the embargo was designed to acquire men and ships for his campaign; see his letter to Governor Fitch of Connecticut, April 12, 1757, LO 3349.

26. Denny to Loudoun, April 19, 1757, LO 3393; Philadelphia merchants to Denny, April 22, 1757, LO 3420; Scott and McMichael to Loudoun, April 27, 1757, LO 3488; and Loudoun to Denny, April 24, 1757, *Pennsylvania Archives,* 1st ser., III, 141-142. Loudoun told Pitt he had sent a warship to patrol the harbor, April 25, 1757 (*Pitt Correspondence,* I, 40).

27. Willing to Maxwell, May 2, 1757, Willing Letter Book.

28. Bezanson et al., *Prices in Colonial Pennsylvania,* pp. 62, 397.

29. *Journals, Massachusetts House,* XXXIII, pt. 2, 463, 448.

30. Hutchinson to Loudoun, April 23, 1757. LO 3437. Hutchinson told the general he would do everything he could to assure the embargo's continuation.

31. Dinwiddie to Loudoun, May 6, 1757, *Dinwiddie Papers,* p. 618. The governor had recently reported to the Lords of the Treasury that revenue due the Crown from a tax on tobacco exports was down over past years because of Loudoun's embargo (*ibid.,* p 624, May 16, 1757).

32. Philadelphia Merchants to the Assembly, June 14, 1757, *Pennsylvania Archives,* 8th ser., VI, 4571-4572.

33. Denny to Assembly, June 16, 1757, *Pennsylvania Colonial Records,* VII, 569.

34. *Ibid.,* VII, 409, 419 ff. (Feb. 8, 27, 1757); *Journals, Massachusetts House,* XXXIII, pt. 2, 249 (Jan. 11, 1757); *Pennsylvania Gazette,* June 30, 1757. Dinwiddie to Loudoun, July 9, 1757, *Dinwiddie Papers,* II, 664-665.

35. Edward Shippen to Joseph Shippen, March 19, 1755, "Military Letters of Captain Joseph Shippen of the Provincial Service, 1756-1758," *Pennsylvania Magazine of History and Biography,* XXXVI (1912), 35.

36. Colden to Pitt, Oct. 27, 1760, *Pitt Correspondence,* II, 348-349; Wentworth to Pitt, Dec. 9, 1760, *ibid.,* p. 343; Morris to Braddock, March 12, 1755, *Pennsylvania Colonial Records,* VI, 306.

37. Frederick B. Tolles, *Meeting House and Counting House: The Quaker Merchants of Colonial Philadelphia, 1682-1783* (New York, 1963), pp. 78-79.

38. MS Minutes of the Philadelphia Monthly Meeting, VI, 171-172, July 3, 1759, *ibid.* See also, John Reynell to John Sherburne, March 12, 1760, John

Reynell Letter Book, 1760-1762 (Historical Society of Pennsylvania).

39. Virginia's Indian corn exports were about one-third below prewar levels according to evidence presented in Walton Bean's "Colonial Farmer," p. 442n. Prices for foodstuffs in Philadelphia were also depressed in 1758 and 1759 owing to the embargoes and other trade restrictions; see Bezanson et al., *Prices in Colonial Pennsylvania*, pp. 398-399. A Philadelphia merchant, Thomas Willing, probably summed up the honest traders' views on smuggling in a letter to the firm of Scott, Pringle & Cheap, May 23, 1758: "the Penaltys are so heavy and an attempt to evade it, so liable to detection that we can't think it prudent to run such Risques where even success would not be equivalent to the Prospect of Danger in attempting" (Willing Letter Book). Arthur L. Jensen (*The Maritime Commerce of Colonial Philadelphia* [Madison, 1968], pp. 143-144) concludes that the "probable predominance of 'fair traders' among the Philadelphia merchants should be strongly emphasized." In Boston and New York merchants formed associations to prevent smuggling (Boston *Evening Post*, Dec. 13, 20, 1756). Twenty American merchant ships were captured by French privateers during the period April 8 to May 9, 1758 (*Pennsylvania Gazette*, June 15, 1758).

40. Hamilton to Pitt, Nov. 1, 1760, *Pitt Correspondence*, II, 351-352. Hamilton's charge is repeated by Nicholas B. Wainwright in "Governor Denny in Pennsylvania," *Pennsylvania Magazine of History and Biography*, LXXXI (1957), 194; by Victor Johnson in "Fair Traders," *ibid.*, LXXXIII, (1959), 146; by Pares in *War and Trade*, p. 448; and by Gipson in *The Coming of the Revolution*, p. 31.

41. The first cleared for Port-au-Prince, June 28, 1759; the second for Hispanola, July 14, 1759. The *Pennsylvania Gazette* carried notices of ship clearances.

42. Riché to Jacob Van Zandt, May 30, 1759, Thomas Riché Letter Book, I. It is interesting to note that Riché had obtained a flag earlier (April 2, 1759) to carry French prisoners to Port-au-Prince; but it took Riché and Van Zandt nearly three months to gather the required number of prisoners in order to clear customs. This is another indication that the flag trade was not as lax as it has been assumed. According to the *Pennsylvania Gazette*, Riché's shipload of prisoners cleared Philadelphia harbor on June 28, 1759. Finally, if flags could be obtained for £20 in Philadelphia in 1759-1760, it would seem extremely unlikely that at the same time Virginia merchants would offer their governor a £420 bribe for issuing a flag, as Governor Fauquier reported to Pitt, Oct. 28, 1760, *Pitt Correspondence*, 349-350. Likewise, John Stevens, a New Jersey merchant, was unable to buy a flag in July 1759 (John Stevens to Charles Read, July 9, 1759, *Calendar of the Stevens Family Papers*, Vol. II [New Jersey Historical Society], p. 90).

43. *Rhode Island Colonial Records*, VI, 173-174; Hopkins to Pitt, Dec. 20, 1760, *Pitt Correspondence*, II, 374.

44. It should be noted, for example, that in Pitt's letter of Aug. 23, 1760, to all colonial governors, he put West Indians in the same category as Americans (*ibid.*, II, 320). Pares (*War and Trade*, pp. 444-468) narrates trade violations and nearly all of those listed took place in 1760 or after; James B. Hedges (*The Browns of Providence Plantation: Colonial Years* [Cambridge, 1952], pp. 50-62) discusses Rhode Island's trade during the war; again, most of the Browns's involvement in illegal trade came in 1760. Gipson offers much the same evidence (*Coming of the Revolution*), pp. 28-33).

45. Governor Thomas of the Leeward Islands reported this incident to the Board of Trade, Nov. 30, 1758, as noted in Beer, *British Colonial Policy,* p. 94. See also Moore to Pitt, March 6, 1759, *Pitt Correspondence,* II, 55.

46. Hardy to Lords of Trade, June 19, 1756, *New York Colonial Documents,* VII, 117; *Connecticut Colonial Records,* X, 500-501 (Sept. 1756). The charge is buttressed by the report of Governor George Thomas of the Leeward Islands. In 1758 he estimated that 60,000 barrels of provisions were sent to St. Eustatius for French buyers by Irish merchants (Beer, *British Colonial Policy,* p. 86n). The average annual value in pounds of Irish exports to the West Indies was £132,000 in 1741-1750, but during the war years it jumped to £178,000 and for 1761-1767 the figure was £226,000 (Francis G. James, "Irish Colonial Trade in the Eighteenth Century," *William and Mary Quarterly,* 3d ser., XX [1963], 577-578).

47. Hamilton recounted this interpretation to Pitt, Nov. 1, 1760, *Pitt Correspondence,* II, 352-353.

48. C. M. Hough, ed., *Reports of Cases in the Vice-Admiralty Court of New York* (New Haven, 1925), p. 203; John Watts to Isaac Barre, Feb. 28, 1762, *Watts Letter Book,* p. 25.

49. 30 George II, c. 9. The Lords of Trade had recommended this procedure to the governors on October 9, 1756 (*New York Colonial Documents,* VII, 162).

50. Edward Long, Dec. 3, 1760, Colonial Correspondence, Jamaica, II, as quoted in Beer, *British Colonial Policy,* p. 107.

51. Willing to Scott, Pringle and Cheap, Sept. 21, 1759, Willing Letter Book. The New York Council argued that to bar Americans from trading with neutrals, while allowing others to do so, "is evidently of prejudice to the trade of the Colonies . . ." (Colden to Pitt, Dec. 27, 1760, *Pitt Correspondence,* II, 378-379).

52. The Irish were prohibited from exporting foodstuff only during 1757 when there was a severe shortage (Pares, *War and Trade,* p. 438).

53. British law required that the writs had to be renewed within six months after a monarch's death. For a survey of the agitation caused by the writs of assistance outside of Massachusetts, see Oliver M. Dickerson, "Writs of Assistance as a Cause of the Revolution," in Richard Morris, ed., *The Era of the American Revolution* (New York, 1939), pp. 40-75.

54. John Watts probably summed up the merchants' dilemma when he wrote to Isaac Barre: "The Lawyers say it [trade with neutrals] is legal and contrary to no Statute. The Men of Warr say it is illegal and both take and condemn them at their own shops — while they are acquited [sic] at others. No two Courts pursue the same Measure. A Stranger to form a judgment has neither Rule, Law or probity and yet the Evil is suffered to go without determination" (Feb. 28, 1762, *Watts Letter Book,* p. 25).

55. Samuel M. Quincy, ed., *Reports of Cases Argued and Adjudged in the Superior Court of Judicature of the Province of Massachusetts Bay . . .* (Boston, 1865), p. 475n. See also Bernhard Knollenberg, *Origin of the American Revolution, 1759-1766* (New York, 1965), pp. 69-70.

56. Bernard Bailyn, *The Ideological Origins of the American Revolution* (Cambridge, 1957), pp. 233-234.

57. Boston *Gazette,* Jan. 4, 1762.

58. Hutchinson to Loudoun, April 23, 1757, LO 3437; Hutchinson to Henry Conway, Oct. 1, 1765, as quoted in Quincy, ed., *Reports of Cases Argued and Adjudged . . .* p. 415n.

59. Pennsylvania Assembly to Governor Denny, June 15, 1757, LO 3836.

60. G. B. Warden, "The Proprietary Group in Pennsylvania, 1754-1764," *William and Mary Quarterly*, 3d ser., XXI (1964), 377, 382, lists some of the proprietary and antiproprietary merchants who were active politically. See also, Jensen, *Commerce of Colonial Philadelphia*, pp. 133, 144; Watts to Sir William Baker, Oct. 16, 1762, to Moses Franks, Oct. 27, 1762, and to John Kennion, Jan. 27, 1763, in *Watts Letter Book*, pp. 89, 92, 116-117; Pares, *War and Trade*, p. 467; Johnson, "Fair Traders," pp. 148-149.

CHAPTER IX

1. Governor William Shirley of Massachusetts had proposed late in 1754 that the governors of each colony be permitted to command the troops raised in that colony. America's most perceptive politician, Benjamin Franklin, strongly disagreed. He wrote Shirley that "a power in Governors to march the Inhabitants from one end of the British and French Colonies to the other . . . without the Approbation or Consent of their Representatives first obtained to such Expeditions, might be grievous and ruinous to the People, and would put them on a Footing with the Subjects of France in Canada, that now groan under such Oppression from their Governor. . . ."

The Assemblies were also concerned about who would command the soldiers they raised, as we saw in Chapter VI. For a contrary view, see Lawrence Henry Gipson, *The British Empire before the American Revolution*, (15 vols. New York, 1936-1970), VI, 12-13, 15-16, and Daniel Boorstin, *The Americans: The Colonial Experience* (New York, 1958), pp. 361-362. These two historians argue that the colonies were chiefly motivated by a shortsighted isolationist impulse fostered by Britain's willing protection of the colonies, according to the former, and by the peculiar American condition, according to the latter.

2. More than sixty years ago E. I. McCormac looked at the impact of the war on the assemblies. The work fails to provide either an ideological context or a theoretical framework for understanding the development of political power in the lower houses, or to explore the impact of the war on other segments of American society (*Colonial Opposition to Imperial Authority during the French and Indian War* [Berkeley, 1911]). For an excellent general discussion of the rise of the lower houses of assembly, see Jack P. Greene, "The Role of the Lower Houses of Assembly in Eighteenth Century Politics," *Journal of Southern History*, XXVII (1961), 451-474.

3. The minutes of the Alexandria conference may be found in E. B. O'Callaghan, ed., *The Documentary History of the State of New York* (4 vols.; Albany, 1849-1851), I, 378-379.

4. PRO/WO, 34/71, Nov. 23, 1754.

5. Aug. 23, 1755, as quoted in John A. Schutz, *William Shirley, King's Governor of Massachusetts* (Chapel Hill, 1961), pp. 227-228. The Massachusetts House of Representatives politely reminded Governor Shirley that the French were continually sending troops to North America and, therefore, it hoped "that equal Strength and Treasure will be graciously afforded by his

Majesty . . . and that too great Dependence will not be placed upon the Ability of his Majesty's Subjects in America, for their own Defense" (*Journals, Massachusetts House*, XXXII, 84-85).

6. *Connecticut Colonial Records*, X, 341; *Journals, Massachusetts House*, XXXI, 266-267, XXXII, 17-18; *Votes . . . N.Y.*, PRO/CO 5/1216.

7. Alison Gilbert Olson ("The British government and Colonial Union," *William and Mary Quarterly*, 3d ser., XVII [1960], 22 ff.) suggests that the Newcastle government decided not to propose a colonial union because it feared that the ensuing controversy would undermine its Parliamentary consensus.

8. Shirley to Sir Thomas Robinson, Aug. 15, 1755, PRO/CO 5/46. Shirley did suggest that the King establish the following optimistic quotas for each colony: Virginia 2,500; Maryland 1,000; Pennsylvania 2,000; New Jersey 1,000; New York, 1,200; Connecticut 1,200; Massachusetts 2,000; Rhode Island 500; and New Hampshire 300.

9. James De Lancey to Shirley, Aug. 15, 1755, *Shirley Correspondence*, II, 251-252n; *Pennsylvania Colonial Records*, VII, 24-29.

10. Jan. 27, 1756, *Votes . . . N.Y.*, PRO/CO 5/1216.

11. Hardy to Assembly, March 4, 1756; House vote, March 16, 1756; Assembly to Hardy, July 2, 1756, *ibid.*

12. The previous year Shirley had been able to persuade the House to undertake a campaign against Niagara, arguing that it was in the common interest (*Journals, Massachusetts House*, XXXII, 17-18, June 2, 1755). The ineffectiveness of that campaign, however, apparently led legislators to insist that Crown Point be the prime target once again (Jan. 14, 1756, LO 759). See also *Journals, Massachusetts House*, XXXII, pt. 2, 387, March 3, 1756, for details about the debate over raising more men.

13. *Ibid.*, 312, Feb. 5, 1756.

14. *Ibid.*, 317-318, Feb. 15, 1756. The rumor became reality later in the year. Parliament appropriated £115,000 to be divided among the colonies who took part in the 1755 campaign (Shirley to James Fox, June 14, 1756, PRO/CO 5/46).

15. Loudoun to Henry Fox, Aug. 19, 1756, LO 1522, blamed Shirley for encouraging the lower houses to put restrictions on the use of provincial soldiers; Loudoun to the Duke of Cumberland, Aug. 27, 1756, LO 1626; Loudoun to Governor Robert Morris, Aug. 20, 1756, *Pennsylvania Colonial Records*, VII, 234; Governor Thomas Fitch to Loudoun, Sept. 11, 1756, LO 1771. Schutz (*Shirley*, pp. 235-239), discusses Shirley's feelings.

16. Loudoun to Fitch, Sept. 13, 1756, *Fitch Papers*, I, 256-257.

17. "Resolve for Raising Additional Troops," Sept. 1756, *ibid.*, p. 262; Fitch to Loudoun, Oct. 8, 1756, LO 1990. The Massachusetts lower house framed a bill similar to Connecticut's. It stipulated, however, that the legislature — not Loudoun or Shirley — would determine if an emergency existed (Sept. 8, 1756, LO 1741).

18. Loudoun to Lieutenant Governor Spencer Phips, Oct. 24, 1756, LO 2076; Sept. 16, 1756, LO 1820; see also Loudoun's complaint to Henry Fox: "I find not only a general backwardness in every Colony but even, almost in every individual on this Continent to aid in carrying on the Publick Service" (Oct. 3, 1756, LO 1961).

19. Loudoun to Henry Fox, Nov. 22, 1756, LO 2263. Loudoun maintained that the lower houses should not put any restrictions on the use of their troops; they should not ask how the troops were to be used; they should immediately

acknowledge the King's right to appoint generals; and they should respond immediately whenever the commander in chief demanded reinforcements.

20. Israel Williams to Joseph Dwight, July 7, 1756, Israel Williams Letters and Papers (Massachusetts Historical Society).

21. It should be noted that Loudoun still believed he could exploit the conference and so achieve what he wanted — to confuse the French. "The use I propose to make of the meeting," he wrote, "is without opening my mind fully to any Body, to sett a Foot the appearance of a Campaign to the South, without being at great Expence by which I hope to oblige the Enemy to divide their Force . . ." (Loudoun to Hardy, Nov. 6, 1756, LO 2165: *Connecticut Colonial Records*, X, 593; *Journals, Massachusetts House*, XXXIII, pt. 2, 273; "Resolves of the Rhode Island Assembly," Jan. 18, 1757, LO 2682; Governor Benning Wentworth to Loudoun, Jan. 12, 1757, LO 2670).

22. Jan. 29, 1757, LO 2728. It is true, of course, that Loudoun probably had more than the preservation of the Crown's prerogative in mind; he was especially eager to put the blame on the colonists in order that he might escape the onus of failure.

23. New England Commissioners to Loudoun, Jan. 31, 1757, LO 2738.

24. Loudoun to Governors and Commissioners, Feb. 1, 1757, LO 2748. The general's vague assurances about where he would or would not use colonial troops did not please everyone. In Massachusetts, Samuel P. Savage caustically observed that Loudoun asked for 4,000 troops "for an Expedn. we knew not when and to do we knew not what . . ." (Savage to George Whitefield, Sept. 22, 1757, Samuel P. Savage Papers [Massachusetts Historical Society]).

25. *Rhode Island Colonial Records*, VI, 28; Nathaniel Bouton et al., eds., *Documents and Records Relating to the Province of New Hampshire* (40 vols.; Concord, 1867-1943), VI, 556.

26. *Connecticut Colonial Records*, X, 593; "Resolves of the Massachusetts General Assembly," Feb. 2, 1757, LO 2756. The Massachusetts commissioners were instructed to agree to Loudoun's proposal that 4,000 troops be raised, but only if the proportions were equitably divided.

27. Loudoun to Henry Fox, Feb. 8, 1757, LO 2802.

28. Rhode Island Commissioners to Loudoun, Feb. 4, 1757, LO 2776; Thomas Hutchinson to Loudoun, Feb. 5, 1757, LO 2778. The people of Rhode Island decided that the quota Governor Stephen Hopkins agreed to was much too high; early in April 1757 he was "removed from the Government by a great Majority of Voices" (Hopkins to Loudoun, April 26, 1757, LO 3482).

29. Jeremiah Gridley to Christopher Kilby, Jan. 19, 1758, LO 5421, and Jan. 28, 1758, LO 5485. In the latter, Gridley noted that some Bostonians were hailing Pownall's conference as the beginning of a new approach to American defense. Governor Thomas Fitch and the Connecticut legislature suggested that New York be invited to send delegates to the Boston conference, but Massachusetts politicians rejected the idea, arguing that "the more extensive the Plan is the more difficult it will be to settle and pursue to effect the several parts of it" (*Fitch Papers*, I, 319).

30. Loudoun made his opposition to the conference widely known; he wrote to political leaders both in America and England (Loudoun to Pitt, Feb. 14, 1758, LO 5598; John A. Schutz, *Thomas Pownall, British Defender of American Liberty* [Glendale, Calif., 1951], pp. 119-121).

31. *Fitch Papers*, I, 325-327. The Massachusetts commissioners were:

Thomas Hutchinson, William Brattle, John Choate, John Tyng, and Benjamin Pratt; the representatives from Connecticut: Jonathan Trumble, Ebenezer Silliman, and William Woolcot. Hutchinson presided over the meetings.

32. Massachusetts House of Representatives to Pownall, Jan. 5, 1758, LO 5338.

33. Jeremiah Gridley to Christopher Kilby, Jan. 18, 19, 1758, LO 5419, 5421; Pownall to Loudoun, Jan. 19, 1758, LO 5420. Gridley charged that Pownall had not done much to win the house's approval (James Abercromby to Loudoun, Jan. 22, 1758, LO 5443).

34. Jeremiah Gridley reported to Loudoun, March 12, 1758, that the debate lasted all one Saturday, though ultimately those who favored raising the troops carried the day (LO 5748).

35. Loudoun to Pownall, March 8, 1758, LO 5731; and Pownall's reply, March 9, 1758, LO 5736.

36. William Pitt to the Colonial Governors of North America, Dec. 30, 1757; *Connecticut Colonial Records,* XI, 93.

37. AB 846; Clarence J. Webster, ed., *The Journal of Jeffery Amherst* (Chicago, 1931), pp. 327-329.

38. Fitch to Amherst, Dec. 23, 1758, PRO/SP 109/70; Governor Benning Wentworth to Amherst, Dec. 25, 1758, *ibid.; Pennsylvania Archives,* 8th ser., VI, 5236, March 17, 1762. The Pennsylvania Assembly voted unanimously to deny Amherst's request for 482 more soldiers.

Christopher Kilby noted this phenomenon in Connecticut in 1756. He wrote Loudoun that the "Governor and the members of the Assembly are brought together and the whole body seems to be Administrators as well as Legislators for the Community" (Dec. 17, 1756, LO 2360).

39. Although the war accelerated the trend toward the absorption of executive authority by the lower houses, the process had been going on for some time, of course. On the very eve of the war, for example, the Lords of Trade observed that the New York Assembly "have taken to themselves not only the management and disposal of such publick money but have also wrested from your Majesty's Government ... almost every other executive part of Government" (Lords of Trade to Governor James De Lancey, April 4, 1754, *New York Colonial Documents,* VI, 831-832; the New Jersey lower house extended its authority over financial affairs during the war, winning the right to issue and distribute the revenue it had earlier raised (W.A. Whitehead et al., eds., *Archives of the State of New Jersey,* [30 vols.; Newark, 1880-1906], XVII, 158).

40. Historians of the Great War for Empire have advocated a wide variety of interpretations to explain the struggle in Pennsylvania over financial matters. Gipson *(British Empire,* VII, 47-60) and Stanley Pargellis *(Lord Loudoun in North America* [New Haven, 1933], pp. 200-202, 222-224) argue that the Quakers who controlled the Pennsylvania Assembly—whatever their principles—were obstructionists whose partisan bickerings undermined the war effort in America. But in his *Pennsylvania Politics and the Growth of Democracy, 1740-1776* (Harrisburg, 1953), pp. 47, 56-57, 65, Theodore Thayer contends that the Quaker party used the wartime need for money to foster the growth of democracy. The contest for financial control is also discussed by John J. Zimmerman, "Benjamin Franklin and the Quaker Party, 1755-1756," *William and Mary Quarterly,* 3d ser., XVII (1960), 291-313, and, most

perceptively, by James H. Hutson, "Benjamin Franklin and Pennsylvania Politics, 1751-1755: A Reappraisal," *Pennsylvania Magazine of History and Biography,* XCIII (1969) 303-371.

41. *Votes and Proceedings of the House of Representatives of the Province of Pennsylvania* for 1754-1755, (Philadelphia, 1755), pp. 9-17; Hutson, "Franklin and Pennsylvania Politics," pp. 331-334.

42. *Pennsylvania Archives,* 8th ser., V, 3856, Jan. 10, 1755.

43. The first version of the bill was passed on March 25, 1755, *ibid.,* V, 3870-3871.

44. Morris's last veto came on May 16, 1755 (*Pennsylvania Colonial Records,* VI, 386-387; Hutson, "Franklin and Pennsylvania Politics," pp. 340-343).

45. *Pennsylvania Archives,* 8th ser., V, 3877, April 1, 1755. The scheme was devised by Benjamin Franklin.

46. *Votes and Proceedings of the House of Representatives of the Province of Pennsylvania* for 1754-1755, pp. 144-152, 169-176. The land tax was to be twelve pence per pound of the land's value and was to be in effect for two years.

47. Hutson, "Franklin and Pennsylvania Politics," pp. 358-359.

48. *Votes and Proceedings of the House of Representatives of the Province of Pennsylvania,* V (1755), 3947; Hutson, "Franklin and Pennsylvania Politics," pp. 358-359.

49. Penn to Morris, Oct. 4, 1755, *Pennsylvania Colonial Records,* VI, 730-733. Penn said his gift was motivated by Braddock's defeat. The Assembly considered the gift money due the province in lieu of a tax on proprietary lands. It should be noted that the Penns' gift had to be collected from arrears in quitrents — a very difficult thing to do (*Pennsylvania Archives,* 8th ser., V, 4150, 4159). Governor Morris realized, of course, that the Assembly's bill swept away a basic prerogative of the executive; see his letter to Governor Robert Dinwiddie, Dec. 29, 1755, *Pennsylvania Archives,* 1st ser., II, 530.

50. *Votes and Proceedings of the House of Representatives of the Province of Pennsylvania,* for 1756-1757 (Philadelphia, 1757), pp. 31-32, 47, 57-59.

51. *Ibid.,* pp. 69-71.

52. Richard Peters to Thomas Penn, Jan. 27, 1757, Penn Papers (Historical Society of Pennsylvania); *Votes and Proceedings,* for 1756-1757, pp. 73-74.

53. *Pennsylvania Colonial Records,* VII, 441, 453-454.

54. *Ibid.,* VIII, 325-326. General John Stanwix told Denny that if he disregarded his instructions and passed the House's supply bill, General Amherst "will justify it to the King's Ministers" (*Pennsylvania Archives,* 1st ser., III, 631-632).

55. In 1760 the proprietors brought their objections to the Assembly's action before the Privy Council. The Lords declared that Pennsylvania's taxing of the proprietary lands was "fundamentally wrong and unjust and ought to be repealed" (*Acts of the Privy Council, Colonial Series, 1745-1766,* pp. 439-442.

56. See, for example, *Votes . . . N.Y.,* PRO/CO 5/1215, April 30, Dec. 3, Dec. 5, 1754; and James De Lancey to Lords of Trade, March 18, 1755, *New York Colonial Documents,* VI, 940-941; "Representation of the Lords of Trade," Feb. 4, 1756, *ibid.,* VII, 32-33, and Charles Hardy to Lords of Trade, Dec. 2, 1756, *ibid.,* VII, 202-203.

57. *Journals, Massachusetts House,* XXXI, 270-271, March 29, 1755; *ibid.,* XXXII, pt. 2, 368, Feb. 25, 1756.

58. Jack P. Greene, *The Quest for Power: The Lower Houses of Assembly in*

the *Southern Royal Colonies, 1689-1776* (Chapel Hill, 1963), pp. 104-107, 305-309. The House of Burgesses agreed in 1758 to work with the governor in the application of funds. This move was made because the Burgesses decided that the system of commissioners was too costly, and not because Pitt's management of the war had created greater imperial harmony and unity.

59. *Votes and Proceedings,* for 1755-1756, appendix, pp. i-iii.

60. William Smith, *History of New York* (Albany, 1757), p. 368.

61. See, for example, the claim of the Pennsylvania Assembly in *Votes and Proceedings,* for 1755-1756, p. 173. Max Savelle (*Seeds of Liberty: The Genesis of the American Mind* [Seattle, 1965] pp. 307-308) touches briefly a number of similar examples. The argument that the lower houses in America were equal to the House of Commons was disputed by some colonials. "If the three branches [of the colonial government] united have equal power [with that of Parliament]," the Boston *Gazette and Country Journal* argued on May 10, 1756, "then each of them have separately the same: and so a house of representatives has power equal to the House of Commons, the council to the House of Lords, and a governor to the King, which is absurd. The truth . . . that a government in America is not equal there to the Parliament of Great Britain is evident from this one consideration, that the former have not power to make laws repugnant or contrary to the laws of the latter."

62. In the case of New York, Governor Charles Hardy was specifically instructed not to press the Assembly for the establishment of a permanent fund to pay the salaries of imperial officials because the Lords of Trade feared the controversy would impair the war effort ("Representation of the Lords of Trade," Feb. 4, 1756, *New York Colonial Documents,* VII, 32-33).

CHAPTER X

1. Charles Wilson, *England's Apprenticeship* (New York, 1965), p. 60, quoting Thomas Mun, *England's Treasure by Forraign Trade* (London, 1664).

2. Klaus Knorr, *British Colonial Theories, 1570-1850* (Toronto, 1944), pp. 150-151. See also Thomas C. Barrow, *Trade and Empire: The Customs Service in Colonial America, 1660-1775* (Cambridge, 1967), for the development of that branch of the imperial administration charged with implementing trade policy.

3. Knorr, *British Colonial Theories,* p. 149. Not everyone was satisfied with this new posture. See, for example, Michael Kammen, *Empire and Interest: The American Colonies and the Politics of Mercantilism* (New York, 1970), pp. 91-92, for comments by Englishmen who lamented this new attitude.

4. George L. Beer, *British Colonial Policy, 1754-1765* (New York, 1907), p. 136n, quoting *The Advantages of the Difinitive Treaty,* p. 2.

5. Charles McLean Andrews, *The Colonial Background of the American Revolution* (New Haven, 1961), pp. 101-108. David Fieldhouse ("British Imperialism in the Late 18th Century: Defense or Opulence" in A. F. Madden and K. Robinson, eds., *Essays in Imperial Government* [Oxford, 1963]) dates the change from mercantilism to industrialism in 1750.

6. Matthew Decker, *An Essay on the Cause of the Decline of Foreign Trade* (London, 1751), p. 176, as quoted in Knorr, *British Colonial Theories,* pp. 144-145.

7. Malachi Postlethwayt, *Britain's Commercial Interest Explained and*

Improved (London, 1757), p. 103, as quoted in Richard Koebner, *Empire* (New York, 1965), pp. 101-102.

8. Thomas C. Barrow, ed., "A Project for Imperial Reform: 'Hints Respecting the Settlement of our American Provinces,' 1763," *William and Mary Quarterly*, 3d ser., XXVI (1967), 116-123.

9. Benjamin Franklin, "The Interest of Great Britain Considered with Regard to her Colonies and the Acquisitions of Canada and Guadaloupe. . . . " (London, 1760), in *Franklin Papers*, IX, 62-73.

10. John Shy brilliantly illustrates the change in attitude toward the colonies in his "Thomas Pownall, Henry Ellis and the Spectrum of Possibilities, 1763-1775" in Alison Gilbert Olson and Richard M. Brown, eds., *Anglo-American Political Relations, 1675-1775* (New Brunswick, N.J., 1970), pp. 183-186.

11. Wilson, *England's Apprenticeship*, pp. 284-285.

12. William S. Sachs, "The Business Outlook in the Northern Colonies, 1750-1775" (Ph.D diss., Columbia University, 1957), pp. 144, 147-148. See also Oliver M. Dickerson, *The Navigation Acts and the American Revolution* (New York, 1963), pp. 190-208. The question of the Navigation Acts in particular must begin with Lawrence H. Harper, *The English Navigation Laws* (New York, 1939), and include Dickerson, as well as Roger Ransom, "British Policy and Colonial Growth: Some Implications of the Burden from the Navigation Acts," *Journal of Economic History*, XXVIII (1968), 427-435.

13. Ruth Crandall, "Wholesale Commodity Prices in Boston during the Eighteenth Century," *Review of Economic Statistics*, XVI (1934), 125-127; Arthur H. Cole, *Wholesale Commodity Prices in the United States, 1700-1861* (Cambridge, 1938), pp. 13-14, for prices in New York after the Great War for Empire.

14. Thomas Pownall, *The Administration of the Colonies* (London, 1768), p. 285.

15. Sachs, "Business Outlook," pp. 101-102, for ships leaving Boston for the West Indies, and pp. 103-105 for Pennsylvania's West Indian trade; *Pennsylvania Gazette*, March 21, 1765.

16. Dickerson, *Navigation Acts and American Revolution*, pp. 82-87.

17. Sachs, "Business Outlook," p. 131, for the financial crisis in England. Lawrence Henry Gipson (*The Coming of the Revolution, 1763-1775* [New York, 1954], pp. 63-64) argues that the 6d. duty on molasses was not harmful, claiming that if it were there would have been no legal importation of molasses in 1760 or 1761 when the royal navy was used to prevent smuggling. But this analysis does not take into account the English capture of the French sugar islands, thus making all sugar imports legally clear of duty. Moreover, the slump in the English economy meant that American exports were not in much demand (Sachs, "Business Outlook," pp. 138, 160-161; John Watts to Baker, Aug. 11, 1765, *Watts Letter Book*, p. 368).

18. Stephen Hopkins, *An Essay on the Trade of the Northern Colonies* (1764) in Merrill Jensen, ed., *Tracts of the American Revolution, 1763-1776* (Indianapolis, 1967), p. 10.

19. Edmund S. Morgan and Helen M. Morgan, *The Stamp Act Crisis: Prologue to Revolution* (Chapel Hill, 1953), pp. 28-30.

20. Milton Klein, "The Rise of the New York Bar: The Legal Career of William Livingston," *William and Mary Quarterly*, 3d ser., XV (1958) 335-344.

21. Robert Zemsky, *Merchants, Farmers, and River Gods: An Essay on Eighteenth-Century American Politics* (Boston, 1971), pp. 263-264, 281. The

Connecticut lower house passed a variety of new debtor laws in 1764-1765. (No such legislation had been enacted for the two decades preceding 1764.) See, for example, *Connecticut Colonial Records*, X, 127-133, 228, 296-297, 355-356, 464-465, 560.

22. Jesse Lemisch, "The American Revolution from the Bottom Up," in Barton Bernstein, ed., *Towards a New Past: Dissenting Essays in American History* (New York, 1968), pp. 22-23. For the situation in New England towns, see David Grayson Allen, "The Zuckerman Thesis and the Process of Legal Rationalization in Provincial Massachusetts," *William and Mary Quarterly*, 3d ser., XXIX (1972), 445, 448, 454; Edward M. Cook, Jr., "Social Behavior and Changing Values in Dedham, Massachusetts, 1700 to 1775," *ibid.*, 3d ser., XXVII (1970), 568; Charles H. Levermore, *The Republic of New Haven: A History of Municipal Evolution* (Port Washington, N.Y., 1966; originally published 1886), pp. 195-196.

23. *Acts and Laws Passed by the Great and General Court or Assembly of His Majesty's Province of the Massachusetts Bay* . . . (Boston, 1759), pp. 409-413; *Connecticut Colonial Records*, XI, 214, 235, 255; Lawrence Henry Gipson's "Connecticut Taxation and Parliamentary Aid Preceding the Revolutionary War," *American Historical Review*, XXXVI (1931), 721-739, argues that the colony was in good financial condition after the Great War for Empire and so could afford to help pay for the costs of empire. See also *Pennsylvania Colonial Records*, VIII, 362, 402; Sachs ("Business Outlook," p. 134) comments on the impact of rapid currency contraction.

24. James B. Hedges, *The Browns of Providence Plantation: Colonial Years* (Cambridge, 1952), I, 200, quoting Tench Francis to Nicholas Brown, Sept. 16, 1763, L 63-4 FR. John Watts pointed out proudly and defensively that one-fifth of the male population of New York had participated in the war effort; to tax the colonies "which had over exerted themselves, before they had recover'd . . ." would be an "Injustice" (Watts to William Baker, April 22, 1763, and to General Monckton, May 24, 1764, *Watts Letter Book*, pp. 138, 258).

25. Mark Engal and Joseph A. Ernst, "An Economic Interpretation of the American Revolution," *William and Mary Quarterly*, 3d ser., XXIX (1972), 3, 14, 16-29; John J. McCusker, "Sources of Investment Capital in the Colonial Philadelphia Shipping Industry," *Journal of Economic History*, XXXII (1972), 147, 152-157.

26. Engal and Ernst ("An Economic Interpretation," pp. 16-17) identify opponents of postwar British business practices. The articulation of American political ideology is insightfully and fully discussed by Bernard Bailyn, *The Ideological Origins of the American Revolution* (Cambridge, 1967). The opposite position — that the Revolution was the result of bumbling English politicians and designing American merchants — is discussed by Lawrence Henry Gipson, *The British Empire before the American Revolution* (15 vols.; New York, 1936-1970), XI, 15, 70-82. John Shy ("Pownall and Ellis" in Olson and Brown, *Anglo-American Political Relations*, pp. 181-182), explores and rejects the idea that bumbling English politicians were primarily responsible for causing the American Revolution.

27. Thomas Fitch et al., "Reasons Why the British Colonies in America Should not Be Charged with Internal Taxes by Authority of Parliament" (New Haven, 1764) in Bernard Bailyn, ed., *Pamphlets of the American Revolution, 1750-1776* (Cambridge, 1965), p. 403.

28. Daniel Dulany "Considerations on the Propriety of Imposing Taxes in

the British Colonies for the Purpose of Raising a Revenue" (New York, 1765),
in *ibid.*, p. 622.

29. Stephen Johnson, *Some Important Observations* ... (New London,
Conn., 1765).

30. Morgan and Morgan, *Stamp Act Crisis,* p. 113.

31. Carl Lotus Becker, *The History of Political Parties in the Province of
New York, 1760-1776* (Madison, 1968 edition), pp. 57, 64-71.

32. Henry Moore to Duke of Richmond, Aug. 23, 1766, *New York Colonial
Documents,* VII, 867.

33. Gage to Duke of Richmond, Aug. 26, 1766; Edwin C. Carter, ed., *The
Correspondence of General Thomas Gage with the Secretaries of State, and the
War Office and the Treasury, 1763-1775* (2 vols.; New Haven, 1931), I, 104.

34. Gage to Henry Conway, May 6, 1766, *ibid.,* p. 89. See also, James
Montresor, *Journal,* New York Historical Society, *Collections* (1881), p. 341.

35. Yates Papers, Copy Book and Journal, June 1754-Sept. 1758 (New York
Public Library), Oct. 1757.

36. *Ibid.*

37. Livingston to Yates, Nov. 28, 1757, *ibid.*

38. Livingston to Yates, Feb. 16, 1761, *ibid.;* Yates to Robert Livingston, Jr.,
Feb. 7, 1761, *ibid.*

39. I agree with Bernard Friedman ("The New York Assembly Elections of
1768 and 1769: The Disruption of Family Politics," *New York History,* XLVI
[1965], 11), who argues that the radicals eventually pushed the traditional
factions to the left. For an opposite point of view, see Roger Champagne,
"Family Politics versus Constitutional Principles: The New York Assembly
Elections of 1768 and 1769," *William and Mary Quarterly,* 3d ser., XX (1963),
57-79.

40. Cadwallader Colden to the Earl of Hillsborough, Dec. 16, 1769, *New
York Colonial Documents,* VIII, 194; Colden's estimate was that the Assembly
differed sharply over how to provide the funds for the troops because of "the
attention which many of the Members pay to their popularity." Also, Colden to
Lords of Trade, Jan. 6, 1770, *ibid.,* p. 198: "The supply of the Troops is
unpopular, both in Town and Country."

41. Friedman, "Assembly Elections of 1768 and 1769," pp. 6-7.

42. Friedman contends that the passage of the provisions bill by the De
Lancey faction in 1769 was the event that precipitated a realignment of
political forces in New York *(ibid.,* p. 15). Alexander McDougall's attack on the
Assembly for approving a supply bill for the troops, marking an end to the
radicals' support of the De Lanceys, can be found in Thomas Jones, *History of
New York during the Revolutionary War* (2 vols.; New York, 1879), I, 426-430.

43. Alice P. Kenny (*The Gansevoorts of Albany: Dutch Patricians in the
Upper Hudson Valley* [Syracuse, 1969], pp. 83-88) discusses the transformation
of politics in Albany beginning during the Great War for Empire. By 1760
Albany was the second most important cultural and trade center in the
province.

44. Albany City and County Committee of Correspondence, Dec. 10, 1774,
Yates Papers. Yates also wrote of his experience with the British military in his
antifederalist "Essays on the Constitution." See, for example, his essay of Jan.
5, 1789, p. 26, Yates Papers.

EPILOGUE

1. James Otis, *The Rights of the British Colonies Asserted and Proved* (Boston, 1764), in Merrill Jensen, ed., *Tracts of the American Revolution, 1763-1776* (Indianapolis, 1967), p. 31.

2. John Adams, *A Dissertation on the Canon and the Feudal Law* (Boston, 1765), in *The Works of John Adams* (10 vols.; New York, 1971; originally published Boston, 1851), III, 460. John Dickinson, *Letters From a Farmer in Pennsylvania* (Philadelphia, 1768), in Jensen, *Tracts of the American Revolution,* p. 131.

3. Thomas Paine, *Common Sense Addressed to the Inhabitants of America* (Philadelphia, 1776), in *ibid.,* p. 420.

BIBLIOGRAPHY

I. GUIDES AND CALENDARS

Andrews, Charles M. *Guide to the Materials for American History, to 1783, in the Public Record Office of Great Britain,* 2 vols. Washington: American Historical Association, 1912-1914.

Beers, H. P., comp. "The Papers of the British Commanders in Chief in North America," *Military Affairs,* XIII (1949), 79-94.

Billington, Ray A. "Guides to American History Manuscript Collections in Libraries of the United States," *Mississippi Valley Historical Review,* XXXVIII (1951), 467-496.

Connecticut. *Select List of Manuscripts in the Connecticut State Library.* Hartford: published by the Library, 1920.

Cuthbert, Norma B. *American Manuscript Collections in the Huntington Library for the History of the Seventeenth and Eighteenth Centuries.* San Marino: Henry E. Huntington Library Press, 1941.

Day, Richard E., ed. *Calendar of the Sir William Johnson Manuscripts in the New York State Library.* Albany: The State Library, 1909.

Hays, I. M. *Calendar of the Papers of Benjamin Franklin in the Library of the American Philosophical Society,* 5 vols. Philadelphia: American Philosophical Society, 1908.

Levin, Bruce S., ed. *Guide to the Manuscript Collections of the Historical Society of Pennsylvania.* Philadelphia: Historical Society of Pennsylvania, 1949.

"Manuscript Records of the French and Indian War in the Library of the Society," American Antiquarian Society, *Transactions and Collections,* Vol. XI (1909).

Massachusetts. *Handbook of the Massachusetts Historical Society, 1791-1948.* Boston: Massachusetts Historical Society, 1949.

Morris, Richard B., and Evarts B. Greene, eds. *Guide to the Principal Sources for Early American History (1600-1800) in the City of New York.* New York: Columbia University Press, 1929.

Peckham, Howard, *Guide to the Manuscript Collections in the William L. Clements Library.* Ann Arbor: published by the Library, 1942.

II. PRIMARY SOURCES

A. MANUSCRIPTS

American Philosophical Society
  Burd-Shippen Papers
  Timothy Horsfield's Papers, Chiefly on Indian Affairs of Pennsylvania,
    1733-1761
British Public Record Office
  Colonial Office papers (microfilm)
  War Office papers (microfilm)
Connecticut Historical Society
  French and Indian War Papers
  William Williams Papers
Connecticut State Library
  Connecticut Archives, War
  Collection of Connecticut French and Indian War Papers, 9 vols.
    (1755-1761)
  Jonathan Trumbull, Sr., Papers
  Jonathan Trumbull Papers, Connecticut Colonial Office Papers, 1631-1784
  Jonathan Trumbull Papers, Letter Books
Historical Society of Pennsylvania
  Pemberton Papers
  Clifford Correspondence, Pemberton Papers
  Etting Collection, Pemberton Papers
  Gratz Collection
  Papers of the Shippen Family
  James and Drinker Letter Books (1756-1762)
  Letter Book of John Kidd (1749-1763)
  Letter Books of Isaac Norris, II (1719-1765)
  Thomas Riché Letter Book (1750-1764)
  John Stamper Letter Book (1751-1770)
  Thomas Wharton's Letter Book (1752-1759)
  Letter Book of Charles, Thomas and Morris Willing (1754-1761)
Henry E. Huntington Library
  Abercromby, James, An Examination of the Acts of Parliament Relative to
    the Trade and Government of our American Colonies, Also the Different
    Constitutions of Government in these Colonies Considered . . . (1752?)
  Abercromby Papers
  Agnew Correspondence
  Huntington Manuscripts
  Loudoun Diaries, 6 vols.
  Loudoun Papers
Massachusetts Historical Society
  Thomas Hutchinson Papers
  Letters of Thomas and Richard Penn to Richard Peters, 1750-1758
  Samuel P. Savage Papers
  Israel Williams Letters and Papers
  John Winslow's Journal and Correspondence during the Expedition to Nova
    Scotia, 1755-1756
  Massachusetts State Archives
  Massachusetts Archives

New York City Museum
  Benjamin Floyd Papers
  De Lancey Family Papers
  Peter Livingston Papers
  Philip Livingston Papers
New York Historical Society
  Lord Stirling Papers
  Richard Harison Papers, Letters from Alexander Colden to George Harison, 1755-1767
  New York Public Library
  George Chalmers Collection
  Joseph Hawley Papers
  Yates Papers, Copy Book and Journal, June 1754-September 1758
Private Collections
Bouquet Papers (photostats from the Canadian Archives)
University of California, Santa Barbara
  Louis Knott Koontz Collection
  Penn Manuscripts, Indian Affairs (Microfilm)

B. PRINTED MATERIALS

Annual Register (Great Britain). *A Complete History of the Late War, of Its Rise, Progress and Events, in Europe, Asia, Africa and America* . . . Dublin: John Exshaw, 1763.

Armstrong, Edward, ed. *Correspondence between William Penn and James Logan.* Pennsylvania Historical Society Memoirs, vols. X, XI. Philadelphia: J. B. Lippincott, 1870-1872.

Bailyn, Bernard, ed. *Pamphlets of the American Revolution, 1750-1776.* Cambridge: Harvard University Press, 1965.

Balch, Thomas Willing, ed. *Letters and Papers Relating Chiefly to the Provincial History of Pennsylvania* . . . Philadelphia: Crissy & Markley, 1855.

Bartlett, J. R., ed. *Records of the Colony of Rhode Island and Providence Plantations in New England.* 10 vols. Providence: A.C. Greene, 1856-1965.

Bates, S. A., ed. *Records of the Town of Braintree, 1640-1793.* Randolph, Mass., 1886.

Bouton, Nathaniel, et al., eds. *New Hampshire Provincial Papers.* 40 vols. Concord: Legislature of New Hampshire, 1867-1943.

Brock, R. A., ed. *The Official Records of Robert Dinwiddie, Lieutenant Governor of the Colony of Virginia, 1751-1758. Collections* of the Virginia Historical Society, vol. 2. Richmond: Virginia Historical Society, 1894.

Browne, William Hand, ed. *Archives of Maryland.* 65 vols. Baltimore: Maryland Historical Society, 1883-1952.

Butterfield, L. H., ed. *Diary and Autobiography of John Adams.* 4 vols. Cambridge: Belknap, 1962.

Carter, Edwin Clarence, ed. *The Correspondence of General Thomas Gage with the Secretaries of State, and with the War Office and the Treasury, 1763-1775.* 2 vols. New Haven: Yale University Press, 1931.

Chalmers, George. *An Introduction to the History of the Revolt of the American Colonies* . . . 2 vols. Boston: James Munroe, 1845.

Cobbett, William. *The Parliamentary History of England from the Earliest Period to 1803.* 36 vols. London: His Majesty's Stationery Office, 1806-1820.

Colden, Cadwallader. *The Letters and Papers of Cadwallader Colden.* 9 vols. In the *Collections* of the New York Historical Society. New York: printed for the Society, 1917-1923, 1934-1935.

Crane, Verner W., ed. *Benjamin Franklin's Letters to the Press, 1758-1775.* Chapel Hill: University of North Carolina Press, 1950.

de Forest, Louis E., ed. *The Journals and Papers of Seth Pomeroy, Sometime General in the Colonial Service.* New York: Society of Colonial Wars, 1926.

Dexter, Franklin B., ed. "A Selection of the Correspondence and Miscellaneous Papers of Jared Ingersoll," in *Papers* of the New Haven Historical Society, Vol. IX New Haven: printed for the Society, 1918.

The Diary of Jabez Fitch, Jr. in the French and Indian War, 1757. Rogers Island Historical Association, 1966.

Dickerson, Oliver Morton. *Boston under Military Rule* [1768-1769] *as Revealed in a Journal of the Times.* Boston: Chapman & Grimes, Mount Vernon Press, 1936.

Dobson, John. *Chronological Annals of the War: From Its beginning to the Present Time . . .* Oxford: Clarendon, 1763.

Entick, Rev. John. *The General History of the Late War: Containing Its Rise, Progress and Event, in Europe, Asia, Africa, and America. . . .* 5 vols. London: printed for Edward and Charles Dilly, 1763.

The Fitch Papers: Correspondence and Documents during Thomas Fitch's Governorship of the Colony of Connecticut, 1754-1766. 2 vols. *Collections* of the Connecticut Historical Society, vols. XVII, XVIII. Hartford: Connecticut Historical Society, 1918.

Fitzpatrick, J. C., ed. *Writings of George Washington.* 39 vols. Washington, D.C.: Congress of the United States, 1931-1944.

Fothergill, John. *Considerations Relative to the North American Colonies.* London: printed for Henry Kent, 1765.

Hazard, Samuel et al., eds. Pennsylvania Archives. 9 ser. 138 vols. Philadelphia and Harrisburg: Pennsylvania Historical and Museum Commission, 1853-1949.

Henning, W. W., ed. *The Statutes at Large, Being a Collection of All the Laws of Virginia.* 13 vols. Richmond: Assembly of Virginia, 1809-1823.

Hoadly, Charles J., ed. *The Public Records of the Colony of Connecticut.* 15 vols. Hartford: Press of the Case, 1880.

Hough, C. M., ed. *Reports of Cases in the Vice-Admiralty Court of New York.* New Haven: Yale University Press, 1925.

Hutchinson, Thomas. *The History of the Colony and Province of Massachusetts Bay.* Cambridge, Mass.: Harvard University Press, 1936.

James, Alfred Procter, ed. *Writings of General John Forbes, Relating to His Service in North America.* Menasha, Wisc.: Collegiate Press, 1938.

Journal of Gen. Rufus Putnam, Kept in Northern New York during Four Campaigns of the Old French and Indian War, 1757-1760. Albany: Joel Munsell's Sons, 1886.

Journals of the House of Representatives of Massachusetts, 1715-1761. 37 vols. Boston: Massachusetts Historical Society, 1919-1966.

Kenny, James. "Journal to ye Westward, 1758-1759," *Pennsylvania Magazine of History and Biography,* XXXVII (1913), 395-449.

Kimball, Gertrude, ed. *Correspondence of the Colonial Governors of Rhode Island, 1723-1775*. 2 vols. Boston, 1902-1903.

——, ed. *Correspondence of William Pitt, When Secretary of State with Colonial Governors and Military and Naval Commissioners in America*. 2 vols. New York: Macmillan, 1906.

Koontz, Louis Knott, ed. *Robert Dinwiddie Correspondence, Illustrative of His Career in American Colonial Government and Westward Expansion*. Berkeley and Los Angeles: University of California Press, 1951.

Labaree, Leonard W., ed. *The Papers of Benjamin Franklin*. 15 vols. New Haven: Yale University Press, 1959—.

The Letter Book of John Watts. New York Historical Society *Collections*. Vol. 61. 1928.

Lincoln, Charles Henry, ed. *The Correspondence of William Shirley: Governor of Massachusetts and Military Commander in America, 1731-1760*. 2 vols. New York: Macmillan, 1921.

Luke Gridley's Diary of 1757, While in Service in the French and Indian War. Hartford: Hartford Press, 1907.

McIlwaine, H. R., ed. *Journals of the House of Burgesses of Virginia*. 13 vols. Richmond: Virginia State Library, 1905-1915.

Mante, Thomas. *The History of the Late War in North America . . .* London: printed for W. Strahan and T. Cadell, 1772.

Massachusetts Historical Society *Collections*. 7 ser. 71 vols. Boston: Massachusetts Historical Society, 1792—.

"Military Letters of Captain Joseph Shippen of the Provincial Service, 1756-1758," *Pennsylvania Magazine of History and Biography*, XXXVI (1912), 367-378, 385-463.

Minutes of the Provincial Council of Pennsylvania from the Organization to the Termination of the Proprietary Government. 10 vols. Philadelphia: Pennsylvania Historical and Museum Commission, 1851-1853.

Mitchell, John. *The Contest in America between Great Britain and France, with its Consequences and Importance . . .* London: printed for A. Millar, 1757.

Munro, James, et al., eds. *Acts of the Privy Council, Colonial Series*. 6 vols. Hereford, England: His Majesty's Stationery Office, 1908-1912.

O'Callaghan, E. B., ed. *Documentary History of the State of New York*. 4 vols. Albany: Weed & Parsons, 1850-1851.

——. *Documents Relative to the Colonial History of the State of New York, Procured in Holland, England and France*. 15 vols. Albany: Weed, Parsons & Co., 1856-1907.

Occasional Reflections on the Importance of the War in America . . . London: Whitson & B. White, 1758.

"The Orderly Book of Lieut. William Henshaw," in *Transactions and Collections of the American Antiquarian Society*, XI. Worcester, Mass.: The Society, 1909, 185-254.

Pargellis, Stanley, ed. *Military Affairs in North America, 1748-1765: Selected Documents from the Cumberland Papers in Windsor Castle*. New York: D. Appleton-Century, 1936.

Pownall, Thomas. *The Administration of the Colonies*. 2d ed. London: printed for J. Dodsley, 1765.

Proud, Robert. *The History of Pennsylvania, in North America . . .* 2 vols. Philadelphia: printed by Zachariah Poulson, Jr., 1798.

Publications of the Colonial Society of Massachusetts, *Transactions*. Boston: by the Society, 1895—.

Quincy, Samuel M., ed. *Reports of Cases Argued and Adjudged in the Superior Court of Judicature of the Province of Massachusetts Bay*. Boston: Little, Brown, 1865.

Ramsay, David. *Military Memoirs of Great Britain: Or a History of the War, 1755-1763*. Edinburgh: printed for the author, 1779.

——. *Universal History: Or an Historical View of Asia, Europe, and America, from Their Earliest Records to the Nineteenth Century: With Particular Reference . . . to the United States of America*. 12 vols. Philadelphia: M. Carey and Son, 1818.

Ray, Nicholas. *The Importance of the Colonies of North America, and the Interest of Great Britain with Regard to Them, Considered . . .* London: printed for T. Peat, 1766.

Ricord, Frederick, ed. *Documents Relating to the Colonial History of the State of New Jersey: Journals of the Governor and Council*. Trenton, N.J.: John L. Murphy, 1892.

Sargent, Winthrop, ed. *The History of an Expedition against Fort Du Quesne in 1755; Under Major General Edward Braddock . . .* Philadelphia: Historical Society of Pennsylvania, 1856.

Smith, William. *The History of the Late Province of New York, from Its Discovery to the Appointment of Governor Colden, in 1762*. New York: New York Historical Society, 1829.

Stevens, Sylvester K., and Donald Kent, eds. *The Papers of Colonel Henry Bouquet*. Harrisburg: Pennsylvania Historical and Museum Commission, 1941.

——, eds. *The Papers of Henry Bouquet, The Forbes Expedition*. Vol. II. Harrisburg: Pennsylvania Historical and Museum Commission, 1951.

Sullivan, James, ed. *The Papers of Sir William Johnson*. 12 vols. Albany: The University of the State of New York, 1921-1957.

Trumbull, Benjamin. *A Complete History of Connecticut*. 2 vols. New London, Conn.: H. D. Utley, 1898.

——. *A General History of the United States of America: From the Discovery in 1492 to 1792 . . .* Boston: Farrand, Mallory, 1810.

Webster, Clarence J., ed. *The Journal of Jeffery Amherst, Recording the Military Career of General Amherst in America from 1758 to 1763*. Chicago: University of Chicago Press, 1931.

Welles, Lemuel A., ed. *Letters of Col. Nathan Whiting Written from Camp during the French and Indian War. Papers* of the New Haven Historical Society. Vol. VI. New Haven: The Society, 1900. Pp. 133-150.

Wynne, John. *A General History of the British Empire in America . . .* 2 vols. London: printed for W. Richardson and L. Urquhart, 1770.

Young, Arthur. *Reflections on the Present State of Affairs at Home and Abroad*. London: printed for J. Coote, 1759.

C. PAMPHLETS

Adams, Amos. *The Expediency & Utility of War . . .* Boston: Z. Fowle & S. Draper, 1759.

Adams, William. *A Discourse . . . on the Thanksgiving . . . for the Success of the British Arms . . .* New London: T. Green, 1761.

Anonymous. *To the Freeholders of the Town of Boston.* Boston, 1760.

Appleton, Nathaniel. *A Sermon Preached October 9, Being a Day of Public Thanksgiving Occasioned by the Surrender of Montreal, & All Canada. . . .* Boston: John Draper, 1760.

——. *A Ballad Concerning the Fight between the English and the French at Lake George.* Boston, 1755.

Ballantine, John. *The Importance of God's Presence with an Army, Going against the Enemy . . .* Boston: Edes & Gill, 1756.

Barnard, Thomas. *A Sermon Preached before His Excellency Francis Bernard. . . .* Boston, 1763.

Barton, Thomas. *A Sermon Preached at Carlisle, and Some Other Episcopal Churches in the Counties of York and Cumberland, Soon after General Braddock's Defeat.* Philadelphia: B. Franklin & D. Hall, 1755.

——. *Unanimity and Public Spirit: A Sermon, Preached at Carlisle, and Some Other Episcopal Churches, in the Counties of York and Cumberland, Soon after General Braddock's Defeat . . . To Which is Prefixed, a Letter from the Reverend Mr. Smith, Provost of the College of Philadelphia Concerning the Office and Duties of a Protestant Ministry, Especially in Times of Public Calamity and Danger.* Philadelphia: B. Franklin & D Hall, 1755.

Bland, Humphrey. *An Abstract of Military Discipline.* New York: De Forest, 1754.

Brown, John. *An Address to the Principal Inhabitants of the North American Colonies on Occasion of the Peace.* Philadelphia: Andrew Stuart, 1763.

Burtz, John. *The Mercy of God to His People, in the Vengeance He Renders to Their Adversaries . . .* Newport: J. Franklin, 1759.

C. T., *A Scheme To Drive the French Out of All the Continent of America, Humbly Offered to the Consideration of Esq. . . .* Boston: D. Fowle, 1755.

[Chauncey, Charles]. *A letter to a Friend, Giving a Concise, but Just Account . . . of the Ohio Defeat.* Boston: Edes & Gill, 1755.

——. *A Second Letter to a Friend Giving a More Particular Narrative of the Defeat of the French Army at Lake George by the New England Troops . . .* Boston: Edes & Gill, 1755.

Checkley, Samuel. *A Day of Darkness: A Sermon Preached Before His Excellency, Esq.: The Honorable William Shirley . . .* Boston: May 28, 1755.

——. *The Duty of God's People When Engaged in War, A Sermon Preached at the North Church of Christ in Boston Sept. 21 to Captain Thomas Stoddard and His Company: On Occasion of Their Going against the Enemy.* Boston: D. Fowle, 1755.

Clark, Peter. *Religion To Be Minded, under the Greatest Perils of Life, A Sermon on Psal. CXIX 109, Containing a Word in Season to Soldiers. . . .* Boston: S. Kneeland, 1755.

Clarke, William M.D. *Observations on the Late and Present Conduct of the French with Regard to the Encroachments upon the British Colonies in North America . . .* Boston: S. Kneeland, 1755.

Cogswell, James. *God, the Pious Soldier's Strength and Instructor . . .* Boston: John Draper, 1757.

Conant, Sylvanus. *The Art of War, The Gift of God . . .* Boston: Edes & Gill, 1759.

Cooper, Samuel. *A Sermon Preached before His Excellency Thomas Pownall . . . upon Occasion of the Success of His Majesty's Arms in the Reduction of Quebec.* Boston: Green & Russell, 1759.

——. *Two Letters to a Friend on the Present Critical Conjuncture of Affairs in North America, with an Account of the Action at Lake George.* Boston, 1755.

Cotton, John. *God's Call to His People: Shewing Their Duty and Safety in Days of General Calamity* . . . Boston: B. Mecom, 1757.

The Cruel Massacre of the Protestants in North America, Shewing How the French and Indians Joined Together To Scalp the English and the Manner of Their Scalping. London: printed for Michael Adamson, 1761.

Davies, Samuel. *The Curse of Cowardice* . . . Woodbridge, N.J.: J. Parker, 1759.

——. *An Ode on the Prospect of Peace.* Philadelphia: H. Miller, 1761.

——. *Religion and Patriotism, the Constituents of a Good Soldier, A Sermon Preached to Captain Overton's Independent Company of Volunteers.* . . . Philadelphia: James Chattin, 1755.

——. *Virginia's Danger and Remedy: Two Discourses Occasioned by the Severe Drought in Sundry Parts of the Country; and the Defeat of General Braddock.* Williamsburg: William Hunter, 1756.

Dickinson, John. *A Speech Delivered in the House of Assembly of the Province of Pennsylvania, May 14, 1764.* Philadelphia, 1764.

Dickinson, Moses. *A Sermon Preached before the General Assembly of the Colony of Connecticut.* New London, 1755.

Dunbar, Samuel. *The Presence of God with His People, Their Safety & Happiness.* . . . Boston, 1760.

Eliot, Andrew. *A Sermon Preached October 25th 1759* . . . *for the Success of the British Arms This Year, especially in the Reduction of Quebec, the Capital of Canada.* Boston: S. Kneeland, 1759.

Ellis, Jonathan. *The Justice of the Present War against the French, and the Principles That Should Influence Us in This Undertaking* . . . Newport: James Franklin, 1755.

Emerson, Joseph. *The Fear of God an Antidote against the Fear of Man* . . . Boston: S. Kneeland, 1758.

——. *A Thanksgiving Sermon* . . . Boston: S. Kneeland, 1760.

Evans, Nathaniel. *A Dialogue on Peace* . . . Philadelphia: William Bradford, 1763.

Fish, Joseph. *Angels Ministering to the People of God, for Their Safety and Comfort in Times of Danger and Distress* . . . Newport: James Franklin, 1755.

——. *Christ Jesus the Physician* . . . New London, 1760.

——. *A Sermon Preached at Westerly, in the Colony of Rhode Island, August 27, 1755* . . . *with a More Particular Reference to the Expedition Against Crown Point.* Newport: James Franklin, 1755.

Foxcraft, Thomas. *Grateful Reflections on the Signal Appearances of Divine Providence for Great Britain and Its Colonies in America* . . . Boston: S. Kneeland, 1760.

Frelinghuysen, Theodorus. *War and Rumors of War: A Sermon Preached in the Camp of the New England Forces* . . . New York: Gaine, 1755.

——. *The Gentleman's Compleat Military Dictionary, Containing the Military Art, Explaining the Terms and Phrases Used in the Field and Garrison.* 18th ed. Boston: Greene & Russell, 1759.

Frink, Thomas. *A King Reigning in Righteousness, & Princes Ruling in Judgment.* . . . Boston, 1758.

Graham, Chauncey. *A Sermon against Profane Cursing and Swearing, Delivered to the New York Forces in Their Camp.* New York: H. Gaine, 1761.

Hall, David. *Israel's Triumph* . . . New Haven: J. Parker, 1761.

Hobby, William. *The Happiness of a People Having God for Their Ally* . . . Boston: S. Kneeland, 1758.

Hopkins, Stephen. *Having Been Honored by My Countrymen.* Newport, 1757.

Horrocks, James. *Upon the Peace* . . . Williamsburg: Joseph Royle, 1763.

Huske, Ellis. *The Present State of North America* . . . Boston: D. Fowle, 1755.

Johnson, Stephen. *Some Important Observations, Occasioned by, & Adapted to, the Public Fast, Ordered by Authority, December 18th, A.D., 1765.* New London, 1765.

Judd, Jonathan. *Soldiers Directed and Urged To Inlist under Jesus Christ.* . . . Boston: S. Kneeland, 1759.

Kennedy, Archibald. *Serious Advise to the Inhabitants of the Northern Colonies on the Present Situation of Affairs.* New York, 1755.

Keteltas, Abraham. *The Religious Soldier* . . . New York: H. Gaine, 1759.

Lee, Charles. *Strictures upon a "Friendly Address to All Reasonable Men."* Philadelphia: W. Bradford, 1774.

Lidenius, John. *The Lawfulness of Defensive War* . . . Philadelphia: James Chattin, 1756.

Light, Johannes. *A Soliloquy of Faith Genuine: Or a Dialogue between Self and the Soul; Upon the Nature and Necessity of a True Faith in Order to a Right Warfare Here and Victorious Triumph Hereafter.* New York: H. Gaine, 1755.

Livingston, William. *An Address to His Excellency Sir Charles Hardy, Knt. Captain General and Governor in Chief of the Province of New York* . . . New York: H. Gaine, 1755.

——. *A Review of the Military Operations in North America* . . . New Haven, Conn., 1758.

Lowell, John. *Sermon on the Advantages of God's Presence with His People in an Expedition against Their Enemies.* Boston: Draper, 1755.

——. *A Sermon Occasioned by the Much Lamented Death of Col. Moses Titcomb, Who Fell in Battle Near Lake George September 8th, 1755.* Boston: Edes & Gill, 1760.

MacCarty, Thaddeus. *The Advise of Joab to the Hosts of Israel, Going Forth to War* . . . Boston: Thomas and John Fleet, 1759.

Mayhew, Jonathan. *Two Discourses Delivered November 23rd 1758* . . . *Relating Especially to the Success of His Majesty's Arms* . . . Boston: R. Draper, 1758.

——. *Two Thanksgiving Discourses, October 25, 1759* . . . Boston: R. Draper, 1759.

——. *Two Thanksgiving Discourses, October 9th, 1760* . . . Boston: R. Draper, 1760.

Mellen, John. *A Sermon Preached* . . . *on the General Thanksgiving for the Reduction of Montreal and Total Conquest of Canada* . . . Boston: B. Mecom, 1760.

——. *A Sermon Preached at the West Parish in Lancaster, October 9, 1760 on the General Thanksgiving for the Reduction of Montreal and the Total Conquest of Canada* . . . Boston: B. Mecom, 1760.

Morrill, Isaac. *Sermon to a Company of Soldiers.* Boston: J. Draper, 1755.
——. *The Soldier Exhorted to Courage in the Service of His King and Country, from a Sense of God and Religion* . . . Boston: J. Draper, 1755.
A New Exercise To Be Observed by His Majesty's Troops. New York: Parker & Weymen, 1757.
Parsons, Joseph. *A Sermon Preach'd in the Audience of His Excellency the Governor, His Honor the Lieut.-Governor, and the Honorable His Majesty's Council and House of Representatives* . . . Boston, 1759.
Pemberton, Ebenezer. *A Sermon Preached in the Audience of the Honourable His Majesty's Council and the Honourable Representatives of the Province of Massachusetts Bay* . . . Boston, 1757.
Pollen, Thomas. *The Principal Marks of True Patriotism* . . . Newport: J. Franklin, 1758.
——. *A Sermon Preached in Trinity Church, Newport, Rhode Island,* . . . *upon Occasion of the Embarkation of Some of the Colony's Troops, in Order To Go against the Enemy* . . . Newport: J. Franklin, 1755.
Raynold, Peter. *The Kingdom Is the Lord's, or God the Supreme Ruler and Governor of the World.* New London, 1757.
Reading, Philip. *The Protestant's Danger and the Protestant's Duty: A Sermon on Occasion of the Present Encroachments of the French* . . . Philadelphia: B. Franklin, 1755.
Russell, William. *The Duty of an Army of Professing Christians When Going Forth against Their Enemies* . . . New London: Timothy Green, 1760.
Smith, William. *The Christian Soldier's Duty; the Lawfulness and Dignity of His Office; and the Importance of the Protestant Cause in the British Colonies, Stated and Explained.* Philadelphia: James Chattin, 1757.
Stiles, Isaac. *The Character and Duty of Soldiers Illustrated in a Sermon.* . . . New Haven: James Parker, 1755.
Throop, Benjamin. *Religion and Loyalty: The Duty and Glory of a People* . . . New London, Timothy Green, 1758.
Vinal, William. *A Sermon on the Accursed Thing That Hinders Success and Victory in War, Occasioned by the Defeat of the Hon. Edward Braddock Esq.* . . . Newport: J. Franklin, 1755.
Ward, Samuel. *To the Honorable Stephen Hopkins, Esq.* . . . Newport, 1757.
Webb, Thomas. *A Military Treatise on the Appointments of the Army, Containing Many Useful Hints, Not Touched on Before by any Author* . . . *Which Will Be Particularly Useful in Carrying on the War in North America* . . . Philadelphia: W. Dunlap, 1759.
Webster, Samuel. *Soldiers, and Others, Directed and Encouraged, When Going on a Just and Import, Tho' Difficult Enterprize against their Enemies.* . . . Boston: Edes & Gill, 1756.
Whitefield, George. *A Short Address to Persons of All Denominations, Occasioned by the Alarm of an Intended Invasion.* Philadelphia: B. Franklin, 1756.
Wigglesworth, Samuel. *God's Promise to an Obedient People, of Victory over Their Enemies* . . . Boston: S. Kneeland, 1755.
Williams, Abraham. *A Sermon Preached at Boston before the Great and General Court or Assembly* . . . Boston, 1762.
Williams Eliphart. *God's Wonderful Goodness in Succeeding the Arms of His People* . . . New London: T. Green, 1760.
Williams, Solomon. *The Duty of Christian Soldiers, When Called to War, To Undertake It in the Name of God* . . . New London: T. & J. Green, 1755.
——. *The Relations of God's People to Him and the Engagements and*

Obligations They Are Under To Praise Him and Prepare Him an Habitation. . . . New London: T. Green, 1760.

D. DIARIES, JOURNALS, AND ORDERLY BOOKS

An Account of Sundry Payments Made to Officers and Soldiers in the New York Regiments, 1756-1758. New York Public Library.

Booth, Captain Joseph. Journal. 1760. Connecticut Historical Society.

Bremner, John. Journal. 1756-1764. New York Historical Society.

Bull, John. Orderly Book. May 25-Nov. 1, 1759. Henry E. Huntington Library.

Champion, Henry. Accounts and Journal. 1758. Connecticut State Library.

Comstock, Christopher. Journal. Sept. 8, 1758-Nov. 8, 1758, and July 2, 1759-Nov. 20, 1759. Connecticut Historical Society.

Crown Point Expedition, Journal, 1755-1756. New York Public Library.

Dibble, Ebenezer, of Cornwall, Connecticut. Diary. Campaigns in 1759 and 1762. Connecticut State Library.

Grant, John. Orderly Book. June-October, 1761. Henry E. Huntington Library.

Griswold, Shubal. Journal kept during service in the French and Indian War. Connecticut State Library.

Grubb, Captain Samuel. Orderly Book. June-July, 1759. Henry E. Huntington Library.

Harris, Obadiah. Regimental Journal. May-October, 1758. Henry E. Huntington Library.

Hayward, Benjamin. Journal. 1757. Connecticut Historical Society.

Huse, Carr. Diary. 1758. New York Historical Society.

Knap, Jonathan, of Killingly, Connecticut. Journal. Connecticut State Library.

McKenzie, John, John Petzold, and John de Garmo. Extracts from Orderly Book Crown Point Expedition, Journal. 1755-1756. New York Public Library.

Nichols, Joseph. Diary kept during the Expedition to Ticonderoga. Henry E. Huntington Library.

Upton, Daniel. Diary. 1758. New York Public Library.

Waterman, Asa. Diary. 1760. Connecticut State Library.

Wells, Captain Edmund. Diary. 1756-1757. Connecticut State Library.

Willard, Abijah. Orderly Book and Journal. 1755-1756. Henry E. Huntington Library.

E. NEWSPAPERS AND PERIODICALS

American Magazine

Gentleman's Magazine

Boston Gazette and Country Journal

Boston Evening Post

Connecticut Gazette

Newport *Mercury*

New York *Gazette* or *Weekly Post-Boy*

New York *Mercury*

Pennsylvania Gazette

Pennsylvania Journal

Salem Essex Gazzette

Virginia Gazette

III. SECONDARY MATERIALS
A. BOOKS AND ARTICLES

Alden, John R. "The Albany Congress and the Creation of the Indian Superintendencies," *Mississippi Valley Historical Review,* XXVII (1940), 193-210.

————. *General Gage in America.* Baton Rouge: Louisiana University Press, 1948.

Alexander, James. *A Brief Narrative of the Case and Trial of John Peter Zenger,* ed. Stanley Nader Katz. Cambridge, 1963.

Allen, David Grayson. "The Zukerman Thesis and the Process of Legal Rationalization in Provincial Massachusetts," *William and Mary Quarterly,* 3d ser., XXIX (1972), 443-460. "Michael Zukerman's Reply," pp. 461-468.

Anderson, Niles. "New Light on the 1758 Forbes Campaign," *Western Pennsylvania Historical Magazine,* L (1967), 89-103.

Andrews, Charles McLean. *The Colonial Background of the American Revolution.* New Haven: Yale University Press, 1961.

————. *The Colonial Period.* New York: Henry Holt, 1912.

Bailyn, Bernard. *The Ideological Origins of the American Revolution.* Cambridge: Harvard University Press, 1967.

————. *The Origins of American Politics.* New York: Alfred A. Knopf, 1968.

Baldwin, Alice M. *The New England Clergy and the American Revolution.* New York: Frederick Unger, 1965.

Bancroft, George. *History of the United States of America, from the Discovery of the Continent.* 6 vols. New York: Appleton, 1884.

Barrow, Thomas C., ed. "A Project for Imperial Reform: 'Hints Respecting the Settlement for Our American Provinces,' 1763," *William and Mary Quarterly,* 3rd ser., XXVI (1967), 108-126.

————. *Trade and Empire: The British Customs Service in Colonial America, 1660-1775.* Cambridge: Harvard University Press, 1967.

Baugh, Daniel A. *British Naval Administration in the Age of Walpole.* Princeton: Princeton University Press, 1965.

Baxter, William T. *The House of Hancock: Business in Boston, 1724-1775.* New York: Russell and Russell, 1965.

Bean, Walton. "War and the British Colonial Farmer: A Reevaluation in the Light of New Statistical Records," *Pacific Historical Review,* XI (1942), 439-447.

Becker, Carl Lotus. *Beginnings of the American People.* New York: Houghton, Mifflin, 1915.

————. *The History of Political Parties in the Province of New York, 1760-1776.* Madison: University of Wisconsin Press, 1968.

Beer, George L. *British Colonial Policy, 1754-1765.* New York: Macmillan, 1907.

Berg, Harry. "Economic Consequences of the French and Indian War for the Philadelphia Merchants," *Pennsylvania History,* XIII (1946), 185-193.

Bezanson, Anne, R. D. Gray, and Miriam Hussey. *Prices in Colonial Pennsylvania.* Philadelphia: Historical Society of Pennsylvania, 1935.

Bonomi, Patricia U. *A Factious People: Politics and Society in Colonial New York.* New York: Columbia University Press, 1971.

Boorstin, Daniel. *The Americans: The Colonial Experience.* New York: Random House, 1958.

Bridenbaugh, Carl. *Cities in Revolt: Urban Life in America, 1743-1776.* New York: Capricorn Books, 1955.

Browning, Reed. "The Duke of Newcastle and the Financing of the Seven Years' War," *Journal of Economic History,* XXXI (June 1971), 344-377.

Bruchey, Stuart, ed. *The Colonial Merchant: Sources and Readings.* New York: Harcourt, Brace, and World, 1966.

Bushman, Richard L. *From Puritan to Yankee: Character and the Social Order in Connecticut, 1690-1765.* New York: W. W. Norton, 1970.

Chaffin, Robert J. "The Townshend Acts of 1767," *William and Mary Quarterly,* 3d ser., XXVII (1970), 90-121.

Champagne, Roger. "Family Politics versus Constitutional Principles: The New York Assembly Elections of 1768 and 1769," *William and Mary Quarterly,* XX (1963), 57-59.

———. "Liberty Boys and Mechanics of New York City, 1764-1774" *Labor History,* VIII (1967), 115-135.

Clark, Dora Mae. "The Impressment of Seamen in the American Colonies," *Essays in Colonial History Presented to Charles McLean Andrews by His Students.* New Haven: Yale University Press, 1931.

Cole, Arthur Harrison. *Wholesale Commodity Prices in the United States, 1700-1861.* Cambridge: Harvard University Press, 1938.

Cook, Edward M., Jr. "Social Behavior and Changing Values in Dedham, Massachusetts, 1700 to 1775," *William and Mary Quarterly,* 3d ser., XXVII (1970), 546-580.

Crandall, Ruth. "Wholesale Commodity Prices in Boston during the Eighteenth Century," *Review of Economic Statistics,* XVI (1934), 117-128, 171-173.

Crane, Verner W. "Letters to the Editor on the Albany Congress Plan of Union, 1754," *Pennsylvania Magaine of History and Biography,* LXXV (1951), 350-362.

———. "Letters to the Editor on the Drafting of the Albany Plan of Union, 1754," *Pennsylvania History,* XXVII (1960), 126-136.

Darlington, Mary C., ed. *History of Colonel Henry Bouquet and the Western Frontiers of Pennsylvania.* Philadelphia: privately printed, 1920.

Davis, Ralph. *The Rise of the English Shipping Industry in the Seventeenth and Eighteenth Centuries.* London: MacMillan, 1962.

Davisson, William I., and Lawrence J. Bradley, "New York Maritime Trade: Ship Voyage Patterns, 1715-1765," *New York Historical Society Quarterly,* LX (Oct. 1971), 309-317.

de Sola Pool, Ithiel et al. *Symbols of Democracy.* Palo Alto: Stanford University Press, 1952.

Dickerson, Oliver M. *The Navigation Acts and the American Revolution.* New York: A. S. Barnes, 1963.

———. *American Colonial Government, 1696-1765.* New York: Russell and Russell, 1912.

Dillon, Dorothy R. *The New York Triumvirate: A Study of the Legal and Political Careers of William Livingston, John Morin Scott, and William Smith, Jr.* New York: Columbia University Press, 1949.

Edwards, George William. *New York as an Eighteenth Century Municipality.* Port Washington, N.Y.: Ira J. Friedman, 1967; originally published: Columbia University Press, 1917.

Engal, Mark, and Joseph A. Ernst. "An Economic Interpretation of the American Revolution," *William and Mary Quarterly,* 3rd ser., XXIX (1972), 3-32.

Ernst, Joseph Albert. "The Currency Act Repeal Movement: A Study of Imperial Politics and Revolutionary Crisis, 1764-1767," *William and Mary Quarterly,* 3d ser., XXV (1968), 177-211.

Ezell, John. "The Lottery in Colonial America," *William and Mary Quarterly,* 3d ser., V (1948), 185-200.

Franklin, Benjamin. *Autobiography.* New York: Holt, Rinehart & Winston, 1964.

Friedman, Bernard. "The New York Assembly Elections of 1768 and 1769; The Disruption of Family Politics," *New York History,* XLVI (1965), 3-24.

Frothingham, Richard. *The Rise of the Republic of the United States.* Boston: Little, Brown, 1881.

Gerlach, Don. "A Note on the Quartering Act of 1774," *New England Quarterly,* XXXIX (1966), 80-88.

——. *Philip Schuyler and the American Revolution in New York, 1733- 1777.* Lincoln: University of Nebraska Press, 1964.

Gipson, Lawrence Henry. "The American Revolution as an Aftermath of the Great War for the Empire, 1754-1763," *Political Science Quarterly,* LXV (1950), 86-104.

——. *The British Empire before the American Revolution,* 15 vols. New York: Alfred Knopf, 1936-1970.

——. *The Coming of the Revolution, 1763-1775.* New York: Harper & Row, 1954.

——. "Connecticut Taxation and Parliamentary Aid Preceding the Revolutionary War," *American Historical Review,* XXXVI (1931), 721-739.

——. "The Drafting of the Albany Plan of Union: A Problem in Semantics," *Pennsylvania History,* XXVI (1959), 290-316.

——. "Massachusetts Bay and American Colonial Union, 1754," *Proceedings* of the American Antiquarian Society, vol. 71, pt. 1 (1961), pp. 63-92.

——. "The Taxation of the Connecticut Towns, 1750-1775," in *Essays in Colonial History Presented to Charles McLean Andrews by his Students.* New Haven: Yale University Press, 1931.

——. "Thomas Hutchinson and the Framing of the Albany Plan of Union," *Pennsylvania Magazine of History and Biography,* LXXIV (1950), 3-35.

Greene, Jack P. *The Quest for Power: The Lower Houses of Assembly in the Southern Royal Colonies, 1689-1776.* Chapel Hill: University of North Carolina Press, 1963.

——. "The Role of the Lower Houses of Assembly in Eighteenth-Century Politics," *Journal of Southern History,* XXVII (1961), 451-474.

——. "Search for Identity: An Interpretation of the Meaning of Selected Patterns of Social Response in Eighteenth-Century America," *Journal of Social History,* III (1970), 189-224.

——. "The South Carolina Quartering Dispute, 1757-1758," *South Carolina Historical and Genealogical Magazine* n.v. (1959), 193-204.

Hacker, Louis. *The Triumph of American Capitalism: The Development of Forces in American History to the End of the Nineteenth Century.* New York: Columbia University Press, 1947.

Hanna, William S. *Benjamin Franklin and Pennsylvania Politics.* Palo Alto: Stanford University Press, 1964.

Harper, Lawrence H. *The English Navigation Laws.* New York: Columbia University Press, 1939.

Harrington, Virginia. *New York Merchants on the Eve of the Revolution.* New York: Columbia University Press, 1935.

Hart, Albert B. *The Commonwealth History of Massachusetts.* 5 vols. New York: States History, 1927-1930.

Hedges, James B. *The Browns of Providence Plantation: Colonial Years.* Cambridge: Harvard University Press, 1952.

Hobsbawn, E. J. *Primitive Rebels: Studies in Archaic Forms of Social Movement in the 19th and 20th Centuries.* New York: Frederick Praeger, 1963.

Hutson, James. "Benjamin Franklin and Pennsylvania Politics, 1751-1755: A Reappraisal," *Pennsylvania Magazine of History and Biography,* XCIII (1969), 303-371.

Jacobs, Wilbur R. *The Appalachian Frontier: The Edmund Atkin Report and Plan of 1755.* Lincoln: University of Nebraska Press, 1967.

———. "British-Colonial Attitudes and Policies toward the Indian in the American Colonies," in Howard Peckham and Lawrence Henry Gipson, eds., *Attitudes of Colonial Powers toward the American Indian.* Salt Lake City: University of Utah Press, 1969. Pp. 81-106.

———. "Was the Pontiac Uprising a Conspiracy?" *Ohio Archeological and Historical Society Quarterly,* LIX (1950), 26-37.

———. *Wilderness Politics and Indian Gifts: The Northern Colonial Frontier, 1748-1763.* Lincoln: University of Nebraska Press, 1966.

Jacobson, David L. *John Dickinson and the Revolution in Pennsylvania, 1764-1776.* Berkeley and Los Angeles: University of California Press, 1965.

James, Francis G. "Irish Colonial Trade in the Eighteenth Century," *William and Mary Quarterly,* 3d ser., XX (1963), 574-584.

Jensen, Arthur R. *Maritime Commerce of Colonial Philadelphia.* Madison: University of Wisconsin Press, 1963.

John, A. H. "War and the English Economy, 1700-1763," *Economic History Review,* 2d ser., VII (1955), 329-344.

Johnson, Victor. "Fair Traders and Smugglers in Philadelphia, 1754-1763," *Pennsylvania Magazine of History and Biography,* LXXXIII (1959), 125-149.

Jones, Thomas. *History of New York during the Revolutionary War,* 2 vols. New York: New York Historical Society, 1879.

Judges, A. V. "The Idea of a Mercantile State," *Transactions* of the Royal Historical Society, 4th ser., XXI (1939), 41-69.

Kammen, Michael. *Empire and Interest: The American Colonies and the Politics of Mercantilism.* New York: J. P. Lippincott, 1970.

Katz, Stanley Nider. *Newcastle's New York: Anglo-American Politics, 1732-1753.* Cambridge: Harvard University Press, 1968.

Kenny, Alice P. *The Gansevoorts of Albany: Dutch Patricians in the Upper Hudson Valley.* Syracuse: Syracuse University Press, 1969.

Ketcham, Ralph L. "Conscience, War and Politics in Pennsylvania, 1755-1757," *William and Mary Quarterly,* 3d ser., XX (1963), 416-439.

Klein, Milton M. "Democracy and Politics in Colonial New York," *New York History,* XL (1959), 221-246.

———. "The Rise of the New York Bar: The Legal Career of William Livingston," *William and Mary Quarterly,* 3d ser., XV (1958), 334-358.

Knollenberg, Bernhard. *Origin of the American Revolution, 1759-1766.* New York: Free Press, 1965.

Knorr, Klaus E. *British Colonial Theories, 1570-1850.* Toronto: University of Toronto Press, 1944.

Koebner, Richard. *Empire.* New York: Grosset & Dunlap, 1965; originally published: Cambridge University Press, 1961.

Konkel, Burton Alva. *Benjamin Chew, 1722-1810: Head of the Pennsylvania Judiciary System under Colony and Commonwealth.* Philadelphia: University of Pennsylvania Press, 1932.

Koontz, Louis K. *Robert Dinwiddie; His Career in American Colonial Government and Westward Expansion.* Glendale: Arthur H. Clark, 1941.

Leder, Lawrence H. *Liberty and Authority: Early American Political Ideology, 1689-1763.* Chicago: Quadrangle Books, 1968.

————. "The New York Elections of 1769: An Assault on Privilege," *Mississippi Valley Historical Review,* XLIX (1963), 675-682.

Lemisch, Jesse. "The American Revolution from the Bottom Up," in Barton J. Bernstein, ed., *Towards a New Past: Dissenting Essays in American History.* New York: Pantheon Books, 1968. Pp. 3-45.

————. "Jack Tar in the Streets: Merchant Seamen in the Politics of Revolutionary America," *William and Mary Quarterly,* 3d ser., XXV (1968), 371-407.

Levermore, Charles H. *The Republic of New Haven: A History of Municipal Evolution.* Port Washington, N.Y.: Kennikat, 1966; first published 1886.

Lokken, Roy. *David Lloyd, Colonial Lawmaker.* Seattle: University of Washington Press, 1959.

Long, John C. *Lord Jeffery Amherst: A Soldier of the King.* New York: Macmillan, 1933.

Lovejoy, David S. *Rhode Island Politics and the American Revolution, 1760-1776.* Providence, R.I.: Brown University Press, 1958.

McAnear, Beverly, ed. "Personal Accounts of the Albany Congress of 1754," *Mississippi Valley Historical Review,* XXXIX (1953), 727-746.

McCormac, E. I. *Colonial Opposition to Imperial Authority during the French and Indian War.* Berkeley: University of California Press, 1911.

McCusker, John J. "Sources of Investment Capital in the Colonial Philadelphia Shipping Industry," *Journal of Economic History,* XXXII (March 1972), 146-157.

McDonald, Forrest, ed. *Empire and Nation: Letters from a Farmer in Pennsylvania . . . Letters from the Federal Farmer.* Englewood Cliffs, N.J.: Prentice-Hall, 1962.

Maier, Pauline. "Popular Uprisings and Civil Authority in Eighteenth-Century America," *William and Mary Quarterly,* 3d ser., XXVII (1970), 3-35.

Mark, Irving. *Agrarian Conflicts in Colonial New York, 1711-1775.* Port Washington, N.Y.: Ira J. Friedman, 1965.

Massachusetts Historical Society. *Collections.* 6th ser. Vol. IX. Boston: The Society, 1897.

Merrit, Richard. "The Colonists Discover America: Attention Patterns in the Colonial Press, 1735-1775," *William and Mary Quarterly,* 3d ser., XXI (1964), 270-287.

————. *The Growth of American Community, 1735-1775.* New Haven: Yale University Press, 1966.

Morgan, Edmund, and Helen M. Morgan. *The Stamp Act Crisis: Prologue to Revolution.* Chapel Hill: University of North Carolina Press, 1953.

Morris, Richard B. ed. *The Era of the American Revolution.* New York: Columbia University Press, 1939.

Morton, Richard L. *Colonial Virginia.* 2 vols. Chapel Hill: University of North Carolina Press, 1960.

Nettles, Curtis P. "British Mercantilism and the Economic Development of the Thirteen Colonies," *Journal of Economic History,* XII (1952), 105-114.

Newbold, Robert C. *The Albany Congress and Plan of Union in the Colonies.* New York: Vantage Press, 1955.

Nixon, Lily L. "Colonel James Burd in the Campaign of 1759," *Western Pennsylvania Historical Magazine,* XVII (1934), 235-246.

———. "Colonel James Burd in the Forbes Campaign," *Pennsylvania Magazine of History and Biography,* LIX (1935), 106-133.

O'Conor, Norreys Jephson. *A Servant of the Crown, in England and in North America, 1756-1761.* New York: Appleton-Century, 1938.

Olson, Allison Gilbert. "The British Government and Colonial Union," *William and Mary Quarterly,* 3d ser., XVII (1960), 22-34.

Olson, Allison Gilbert, and Richard Maxwell Brown, eds. *Anglo-American Political Relations, 1675-1775.* New Brunswick, N.J.: Rutgers University Press, 1970.

Omond, J. S. *Parliament and the Army, 1642-1904.* Cambridge: Cambridge University Press, 1933.

Osgood, Herbert L. *The American Colonies in the Eighteenth Century.* 4 vols. New York: Columbia University Press, 1924-1925.

Palmer, R. R. *The Age of the Democratic Revolution: A Political History of Europe and America, 1760-1800.* 2 vols. Princeton: Princeton University Press, 1959.

Pares, Richard. "The Economic Factors in the History of the Empire," *Economic History Review,* VII (May 1937), 119-144.

———. "The Manning of the Navy in the West Indies, 1702-1763," *Transactions* of the Royal Historical Society, 4th ser., XX (1937), 31-60.

———. *War and Trade in the West Indies, 1739-1763.* London: F. Cass, 1963.

Pargellis, Stanley M. *Lord Loudoun in North America.* New Haven: Yale University Press, 1933.

Parkman, Francis. *The Conspiracy of Pontiac and the Indian War after the Conquest of Canada.* 2 vols. Boston: Little, Brown, 1901.

———. *Montcalm and Wolfe.* 3 vols. Boston: Little, Brown, 1902.

Peckham, Howard. *Pontiac and the Indian Uprising.* Princeton: Princeton University Press, 1947.

———. "Speculations on the Colonial Wars," *William and Mary Quarterly,* 3d ser., XVII (1960), 463-472.

Plumb, J. H. "The Mercantile Interest: The Rise of the British Merchant after 1689," *History Today,* V (1955), 762-767.

Plummer, Wilbur C. "Consumer Credit in Colonial Philadelphia," *Pennsylvania Magazine of History and Biography,* LXVI (1942), 385-409.

Ransom, Roger. "British Policy and Colonial Growth: Some Implications of the Burden from the Navigation Acts," *Journal of Economic History,* XXVIII (Sept. 1968), 427-435.

Robbins, Caroline. *The Eighteenth-Century Commonwealthman: Studies in the Transmission, Development and Circumstance of English Liberal Thought from the Restoration of Charles II until the War with the Thirteen Colonies.* Cambridge: Harvard University Press, 1961.

Robertson, C. H. "The Imperial Problem in North America in the Eighteenth Century (1714-1783)," *"Historical Journal of the University of Birmingham,* I (1947), 134-157.

Root, Winfred. *The Relations of Pennsylvania with the British Government, 1696-1765.* Philadelphia: University of Pennsylvania, 1912.

Rudé, George. *The Crowd in History: A Study of Popular Disturbances in France and England, 1730-1848.* New York: John Wiley & Sons, 1964.

Savelle, Max. *Seeds of Liberty: The Genesis of the American Mind.* Seattle: University of Washington Press, 1965.

Schutz, John A. *Thomas Pownall, British Defender of American Liberty: A Study of Anglo-American Relations in the Eighteenth Century.* Glendale: Arthur H. Clark, 1951.

———. *William Shirley, King's Governor of Massachusetts.* Chapel Hill: University of North Carolina Press, 1961.

Shafroth, John. "The Capture of Louisbourg in 1758," United States Naval Institute, *Proceedings,* LXIV (1938), 78-96.

Shepherd, James F., and Gary M. Walton. "Trade, Distribution, and Economic Growth in Colonial America," *Journal of Economic History,* XXXII (March 1972), 128-145.

Sherrard, O. A. *Lord Chatham: Pitt and the Seven Years' War.* London: Garden City Press, 1935.

Shy, John. "A New Look at Colonial Militia," *William and Mary Quarterly,* 3d ser., XX (1963), 175-185.

———. "Quartering His Majesty's Troops in New Jersey," New Jersey Historical Society, *Proceedings,* LXXVIII (1960), 82-94.

———. *Toward Lexington: The Role of the British Army in the Coming of the American Revolution.* Princeton: Princeton University Press, 1965.

Smith, Page. *John Adams.* 2 vols. New York: Doubleday, 1962.

Sosin, Jack M. *Whitehall and the Wilderness: The Middle West in British Colonial Policy, 1760-1775.* Lincoln: University of Nebraska Press, 1961.

Stout, Neil. "Manning the Royal Navy in North America, 1763-1775," *American Neptune,* XXIII (1963), 174-185.

Sumner, William G. "The Spanish Dollar and the Colonial Shilling," *American Historical Review,* III (1898), 607-617.

Thayer, Theodore. "The Army Contractors for the Niagara Campaign, 1755-1756," *William and Mary Quarterly,* 3d ser., XIV (1957), 31-46.

———. *Pennsylvania Politics and the Growth of Democracy, 1740-1776.* Harrisburg: Pennsylvania Historical and Museum Commission, 1953.

———. "The Quaker Party of Pennsylvania, 1755-1765," *Pennsylvania Magazine of History and Biography,* LXXI 1947), 19-43.

Thomas, Robert Paul. "British Imperial Policy and the Economic Interpretation of the American Revolution," *Journal of Economic History,* XXVIII (1968), 436-440.

———. "A Quantative Approach to the Study of the Effects of British Imperial Policy upon Colonial Welfare," *Journal of Economic History,* XVIII (1965), 615-638.

Thompson, Mack E. "The Ward-Hopkins Controversy and the American Revolution in Rhode Island: An Interpretation," *William and Mary Quarterly,* 3d ser., XVI (1959), 363-375.

Tolles, Frederick. *Meeting House and Counting House: The Quaker Merchants of Colonial Philadelphia, 1682-1783.* New York: W. W. Norton, 1963.

Trask, Roger R. "Pennsylvania and the Albany Congress, 1754," *Pennsylvania History,* XXVII (1960), 273-290.

Van Doren, Carl. *Benjamin Franklin.* New York: Viking Press, 1938.

Van Schaack, Henry C. *Memoirs of the Life of Henry Van Schaack.* Chicago, 1892.

Wainwright, Nicholas B. *George Croghan, Wilderness Diplomat.* Chapel Hill: University of North Carolina Press, 1959.

———. "Governor Denny in Pennsylvania," *Pennsylvania Magazine of History and Biography,* LXXXI (1957), 170-198.

Warden, G. B. "The Proprietary Group in Pennsylvania, 1754-1764," *William and Mary Quarterly,* 3d ser., XXI (1964), 367-389.

Waters, John J., Jr. *The Otis Family in Provincial and Revolutionary Massachusetts.* Chapel Hill: University of North Carolina Press, 1968.

White Phillip L., *The Beekmans of New York in Politics and Commerce, 1647-1877.* New York: New York Historical Society, 1956.

Whitfield, Bell, and Leonard Labaree. "Franklin and the Wagon Affair," American Philosophical Society, *Proceedings,* CI (1957), 551-558.

Wiener, Frederick Bernays. *Civilians under Military Justice: The British Practice since 1689, Especially in North America.* Chicago: University of Chicago Press, 1968.

Willson, Beckles. *The Life and Letters of James Wolfe.* London: William Heinemann, 1909.

Wilson, Charles. *England's Appreticeship.* New York: St. Martin's Press, 1965.

————. "The Other Face of Mercantilism," Royal Historical Society, *Transactions,* 5th ser. IX (1959), 81-101.

Wood, Gordon S. "A Note on Mobs in the American Revolution," *William and Mary Quarterly,* 3d ser., XXIII (1966), 635-642.

Wood, R. F. "Jesse Platt," *New York Genealogical and Biographical Record,* n.v. (Oct. 1939), 6-10.

Zemsky, Robert. *Merchants, Farmers, and River Gods: An Essay on Eighteenth-Century American Politics.* Boston: Gambit, 1971.

Zimmerman, John J. "Benjamin Franklin and the Quaker Party, 1755-1756," *William and Mary Quarterly,* 3d ser., XVII (1960), 291-313.

Zukermann, Michael. *Peaceable Kingdoms: New England Towns in the Eighteenth Century.* New York: Alfred A. Knopf, 1970.

B. UNPUBLISHED DISSERTATIONS

Foote, William Alfred. "The American Independent Companies of the British Army, 1664-1764." University of California, Los Angeles, 1966.

Hayes, James W. "The Social and Professional Background of the Officers of the British Army, 1714-1763." University of London, 1956.

Lemisch, Jesse. "Jack Tar vs John Bull: The Role of New York's Seamen in the Precipitating of the Revolution." Yale University, 1962.

McAnear, Beverly. "Politics in Provincial New York, 1689-1761." Stanford University, 1935.

Marshall, Peter. "The Rise and Fall of Imperial Regulation of American Indian Affairs." Yale University, 1959.

Sachs, William S. "The Business Outlook in the Northern Colonies, 1750-1775." Columbia University, 1957.

Smith, William A. "Anglo-Colonial Society and the Mob, 1740-1775." Claremont Graduate School, 1965.

Stout, Neil Ralph. "The Royal Navy in American Waters, 1760-1775." University of Wisconsin, 1962.

INDEX